# THE NEW YANKEE WORKSHOP

## OUTDOOR PROJECTS

Norm Abram

# THE NEW YANKEE WORKSHOP

## OUTDOOR PROJECTS

Little, Brown and Company

Boston   New York   Toronto   London

*First Edition*

Illustrations: John Murphy
Photographs: Richard Howard

*Library of Congress Cataloging-in-Publication Data*
Abram, Norm.
    The New Yankee workshop outdoor projects / Norm Abram with
Roland Walker. — 1st ed.
      p.    cm.
    Includes index.
    ISBN 0-316-00485-5. — ISBN 0-316-00486-3 (pbk.).
    1. Outdoor furniture. I. Walker, Roland. II. New Yankee work-
shop (Television program). III. Title.
TT197.5.09A27    1994
684.1'8 — dc20               93-42574

10  9  8  7  6  5  4  3  2  1

RRD-OH

Published simultaneously in Canada by Little, Brown & Company
(Canada) Limited

Printed in the United States of America

To Dick Holden,
television cameraman for fifteen
years for *New Yankee
Workshop* and *This Old House,*
and to
Richard Howard,
photographer for most of my
*New Yankee Workshop*
books, in appreciation for their
craftsmanship and with
thanks for their assistance in
illuminating the steps of
woodworking with
power tools.

# Contents

Acknowledgments    ix

Introduction    3

1   Sandbox    9

2   Gardener's Workbench    27

3   Wooden Wheelbarrow    47

4   Picnic Table    73

5   Garden Swing    85

6   Outdoor Planters    107

7   Child's Wagon    123

8   Outdoor Lidded Bench    145

9   Four Colonial Fences    163

10  Redwood Arbor    183

Index    202

New Yankee Workshop Project Index    204

# Acknowledgments

AS THIS fourth book of projects from *The New Yankee Workshop* on public television goes to press, we are about to begin producing programs for the seventh season. By now we have it down to a system. Russell Morash is the visionary behind this series and its executive producer. The coordinating producer, Nina Sing Fialkow, provides invaluable research and scheduling assistance. Marian Morash keeps the finances in order with infectious cheerfulness.

Russ Morash and I select the projects for each season, and I design and make a prototype for each piece. Then I make a second example of the same piece while Russ and his crew videotape the process for subsequent broadcast. Each member of the crew is a professional and a friend, but I want especially to thank Dick Holden, the ingenious cameraman since the beginning of the series, who is retiring before our seventh season.

After each project is videotaped I make measured drawings of the piece and its major parts. John Murphy takes my drawings and converts them into the final fine drawings for the book. Eventually I go back into the workshop and make a third copy of each piece. This time Richard Howard takes crystal clear still photographs of the steps and techniques essential to making the piece; these will go into the book with John Murphy's drawings. Richard also takes photographs of the finished pieces.

A writer — Roland Walker for this volume — helps transform the steps of making each piece into crisp how-to prose. Then we are ready to deliver text, photos, and drawings to our publisher, Little, Brown and Company, whose editor in chief, William D. Phillips, has lent his enthusiasm to all of our woodworking books. Catherine Crawford has been the working editor on this volume. Pamela Marshall copyedited all of the material for accuracy and style. Donna Peterson supervised production, and Barbara Werden and Mary Reilly executed the design.

The preparation of this book, as you can see, has required the combined efforts of many people, beginning with the moment when Russ Morash and I first began discussing the content of another season's programs. I am sincerely grateful to each and every one of them.

At WGBH Educational Foundation in Boston, station manager David Liroff has been a forceful supporter of *The New Yankee Workshop* from its beginning. The series could not survive without the financial support of national underwriters; in the period during which the projects in this book were filmed, the Parks Corporation, Vermont American Tool Company, Ace Hardware Corporation, and Delta International Machinery Corporation provided generous support.

Many of the pieces I make on *The New Yankee Workshop* are inspired by and adapted from pieces found in museums and homes, and so the series is a testimonial to many craftsmen of the past. The wagon in this book was inspired by one I saw in the Margaret Woodbury Strong Museum in Rochester, New York, and the wheelbarrow by one in the Sloane/Stanley Museum in Kent, Connecticut. The fences were inspired by examples from colonial Williamsburg. Walpole Woodworkers consulted with me on the design of the arbor. The lidded bench, garden swing, and picnic table were adapted from outdoor furniture in Russ Morash's yard. Kip Anderson and Roger Swain from another of Russ's productions, *The Victory Garden,* offered suggestions about the gardener's workbench that Russ and I designed. The planters are my own design. The sandbox is based on a childhood photograph provided by my parents of me in my sandbox.

## 1

## SANDBOX

*page 9*

"*When I was just a little boy, my father built
a very special sandbox for my sister and me.
. . . This is a 1990s version of my old
childhood favorite.*"

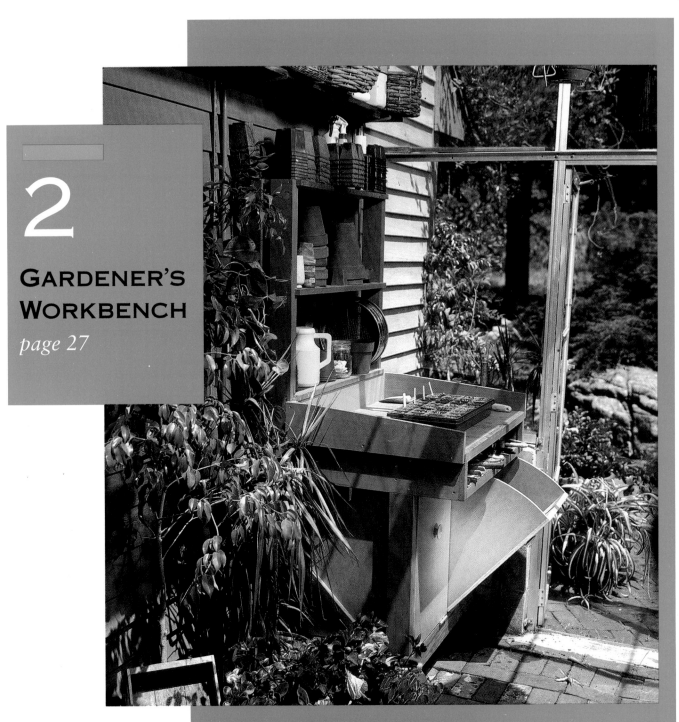

## 2

## GARDENER'S WORKBENCH

*page 27*

*"Every gardener deserves a good workbench with some shelves for storing pots, a good-sized work surface, and ample storage for potting soil."*

# 3

# WOODEN
# WHEEL-
# BARROW

*page 47*

*"The humble wooden wheelbarrow was an important tool in New England history. For the one shown here, I borrowed the best features of some of the antique wheelbarrows and added a modern pneumatic tire for practicality and usefulness."*

# 4

## PICNIC TABLE

*page 73*

*"Over the years I've had the opportunity to sit at many different styles of picnic tables. This one takes into account some of the best features I've seen."*

# 5

## GARDEN SWING

*page 85*

*"Around the turn of the century, garden swings like this one were a common sight in the backyards of America, and people would while away a summer evening just swinging and talking for hours on end. My garden swing is based on an antique garden swing that must be at least seventy-five years old."*

# 6

## OUTDOOR PLANTERS

*page 107*

*"Every home can use a couple of good-looking outdoor planters. Here are two that will look great on a porch or deck, or any-where around the yard."*

# 7

## CHILD'S WAGON

*page 123*

*"Times may have changed, but kids are still
kids, and this little wagon is guaranteed to
put a grin on any young face."*

# 8

## OUTDOOR LIDDED BENCH

*page 145*

*"This outdoor lidded bench is an improved version of one that's been sitting on the grounds of the New Yankee Workshop for years. The seat lifts off to reveal a storage compartment underneath — a good place for storing the dog's leash, the garden hose, or maybe some garden tools."*

# 9

## FOUR COLONIAL FENCES

*page 163*

*"For the four different fence styles featured in this chapter, there was no question where I would turn for inspiration: the re-created eighteenth-century colonial village of Williamsburg, Virginia."*

# 10

## REDWOOD ARBOR

*page 183*

*"While strolling around Nantucket one summer, I was so intrigued by the number of arbors I found that I decided to build one for my own garden. For mine, I added a bench so we could relax and enjoy our garden on a balmy summer evening."*

# THE NEW YANKEE WORKSHOP

## OUTDOOR PROJECTS

# Introduction

AS a carpenter and contractor for almost twenty-five years, I've built more than my share of outdoor structures and furniture. I've watched many of these projects weather with the years and I've witnessed firsthand what nature can do to wood. I've learned from experience which woods resist rot, which glues take a soaking, and which finishes hold up longest after years of exposure to showers, sunshine, and snow.

The outdoor projects in this book (the fourth in the *New Yankee Workshop* series) are designed to look good, of course, but I also designed them to last. These projects are built mostly with wood that is naturally resistant to decay. I've used pressure-treated lumber only for a few ground-contact applications, where it makes the most sense. Each project is built with water-resistant glue and rust-resistant fasteners — either zinc-plated or stainless steel. I think you'll find that the projects you build from this book will provide many years of pleasure for you and your family.

## Weather and Wood

When a big tree topples to the forest floor, it's attacked by a legion of wood-eating insects, borers, and fungi intent on making a meal. With a little moisture and oxygen to get the thing cooking, these hungry organisms soon turn the tree into compost.

Some trees are slower to rot than others. Our colonial ancestors noticed this and they selected the heartwood of these trees for fence posts, bridges, waterwheels, barrels, and the like. Back in America's "wooden age," every farm boy knew that black locust made the best fence posts, white oak the best barn sills, and cedar the best shingles and shakes for a roof.

Today we rely upon pressure-treated southern yellow pine for most outdoor applications. It's easy on the pocketbook, resists rot for decades, and has revolutionized the way we build outdoor structures. Pressure-treated lumber is impregnated with chemical preservatives like chromated copper arsenates (CCA), pentachlorophenol and copper, or zinc naphthenate. These chemicals work by poisoning the wood to make it unappetizing to fungi and insects. The jury's still out on how these chemicals affect humans, but until we know for sure, I avoid using pressure-treated wood for children's playthings or projects like tables, where food might come in contact with the wood.

If you work with pressure-treated wood, play it safe. Be sure to wear a dust mask when sawing or sanding and always wash your hands before eating or smoking. Discard pressure-treated scraps in the trash or bury them in a landfill. Never burn pressure-treated wood in a wood stove or fireplace — the smoke is toxic.

In spite of the precautions required in using this material, pressure-treated wood is still the best choice for ground-contact applications. But for most other situations, I prefer to use woods that are naturally resistant to decay: redwood, cedar, swamp cypress (also called bald cypress), white oak, or plantation-grown teak.

The premium choice is plantation-grown teak. It's very pricey and, because the wood has abrasive silica in it, it's tough on the tools. But teak is a beautiful, durable hardwood that's highly resistant to rot. Domestic, North American woods are more economical than teak, although price and availability can vary widely from one region to another. Redwood, for example, costs far more in New England, where I live, than it does on the Pacific coast, where it grows.

## Waterproof Glues

Outdoor furniture often stays out all year and gets rained or snowed upon for days on end. Water works its way into glue joints, so you want to choose an adhesive that won't come apart when it's wet.

Many woodworkers I talk to seem confused by the use of the terms "waterproof" and "water-resistant." I haven't heard a better explanation than this one: water-*resistant* glues will hold up to an occasional soaking but they aren't designed for long-term immersion in water. Regular yellow glue (aliphatic resin) is fairly water-resistant, but it won't hold up under constant exposure to moisture. Water*proof* glues, on the other hand, can be soaked for long periods without losing their grip.

I know of only two glues that are guaranteed waterproof — epoxy and resorcinol. Both are expensive, two-part adhesives that must be mixed together before use. Both will hold up under water and are widely used by boat builders.

Epoxy is sold as two liquids — a resin and a hardener — and is available in fast-set or slow-set formulas as well as in different viscosities for special applications. Resorcinol is a dark, reddish-brown glue that's sold as a little kit containing two cans: one can of resin and one can of catalyst. It cures very slowly and requires a minimum drying temperature of 70 degrees F. Because you have to mix them, neither of these glues is very convenient to use.

I've had really good results with a one-part water-resistant glue that's recently come on the market. It's a special type of yellow, aliphatic-resin glue that's easy to use. Though, unlike epoxy and resorcinol, it isn't completely waterproof, it's highly water-resistant. What's more, unlike epoxy, glue spills and brushes clean up with water.

Occasionally on some outdoor projects, I use construction adhesive to supplement screws, bolts, or other mechanical fasteners. Construction adhesive comes in two basic types — a regular formula for use on wood, and a special pressure-treated formula designed for gluing pressure-treated wood.

## Outdoor Finishes

You can't prevent wood from decaying by applying paint, water repellents, or varnish. In the presence of moisture (such as contact with the ground), the wood will eventually begin to rot. And while no finish will keep wood looking 100 percent new, some finishes do offer some protection from water and ultraviolet radiation from the sun. Trouble is, no matter what type of finish you use, the wood needs to be refinished every few years to look good.

The Forest Products Lab of the U.S. Department of Agriculture has an outdoor site in Madison, Wisconsin, where they test different finishes by exposing them to the weather year in and year out. Their research has shown that multiple coats of oil-based paint or marine spar varnish protect wood best against the effects of sunshine and rain. And while they found that no finish keeps wood looking new indefinitely, wood in outdoor applications looks best if finished promptly, before it has a chance to weather.

I'm not a big fan of paint for outdoor projects. Even the best paint peels eventually and has to be recoated. Instead, when I want to color the wood, I prefer to use a pigment stain especially formulated for outdoor use. These stains — designed for exterior siding and trim — are fade-resistant and don't peel like paint. I usually apply them over a primer according to the manufacturer's instructions.

But for most furniture projects that will remain outdoors, I prefer to let the wood weather naturally. Left unfinished, most wood weathers to a pleasing, natural color, thanks to the bleaching effect of the sun. Cypress and cedar, after several years, turn a beautiful silvery-gray. I find the natural look attractive and it saves me the trouble of refinishing every few years. One place wood seems to age beautifully is by the ocean. Perhaps it's the combination of sun, wind, and salt air.

A word of advice about unfinished wood: in shady or damp conditions, which foster the growth of mildew, unfinished wood will darken until it becomes almost black.

*Fasteners*

Rust-resistant fasteners are essential for outdoor projects. Stainless steel is the ultimate choice but fasteners made from this material are very expensive. I usually use zinc-plated nuts, bolts, washers, and screws, and galvanized nails. These are inexpensive and widely available. I prefer to use hot-dipped galvanized nails because the irregularities in the rough galvanized coating increase the holding power of the nails.

That's enough theory for now. This book is about woodworking, and if you're like me, you can't wait to get down to the shop. I hope you enjoy the outdoor projects that follow. I've had a lot of fun building them here in the New Yankee Workshop. I know you will too.

NORM ABRAM
*The New Yankee Workshop*

# 1

# *Sandbox*

## PROJECT PLANNER

*Time:* 2 days

*Special hardware, tools, and materials:*

(1) tube of construction adhesive

(1) tube of construction adhesive for pressure-treated lumber

(1) box of 3/8-in. staples

caulking gun

staple gun

hot-melt glue gun

single-edge razor blades or utility knife

(100) 1¼-in. galvanized bugle-head screws

(50) 1⅝-in. galvanized bugle-head screws

(32) 2-in. galvanized bugle-head screws

(1) 5-ft. by 7-ft. piece of waterproof canvas (often sold as awning material)

4d galvanized finishing nails

5d galvanized finishing nails

*Wood:*

(2) 12-ft. 1 × 10 cedar

From each board, cut 2 pieces 48 in. long with a 45-degree miter cut on both sides for sandbox sides (4 pieces required). Cut remaining pieces according to plan for gables (2 required).

(1) 5-ft. 1 × 8 cedar

Cut in half and rip each piece into two 3-in.-wide pieces for rafters (4 required).

(1) 8-ft. 1 × 8 cedar

Rip one piece 3½ in. wide and cut to 46½ in. long for roof ridge. Bevel top edge according to plan. Rip 13-degree bevel on one edge of remaining piece according to plan and cut into 2 pieces 48 in. long for fascia boards.

(1) 5-ft. 1 × 12 cedar

Cut 4 pieces according to plan for seats.

(1) 8-ft. 2 × 4 cedar or redwood

Cut into 2 pieces 47⅞ in. long for standards.

(1) 8-ft. 2 × 4 pressure-treated pine

WHEN I was just a little boy, my father built a very special sandbox for my sister and me. I remember it well, with its striped canvas canopy and triangular seats. I spent many happy hours playing in that old sandbox and I thought it would be fun to build one like it for the young kids in my family. My mother and father found an ancient black-and-white photo of the sandbox to work from, and I picked my father's brain for the dimensions and construction details. The result? A 1990s version of my old childhood favorite.

While the design is the same, the materials have changed. My father would never have bought cedar to make the sides and the seats, for example. It was just too expensive in the early 1950s. But today, cedar is available at a reasonable cost. It resists rot and weather well and you don't have to paint it. For the legs and the bottom of the sandbox I chose pressure-treated lumber — a material that didn't even exist in the '50s. Damp sand can sit in contact with that stuff forever without the slightest hint of rot. For the canopy, I used an "improved" awning-type canvas, which is resistant to the sun's ultraviolet rays and rot and will last a long time.

## *Making the Legs*

To get started, I cut the legs from some pressure-treated wood. At my building supply center, I bought some 5/4 × 6 pressure-treated decking (referred to as "five quarter"). I can cut all 8 legs from a single 10-ft. board (see Project Planner).

On my radial-arm saw table, I set up a stop block 13¼ in. to the right of the blade. The stop block guarantees that all 8 legs will be exactly the same length. I angle the stop block so that only one corner of

Rip into 2 pieces 1⅝ in. wide. Cut to fit for deck cleats (4 required).

(3) 12-ft. 5/4 × 6 pressure-treated decking

Cut 6 pieces 46½ in. long and 2 pieces 44½ in. long for decking. From remainder, cut 7 strips 1/4 in. × 1 in. × 46½ in. for splines. Use remaining scrap for stiffener.

(1) 10-ft. 5/4 × 6 pressure-treated decking

Cut 8 pieces 13¼ in. long for legs.

it touches the workpiece. Because only the corner touches the wood, it's impossible for sawdust to build up between the stop block and the workpiece, which could alter the lengths of the legs.

First, I square up the right end of the workpiece. Then I butt this squared end against the stop block and cut the first leg to length (13¼ in.). I cut 7 more legs in the same way.

The next step is to join the leg pieces together in pairs with right-angle butt joints (see *Leg Assembly Detail*). If I join them just as they are, one side of the finished leg will appear wider, like a capital L. The legs will be better looking if the 2 sides appear equal. To do this, I have to reduce the width of one board by the thickness of the stock. On my table saw, I set the rip fence 4½ in. from the blade and rip a strip from 4 of the leg pieces.

To assemble the legs, I clamp a narrow piece in the bench vise (sawn edge up), place one of the wider leg pieces on top at right angles, and line it up at the ends. Because the edges of the decking boards are rounded, it's hard to tell when the top board's edge is flush with the face of the narrow board underneath. I hold a square on the narrow board's face and butt the edge of the top board against it.

When the boards are lined up, I predrill holes for the screws that will hold the 2 boards together. Then I install three 2-in. galvanized bugle-head screws in the joint. I complete the other 3 pairs of legs in the same way.

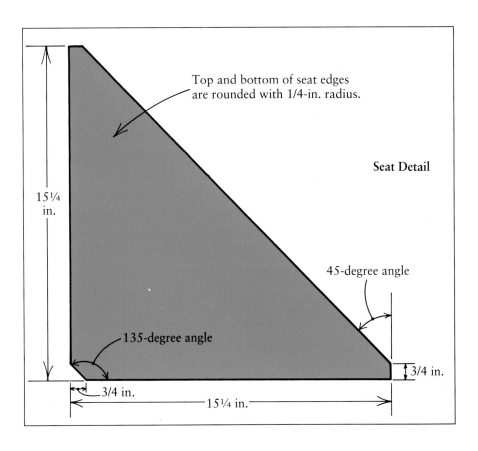

Top and bottom of seat edges are rounded with 1/4-in. radius.

Seat Detail

15¼ in.

45-degree angle

135-degree angle

3/4 in.

3/4 in.

15¼ in.

## 1-A  *Major Anatomy and Dimensions*

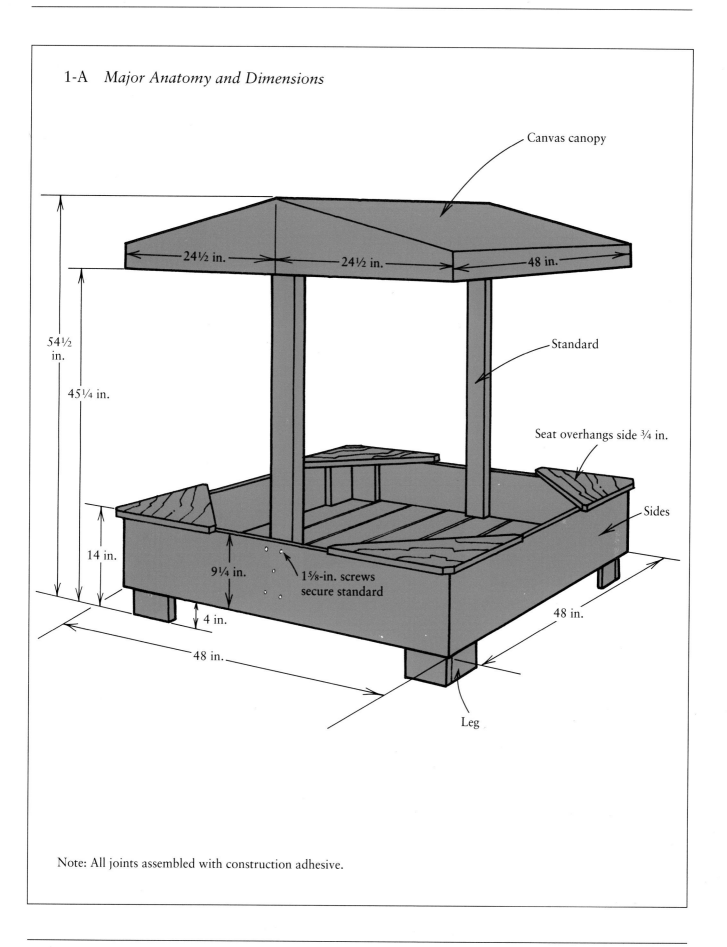

Canvas canopy

24½ in.  24½ in.  48 in.

54½ in.

45¼ in.

Standard

Seat overhangs side ¾ in.

Sides

14 in.

9¼ in.

1⅝-in. screws secure standard

4 in.

48 in.

48 in.

Leg

Note: All joints assembled with construction adhesive.

## Mitering the Sides

The cedar sandbox sides are mitered at the corners. Miter joints look good but they aren't very strong because end grain–to–end grain glue joints are weak. But since these corner joints will be reinforced by the legs (*drawing 1-B*), I'm not too concerned about the strength of the miters. They don't have to play any structural role.

The radial-arm saw is the ideal tool for mitering relatively long boards like these because the board stays put while the saw blade moves. I tilt the blade of my saw 45 degrees and cut all 4 sides with a miter on each end. The sides measure 48 in. from long point to long point.

Before I nail these miters together, I run a bead of construction adhesive along the joint. This will make the joint a lot stronger. I assemble one of the corners and, holding the joint together with one hand, hammer some 5d galvanized siding nails into the joint to hold it together (*photo 1-1*). I do the same for the other 3 corners of the box.

With the sides nailed together, I want to make sure that the sandbox is square. The easiest way to do this is to measure diagonally from corner to corner. If the two diagonals are equal, the box is square. I screw a temporary scrap-wood brace across 2 of the corners to keep the box square until after the decking boards are installed.

## Installing the Legs

Now I'm ready to put on the legs. With the box on one side on my bench, I spread some construction adhesive in the corner where one of the legs will go. Here I use a special type of construction adhesive formulated for use on pressure-treated wood. I put a leg in place, flushing up the top end with the top edge of the box side.

With my combination drill/countersink tool, I predrill through the leg for the 5 screws that will fasten the leg to the side. I countersink about 3/8 in. deep — enough for the screw to get a good bite. I drill 4 screw holes in the corners and one in the center like 5 dots on a die, and screw the leg down with 1¼-in. galvanized screws.

## Deck Cleats

With the legs all installed, I'm ready to make the 4 deck cleats that support the bottom of the sandbox (*drawing 1-B*). I cut these cleats from a pressure-treated 2 × 4, ripping it into two 1⅝-in-wide pieces (see Project Planner).

I cut and fit the cleats one at a time. I measure between the legs on one side and crosscut a cleat to fit. I have to cut notches in the ends of the cleat to fit around the legs. To lay out the notch, I place the cleat in position across the legs and mark off the width of each leg with a combination square (*photo 1-2*). Next, I turn the cleat 90 degrees and, with my combination square and a pencil, mark off the 1-in. thickness

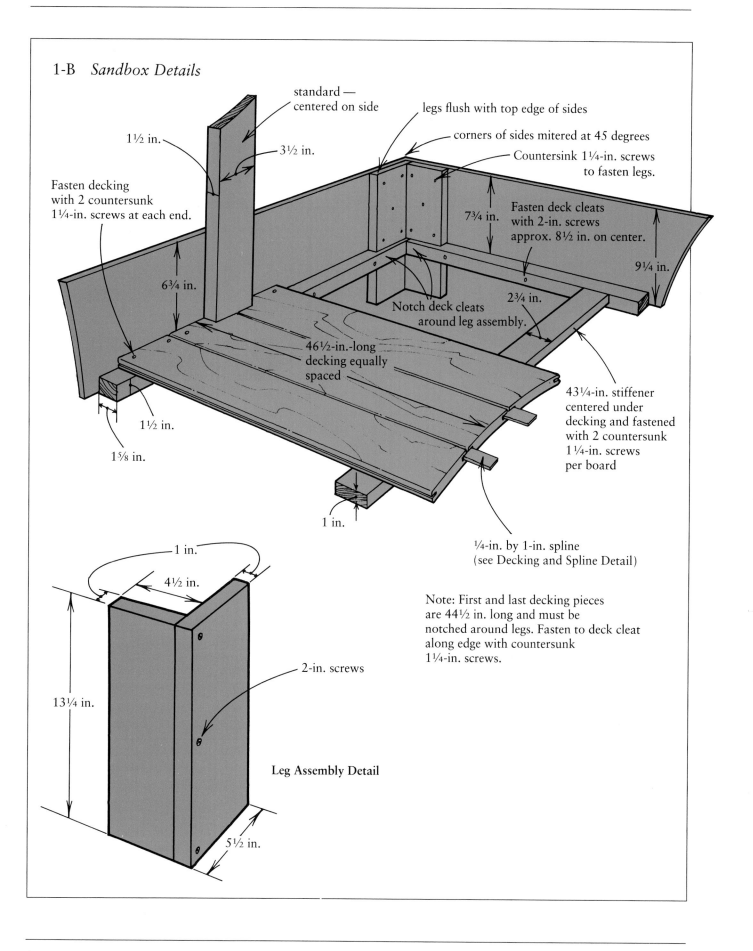

standard — centered on side

legs flush with top edge of sides

corners of sides mitered at 45 degrees

Countersink 1¼-in. screws to fasten legs.

1½ in.

3½ in.

Fasten decking with 2 countersunk 1¼-in. screws at each end.

7¾ in.

Fasten deck cleats with 2-in. screws approx. 8½ in. on center.

9¼ in.

6¾ in.

Notch deck cleats around leg assembly.

2¾ in.

46½-in.-long decking equally spaced

1½ in.

43¼-in. stiffener centered under decking and fastened with 2 countersunk 1¼-in. screws per board

1⅝ in.

1 in.

¼-in. by 1-in. spline (see Decking and Spline Detail)

Note: First and last decking pieces are 44½ in. long and must be notched around legs. Fasten to deck cleat along edge with countersunk 1¼-in. screws.

1 in.

4½ in.

2-in. screws

13¼ in.

5½ in.

Leg Assembly Detail

**1-1** To assemble the sandbox side miters I run a bead of construction adhesive along the joint and secure it with some 5d galvanized siding nails.

**1-2** I have to cut notches in the deck cleats to fit around the legs. To lay out the notch, I place the cleat in position across the legs and mark off the width of the leg with a combination square.

**1-3** Next, I turn the cleat 90 degrees and, with my combination square and a pencil, mark off the 1-in. thickness of the leg on each end of the cleat.

of the leg on each end of the cleat (*photo 1-3*). I cut out the notches with my jigsaw.

To install the cleat, I run a bead of construction adhesive along the entire length and place it in position flush with the bottom edge of the cedar side. I screw it to the sides and legs with 2-in. galvanized screws spaced about 8 in. on center (*photo 1-4*). The opposite cleat goes on next, followed by the other 2 cleats, which are slightly shorter.

### Deck Boards

For the bottom of the sandbox, I use some 5/4 × 6 pressure-treated decking (see Project Planner). On my radial-arm saw, I cut 6 boards 46½ in. long, using a stop block to make sure that the lengths are all equal. Next, I cut 2 more boards 44½ in. long. These 2 boards will be the first and last deck boards and must be a little shorter so they'll fit between the legs.

I have to notch the 2 shorter boards so they'll fit around the legs and sit about 3/8 in. from the cedar sides of the box. I use my combination square to mark out these notches just as I did for the cleats. I cut out the notches with my jigsaw.

Pressure-treated wood nearly always shrinks initially when you build something. In this case, that's great for drainage but terrible in terms of the sand running out. To keep the sand from falling through the gaps, I install 1/4-in. by 1-in. splines between the boards (see *Decking and Spline Detail*). The splines fit into grooves milled in the edges of the boards.

On the table saw, I set my rip fence 1/4 in. from the blade and rip the 1/4-in. by 1-in. splines from a piece of 5/4 decking. I cut the splines to length on my miter box — 46½ in.

To mill the spline grooves in the deck boards, I set up the table saw with my stack dado head set for a 1/4-in.-wide cut. I raise the blade 9/16 in. above the table and mill a groove down the middle of each

**1-4** After cutting the cleat notches with my jigsaw, I fasten the cleat to the sides and legs with construction adhesive and 2-in. galvanized screws spaced about 8 in. on center.

**1-5** I mill the 1/4-in.-wide spline grooves in the deck boards with a stack dado head on the table saw. The 2 outer boards get a groove in only one edge (as shown here). The other boards get a groove in both edges.

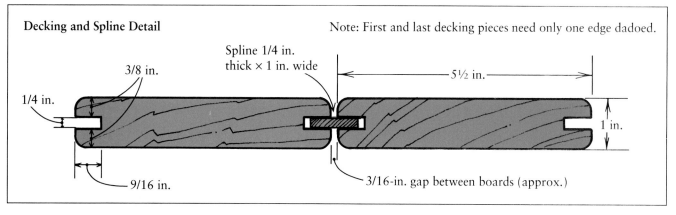

**Decking and Spline Detail**

Note: First and last decking pieces need only one edge dadoed.

Spline 1/4 in. thick × 1 in. wide

3/8 in.

1/4 in.

5½ in.

1 in.

9/16 in.

3/16-in. gap between boards (approx.)

**1-6** I fit the deck boards on top of the cleats, starting with one of the notched outer boards and slipping the splines in the grooves as I go.

**1-7** To add a little strength to the floor, I screw a 2¾-in. by 42¼-in. stiffener to the underside of the deck boards with two 1¼-in. screws in each board.

edge (*photo 1-5*). Then I flip the board end-for-end and make a second pass to cut a perfectly centered groove. The 2 outer deck boards need a groove in only one edge.

Installing the deck boards is a piece of cake. I run a bead of construction adhesive (the type formulated for pressure-treated wood) on the tops of the cleats and fit the boards in place, starting with one of the notched boards and slipping the splines in the grooves as I go (*photo 1-6*). When the boards are all in, I even up the spacing — about 1/4 in. between boards. Then I predrill and countersink for 2 screw holes in the end of each board, angling the drill slightly to give the screws a good bite in the cleats. Then I drive in some 1¼-in. galvanized screws to anchor the deck boards to the cleats. With the deck boards in place, I can remove the temporary brace that kept the box square.

To add a little strength to the floor, I use the scrap left from cutting the splines to make a stiffener approximately 2¾ in. × 43¼ in. (*drawing 1-B*). I fasten it to the underside of the deck boards with two 1¼-in screws in each board (*photo 1-7*).

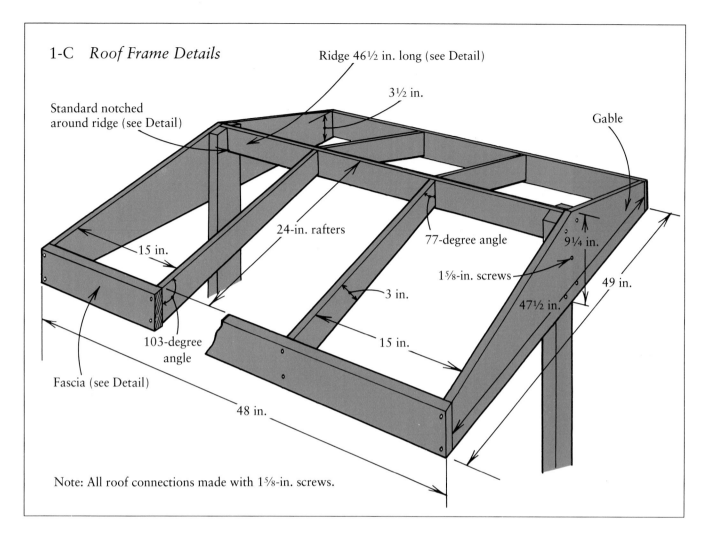

1-C  *Roof Frame Details*

Ridge 46½ in. long (see Detail)

3½ in.

Standard notched around ridge (see Detail)

Gable

24-in. rafters

77-degree angle

9¼ in.

15 in.

1⅝-in. screws

49 in.

3 in.

47½ in.

15 in.

103-degree angle

Fascia (see Detail)

48 in.

Note: All roof connections made with 1⅝-in. screws.

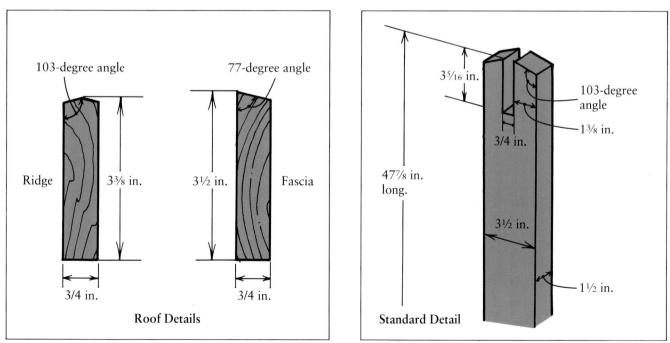

103-degree angle

77-degree angle

Ridge

3⅜ in.

3½ in.

Fascia

3/4 in.

3/4 in.

**Roof Details**

3⁵⁄₁₆ in.

103-degree angle

1⅜ in.

3/4 in.

47⅞ in. long.

3½ in.

1½ in.

**Standard Detail**

**1-8**  I nail 2 pieces of 1 × 10 cedar together, lay out the shape of the gable on the top board, and cut out both gables at the same time with my small circular saw.

**1-9**  The roof ridge must be beveled on both sides to match the pitch of the gable. Without changing the table-saw setup, I simply make 2 passes, flipping the board over for the second pass.

## Framing the Roof

The "roof" on my sandbox is a scaled-down version of the real McCoy. Two gables are connected by a ridge at the peak and by fascia boards at the bottom. Little rafters span the distance from fascia boards to ridge. This whole affair is covered with canvas and suspended over the sandbox on two 2 × 4 standards attached to the sandbox sides (*drawings 1-A and 1-C*).

I start by cutting the gable ends from some 1 × 10 cedar (see Project Planner). Each gable is 47½ in. long and 9¼ in. wide at the peak (*drawing 1-C*). At the ends, the gable slopes down to 3½ in. where it connects to the fascia. I nail 2 pieces of 1 × 10 together so I can cut out both gables at the same time with my circular saw (*photo 1-8*).

The fascia boards that join the 2 gables must have their top edges beveled at the same pitch as the roof. The ridge must be beveled on

both sides to follow the pitch of the roof. I cut these bevels on the table saw. I tilt the blade 13 degrees and set the rip fence 3½ in. from the blade (measured at the table surface). Then I run my fascia boards through, ripping a bevel on one edge.

To bevel the ridge, I don't have to make any adjustments to the saw. I just make 2 passes, flipping the board over for the second pass (*photo 1-9*).

I assemble the gables, fascia, and ridge with some 1⅝-in. screws, predrilling the holes so I won't split the cedar. Two screws in each joint will be plenty strong.

Now to make the 4 little rafters. I rip the rafters 3 in. wide from 1 × 8 cedar (see Project Planner). To mark the length of the rafters, I place one over the ridge and fascia (*photo 1-10*). I mark the length and draw an angled line to make sure I angle the cuts in the proper direction. I swing my miter-saw blade 13 degrees to the left and cut the rafter to the marks. All 4 rafters are the same length.

To install the rafters, I screw 1⅝-in. screws into the ends. To fasten the rafters on the second side of the roof, I have to angle the screws through the ridge board into the end of the rafter as if I were toenailing (*photo 1-11*).

**1-10** To mark the length of the rafters, I place one over the ridge and fascia. I mark the length and draw an angled line to make sure I angle the cuts in the proper direction when I cut them on my miter box.

**1-11** I assemble the roof frame with 1⅝-in. galvanized bugle-head screws. To install the rafters on the second side, I have to angle the screws through the ridge board into the end of the rafter.

## Vertical Standards

To make the 2 standards that hold up the roof, I cut an 8-ft.-long cedar 2 × 4 in half. I pivot the blade of my miter saw 13 degrees and make 2 cuts on one end of each piece to conform to the peak of the gable.

Next, I have to cut a slot at the top of each standard to support the ridge board (see *Standard Detail*). I mark off a 3/4-in. by 3⅜-in. slot and cut out the waste with my jigsaw (*photo 1-12*).

## Raising the Roof

Now I'm ready to attach the standards to the sides of the box. First, I apply a little construction adhesive to strengthen the joint, and then I drill and countersink for five 1⅝-in. screws in each standard. I install the screws through the side into the standard, making sure it's perpendicular to the side.

The roof frame goes on next. I spread some adhesive on the insides of the gables where the standards will go and drill and screw through the gables into the standards.

**1-12** The ridge board fits into a 3/4-in. by 3⅜-in. slot in the top of each of the 2 × 4 standards that hold up the top. I cut the slot with my jigsaw. Note that the top of the standard is angled to match the roof pitch.

## Installing the Seats

Making the seats is the last piece of woodworking to do on this project. The seats are just 45-degree-angle cuts on a piece of 1 × 12 cedar (see Project Planner) measuring 15¼ in. on the sides (see *Seat Detail*). I cut out one seat with my small circular saw and use it as a pattern to mark out the other 3 (*photo 1-13*). Once the seats are cut

**1-13** After cutting one seat from a 1 × 12 board, I use the first seat as a pattern to mark out the other three seats.

**1-14** To cover the gables, I staple the canvas along the gable's top edge, then trim the canvas along the top inside edge of the gable with a razor blade or utility knife. To guide the blade I rest it against the inside of the gable.

**1-15** After trimming off the canvas, I lift up the seam and run a bead of hot-melt glue along the top edge of the gable. I press the canvas into the hot glue and smooth the seam down flat with a small block of wood.

out, I saw off the corners and round over all the edges with a 1/4-in.-radius roundover bit in my router. I don't want any splinters here.

I fasten the seats to the sandbox with construction adhesive and 4d galvanized finishing nails. Screw heads, even if they were countersunk, might get hot enough from the sun to burn a child's legs. The seat overhangs the sides of the sandbox by 3/4 in. (*drawing 1-A*).

*Putting on the Canvas*

To put on the canvas I need a couple of things: a staple gun, some razor blades or a utility knife, and a hot-melt glue gun. I roll up the canvas along its 7-ft. length (see Project Planner) to start.

The first thing I do is cover the gable ends. I partially unroll the canvas over the roof, centering the width of the canvas along the ridge. I pull the 5-ft.-wide end down over one gable, pulling it about 1½ to 2 in. below the bottom edge of the gable. Then I fold the canvas down tight over the top edge of the gable and staple it along the table's top edge.

Next, I take a razor blade or utility knife and trim the canvas along the top inside edge of the gable (*photo 1-14*). I just let the blade rest right up against the wood and trim off the canvas. On the bottom edge of the gable, I pull the canvas tight and staple it to the bottom edge. Then I trim off the bottom edge along the inside of the gable.

At each corner of the fascia board, I make a neat fold, cutting out notches in the canvas so the canvas lies flat on the wood without any puckers.

Once the canvas is stapled in place, I fold back the edges and run a bead of general purpose hot-melt glue along the top and bottom edges of the gable (*photo 1-15*). Before the glue cools and sets up, I press the

**1-16** To cover the top, I start by folding under the edge of the canvas along the top of one gable. I fold it under about 3/4 in. to prevent fraying. I install one staple at the lower corners of the fascia to temporarily hold the canvas in place.

**1-17** I run a bead of hot glue under this folded seam, pressing the canvas down onto the glue and smoothing the seam with a small block of wood.

**1-18**  I go back underneath the roof and squeeze some more glue into the seam along the inside edge of the gable and smooth it down with my wood block.

canvas down on the glue and smooth it down flat with a small block of wood.

After covering both gables, I'm ready to put on the top piece of canvas. I unroll the canvas over the roof, making sure the ends hang below the bottom edges of the fascia boards. Next, to prevent the edges from fraying, I tuck the edges under about 3/4 in. along the top of a gable (*photo 1-16*). I hold the canvas in place temporarily at both ends with a staple at the bottom corner of the fascia. Then I run a bead of hot glue under this folded seam (*photo 1-17*), pressing the canvas down onto the glue on the top edge of the gable and smoothing the seam with the small block of wood. Any glue that squeezes out can be trimmed off after it dries.

Now I can remove the 2 staples and glue the seams down at the corners of the fascia board. With both ends secured, I go back underneath the roof with my hot-melt glue gun and squeeze some glue into the seam along the inside top edge of the gable (*photo 1-18*). Reaching up around to the outside, I smooth the seam down with my wood block.

I repeat this procedure on the other gable, stretching the canvas tight over the roof. When I've secured the canvas to the top of both gables, I stretch the ends down over the fascia boards and staple them in place to the bottom edge of the fascia. I trim off the canvas along the inside edge of the fascia and run some glue under this seam to keep the canvas from fraying. Then I fold in the corners and glue them in place.

Well, that about does it for the 1990s edition of my old childhood sandbox. Now all I have to do is find some sand and a couple of small kids to fill it.

# 2

# *Gardener's Workbench*

EVERY gardener deserves a good workbench with some shelves for storing pots, a good-sized work surface, and ample storage for potting soil. Now, I make no pretense to be a gardener, but I do have access to some of the best gardeners in the country. It was their combined knowledge and suggestions that allowed me to come up with this design. I built one for my wife, the gardener in our family. She loves it.

When I asked the experts what features they'd like in a gardener's workbench they had a few specific requests. They wanted 3 wide shelves at the back with the top shelf no more than 6 ft. high so they could reach it when standing in front of the bench. They asked for a work surface that could stand up to moisture with a backsplash and sides to keep things from falling off. They wanted an area to store markers, scissors, and a few garden tools. And, of course, they needed a place to store potting soil.

I took their suggestions to heart and designed all these features into my workbench. I made the frame of redwood, one of the prettiest and most rot-resistant woods I know of. The work surface and backsplash are made of medium-density overlay (MDO) board. MDO is a special kind of paper-covered plywood. It's very durable, takes paint well, and is so tough that it's used to make road signs. Underneath the work surface, there's a small compartment for tools. And down below, there are 2 ample bins that pivot out and hold about 2 cu. ft. of potting soil each.

The back of the shelves is open but that's not a problem because the workbench will go against the wall of a greenhouse or garage. To keep it rigid, I installed an X-brace on the back (*drawing 2-A*).

## PROJECT PLANNER

*Time:* 3 days
*Special hardware and tools:*
(1) tube of construction adhesive and caulking gun
(4) 3-in by 3-in. brass-plated butt hinges
(2) 2-in.-dia. hardwood knobs
(8) 2½-in. galvanized bugle-head screws
(20) 1⅝-in. galvanized bugle-head screws
(125) 1¼-in. galvanized bugle-head screws
*Wood:*
(3) 6-ft. 2 × 4 redwood
Cut 2 pieces 72 in. long for back legs/standards. Cut one 2 × 4 into 2 pieces 35¾ in. long for lower front crosspiece and stretcher/bin support.
(2) 8 ft. 2 × 4 redwood
Cut one 2 × 4 into 2 pieces 40¼ in. long for shelf standards. Cut one 2 × 4 into 2 pieces 37¼ in. long for front legs.
(1) 12-ft. 1 × 10 redwood
Cut 3 pieces 34 in. long for upper shelves. From remaining piece rip and joint 3 pieces 1¼ in. wide for face frame, and one piece 1½ in. wide for support cleat for back edge of work surface. Rip 2 pieces ½-in. wide for tool-shelf cleats.
(2) 8-ft. 1 × 6 redwood
From each piece cut one piece 33¼ in. long for upper side rail (2 required), one piece 27 in. long for lower side rail (2 required), and one piece 26 in. long for work surface sides (2 required).
(1) 6-ft.-long 1 × 6 redwood
Rip and joint into 2 pieces 2½ in. wide for X-brace.
(1) 4-ft. by 5½-ft. piece of 3/4-in. medium-density overlay (MDO) plywood
Cut one piece 36 in. × 48 in. across the 4-ft. width, then rip: one piece 24¼ in. wide and crosscut to 35¾ in. long for work surface; one

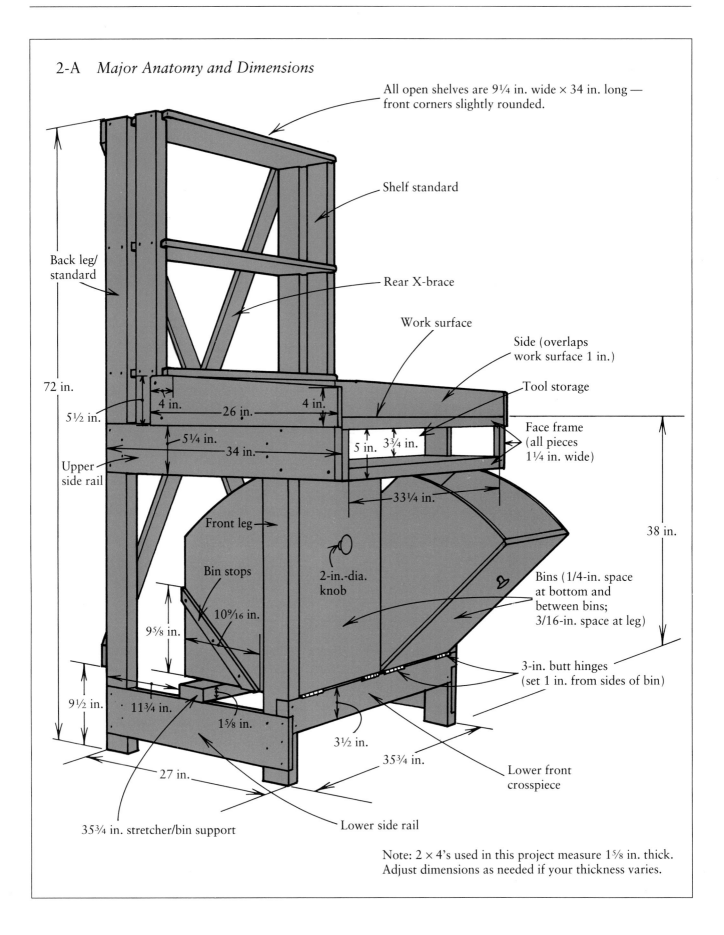

## 2-A  Major Anatomy and Dimensions

All open shelves are 9¼ in. wide × 34 in. long —
front corners slightly rounded.

Shelf standard

Rear X-brace

Work surface

Side (overlaps
work surface 1 in.)

Tool storage

Face frame
(all pieces
1¼ in. wide)

Back leg/
standard

72 in.

5½ in.

4 in.     26 in.     4 in.

5¼ in.

34 in.

5 in.    3¾ in.

Upper
side rail

33¼ in.

Front leg

2-in.-dia.
knob

Bins (1/4-in. space
at bottom and
between bins;
3/16-in. space at leg)

Bin stops

10⁹⁄₁₆ in.

9⅝ in.

38 in.

9½ in.    11¾ in.

1⅝ in.

3-in. butt hinges
(set 1 in. from sides of bin)

3½ in.

35¾ in.

Lower front
crosspiece

27 in.

35¾ in. stretcher/bin support

Lower side rail

Note: 2 × 4's used in this project measure 1⅝ in. thick.
Adjust dimensions as needed if your thickness varies.

## Side Frame Assembly

To get started I want to make the legs and shelf standards from some redwood 2 × 4s (*drawings 2-A and 2-B*). The back leg and back shelf standard are all one piece (*drawing 2-B*). On my power miter box, I cut 2 pieces 72 in. long for the back legs and 2 pieces 37¼ in. long for the front legs. For the shelf standards, I cut 2 pieces 40¼ in. long (see Project Planner).

With these 6 parts cut to length, I'm ready to mill some dadoes and rabbets. I have to cut 3/4-in. by 3/4-in. dadoes for the shelves and some 3/4-in. by 5½-in. dadoes for the upper and lower side rails that tie the legs together (*drawings 2-A and 2-B*). On the bottom ends of the shelf standards and the top ends of the front legs, I mill 3/4-in. by 5½-in. rabbets for the upper rail. And at the top ends of the back legs and shelf standards, I mill 3/4-in. by 3/4-in. rabbets for the top shelf.

There are 3 power tools I could choose from to cut these dadoes and rabbets. One choice would be a router and a straightedge. The problem with this setup is it takes a long time. You have to reposition, square up, and reclamp the straightedge every place you want to cut. The table saw is another alternative that works pretty well but the layout lines have to face down and it's difficult to keep the cut straight and true when cutting with the miter gauge, especially on long stock like the back legs of the workbench. The best choice for cutting dadoes in long stock is the radial-arm saw. The layout lines can face up and the wood stays put while the saw moves.

To cut the dadoes, I install a stack dado head cutter on the radial-arm saw arbor. This tool has 7 components: 2 circular-saw blades with 5 chippers that fit in between the blades. It can cut dadoes up to 13/16 in. wide. Here's how I set it up for a 3/4-in.-wide cut: First, I install one of the blades, which cuts a 1/8-in.-wide kerf. Then, I install 4 chippers, staggering them so the cutter will be balanced. Each chipper makes a 1/8-in.-wide cut. Finally, I put on the second saw blade. The combined widths of both blades and the chippers add up to 3/4 in. I thread the nut on the arbor, put the guard back on, and I'm ready to go.

With a pencil and square, I lay out the dadoes and rabbets. Then I set the radial-arm saw for a 3/4-in.-deep cut and mill all the joints (*photo 2-1*). I have to make multiple crosscuts for the 5½-in.-wide dadoes and rabbets.

I have to cut dadoes in the front legs for the lower front crosspiece (*drawings 2-A and 2-B*). The depth of these dadoes must equal the thickness of the crosspiece — about 1⅝ in. This depth exceeds the capacity of my 7-in. dado head, so I'll have to resort to my table saw for cutting these dadoes. With a regular crosscutting blade on the saw, I make repeated crosscuts to "nibble away" the width of the dado a little at a time (*photo 2-2*). I raise the blade 1⅝ in. above the table and feed the stock with the miter gauge. I push the wood through and

piece 7 in. wide and crosscut to 35¾ in. long for backsplash; one piece 5½ in. wide and crosscut to 34¼ in. long for back of tool storage compartment; one piece 9¾ in. wide and crosscut to 34¼ in. long for tool storage shelf. Rip remaining piece along short side into: 2 pieces 16 in. wide and crosscut to 22 in. long for bin fronts; one piece 15½ in. wide and crosscut into 2 pieces 14¾ in. long for bin bottoms. Use scrap to make stops for bins.

(1) 4-ft. by 4-ft. piece of 1/2-in. MDO plywood

Rip one piece 15½ in. wide and crosscut into 2 pieces 16¾ in. long for bin backs. Rip 2 pieces 15⅝ in. wide and crosscut into 4 pieces 22 in. long for bin sides.

**2-1** The radial-arm saw is ideal for milling the dadoes in the workbench legs. I set my stack dado head for a 3/4-in.-deep cut and make multiple crosscuts to complete the 5½ -in.-wide dadoes and rabbets.

**2-2** The 1⅝-in.-deep dadoes in the front legs for the lower front crosspiece are too deep to cut with the dado head. With a regular table-saw blade, I make repeated crosscuts to "nibble away" the width of the dado a little at a time.

**2-3** I chamfer the bottom corners of the legs with a block plane to keep the corners from chipping when the legs slide across the floor.

move it over a little as I bring it back so that the blade doesn't cut on the backstroke.

Using the same nibbling technique, I mill a 3/4- by 2⅛-in. rabbet on each end of the 35¾-in.-long lower front crosspiece (*drawing 2-B*). These rabbets allow the ends of the crosspiece to fit over the lower side rails (*drawing 2-A*).

Now I'm almost ready to assemble the side frames, but first I want to relieve the sharp corners at the bottom ends of the legs. I learned from experience that these sharp corners will chip and break off when you slide the legs across the floor. To prevent this from happening I chamfer the edges all the way around with a block plane (*photo 2-3*).

With the side rails cut to length (see Project Planner), I'm ready for some assembly. I'm going to put the 2 side frames together, assembling the joints with construction adhesive and 1¼-in. galvanized bugle-head screws. I put the frames together one at a time.

I put a front leg and back leg on the bench and spread some construction adhesive in the rail dadoes. First, I install the lower side rail. I predrill and install 4 screws in each joint. The upper side rail goes on

## 2-B  *Side-Frame Assembly*

(All dadoes and rabbets are 3/4 in. deep except as noted.)

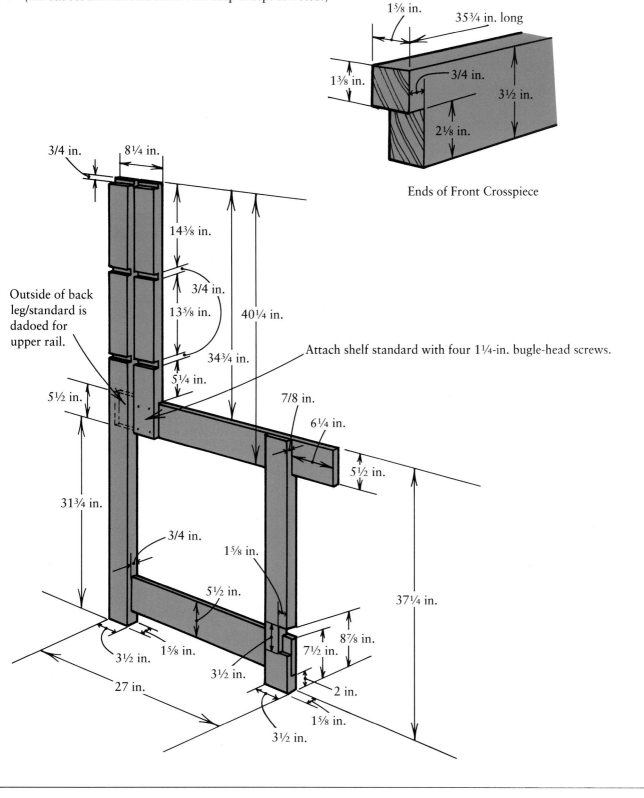

1⅝ in.

35¾ in. long

1⅜ in.

3/4 in.

3½ in.

2⅛ in.

Ends of Front Crosspiece

3/4 in.

8¼ in.

14⅜ in.

3/4 in.

13⅝ in.

40¼ in.

Outside of back leg/standard is dadoed for upper rail.

34¾ in.

Attach shelf standard with four 1¼-in. bugle-head screws.

5¼ in.

5½ in.

7/8 in.

6¼ in.

5½ in.

31¾ in.

3/4 in.

1⅝ in.

5½ in.

37¼ in.

8⅞ in.

7½ in.

3½ in.

1⅝ in.

3½ in.

2 in.

27 in.

1⅝ in.

3½ in.

next with 4 screws in each end. I hold the front leg 6¼ in. back from the front end of the upper side rail (*drawing 2-E*).

The next piece to install is the front shelf standard (*drawings 2-A and 2-B*). The front edge of this piece should be 8¼ in. from the back edge of the back leg/standard (*drawing 2-B*). I glue and attach the standard to the upper rail with four 1¼-in. screws in predrilled countersunk holes, making sure it's square to the rail.

### Installing the Shelves

With both side frames assembled, I'm ready to make and install the shelves. On my radial-arm saw I crosscut three 34-in.-long shelves from 1 × 10 redwood (see Project Planner). Next, I round the front corners of the shelves with a drum sander in the drill press. A belt sander would also work fine.

If the door to your shop is less than 3 ft. wide, don't glue anything from this point on or you won't get the workbench out of your shop. Just preassemble the pieces for now and glue them together later.

To install the shelves, I clamp one of the side frames on edge and spread some construction adhesive in the shelf dadoes and the rabbet for the top shelf. I put the shelves in position, flushing up the back edge of the shelf with the back edge of the back leg/standard. For the 2 lower shelves, I drill through the front and back standards into the ends of the shelves — two 1⅝-in. screws in each standard. The top shelf gets two 1⅝-in. screws in each end. Then, at each end, I drill 2 holes through the top of the shelf and install 1¼-in. screws into the end of the standard.

When the shelves are all in, I can install the other side frame, gluing and screwing the shelves to the standards. The lower front crosspiece goes in next, with adhesive and 2½-in. screws to secure it in place.

Now I can set the workbench frame upright on the floor. Holding my tape on the back edge of the back legs I measure 11¾ in. along each lower side rail to mark the location of the stretcher/bin support (*drawing 2-A*). This piece of 2 × 4 adds some stability to the base but, more important, it supports the backs of the bins when they're closed. I cut this 35¾-in.-long piece from a redwood 2 × 4 and fasten it to the lower side rails with adhesive and 2½-in. screws, positioning the back edge of the stretcher on the layout line.

### X-Brace

The back of the workbench is reinforced with a simple X-brace half lapped in the middle, where the 2 pieces join, and attached to the backs of the shelves and the frame with screws (*drawings 2-A and 2-C*).

From a 6-ft. length of 1 × 6 redwood, I rip and joint 2 pieces 2½ in. wide (see Project Planner). To lay out the X-brace, I put a center mark on both ends of each piece. With the workbench front down on the floor, I clamp one of the X-brace pieces diagonally across the

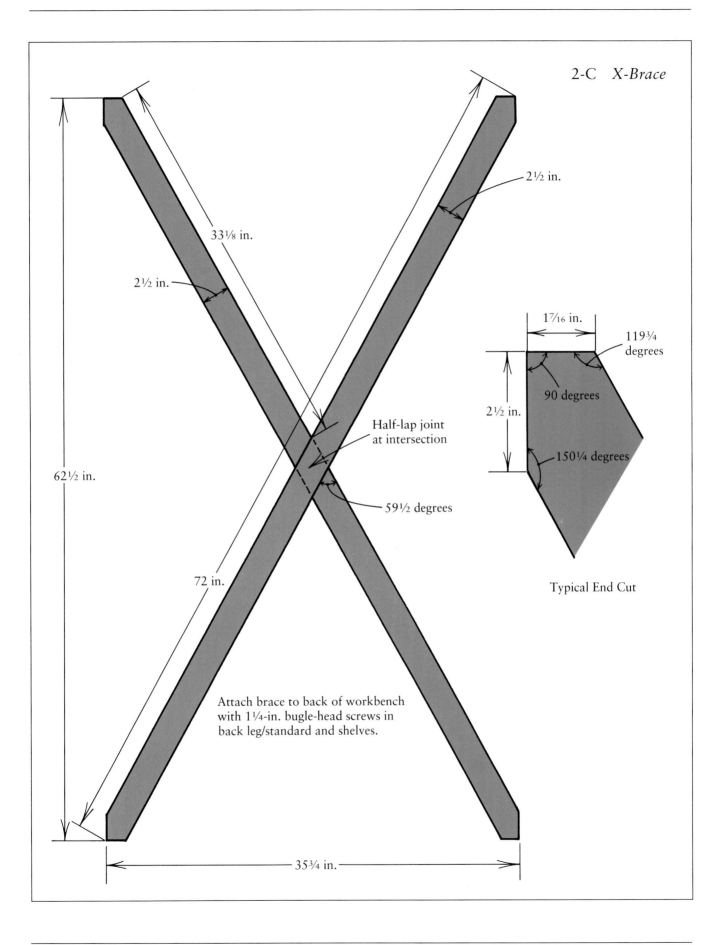

2½ in.

33⅛ in.

2½ in.

62½ in.

Half-lap joint
at intersection

59½ degrees

72 in.

Attach brace to back of workbench
with 1¼-in. bugle-head screws in
back leg/standard and shelves.

35¾ in.

1⁷⁄₁₆ in.

119¾
degrees

90 degrees

2½ in.

150¼ degrees

Typical End Cut

**2-4** With the X-brace clamped to the back of the workbench frame I run a pencil along the sides of each board to mark the angle of the dadoes I'll need to cut for the half-lap joint.

back. At one end, I align the center mark with the corner of the back standard. At the bottom, I align the center mark with a pencil mark 9½ in. up from the bottom of the back leg (*drawing 2-A*). Next, I place the second piece on top of the first and clamp it diagonally across the opposite corners. I align the center marks in the same way and clamp it at the ends.

Now I can mark out the half lap where the 2 pieces cross. I run a pencil along the sides of each board to mark the angle of the dadoes I'll need to cut for the half-lap joint (*photo 2-4*). I also mark off angled cuts at the ends of the brace by running my pencil along the legs and top shelf (*drawing 2-C*).

I cut the half lap with the dado head on my radial-arm saw, setting the saw-arm angle to match the layout lines I marked on the wood (59½ degrees). I adjust the blade height for a 3/8-in.-deep cut and mill a dado in each piece.

I make the angled end cuts on the X-brace pieces with the table saw (*drawing 2-C*). I set the miter gauge to the required angle for each cut. For some cuts, I need to move the miter gauge to the right of the blade. I could also use a jigsaw or a hand saw.

With the half lap completed and the corners all cut, I'm ready to install the X-brace. I spread construction adhesive in the half lap and assemble the joint. Then I attach the brace to the back of the workbench with some 1¼-in. galvanized screws. I put 2 screws at each end of the brace and a couple more into the backs of the 2 lower shelves.

## Work Surface Assembly

On the table saw, I rip the work surface, the backsplash, the back of the tool storage compartment, and the tool shelf from a piece of 3/4-in. MDO board (see Project Planner). I crosscut the work surface and backsplash pieces to 35¾ in. long — the width of the workbench frame — and set the other 2 pieces aside for the moment.

The backsplash needs to have a 3/4-in by 1¾-in. notch cut at each bottom corner to fit over the side rails. I mark out these notches with a pencil and square and make the cuts on the table saw. I make the 1¾-in. cut with the miter gauge. For the little 3/4-in. cut, I use a hand saw.

Now I'm ready to install the backsplash. I drill and install two 1¼-in. screws into each end, fastening the backsplash to the front shelf standards. I decided not to use construction adhesive here or on the work surface. That's because I might have to replace these 2 pieces someday — say maybe 20 years from now — as they deteriorate from moisture and use.

The back of the tool storage compartment goes on next. I measure between the 2 side rails and trim the piece to length — 34¼ in. in this case. I position the compartment back against the backs of the front legs, flush to the top of the rails (*drawing 2-E*). Then I predrill and install two 1¼-in. screws in each end.

The tool storage shelf and the back edge of the work surface will rest on cleats (*drawings 2-D and 2-E*). To make the cleat for the work surface, I rip, joint, and crosscut a 3/4-in. by 1½-in. by 32¾-in. strip of redwood. I screw it to the backsplash with five 1¼-in. screws, holding the top edge of the cleat 5¼ in. below the top edge of the backsplash (*drawing 2-D*).

To make the cleats that support the tool shelf, I rip two 1/2-in by 3/4-in. strips of redwood (see Project Planner). I crosscut one piece 32½ in. long, the distance between the 2 front legs. I run a bead of adhesive along the narrow edge of this back cleat and fasten it to the bottom edge of the tool compartment back with some 1¼-in. galvanized finishing nails. I cut 2 shorter cleats 6¼ in. long and fasten these to the bottom edge of the upper side rails (*photo 2-5*).

I cut the tool shelf to a length of 34¼ in. and cut two 7/8-in. by 3½-in. notches at each back corner to fit around the legs (*drawing 2-E*). Then I run a bead of adhesive along the top edges of the cleats and position the shelf on the cleats. To hold it in place for keeps, I drive a 1¼-in. screw through the side rails into each front corner of the shelf.

2-5   The ends of the tool compartment shelf rest on 1/2-in. by 3/4-in. by 6¼-in. redwood cleats fastened to the upper side rails with construction adhesive and nails.

## 2-D  *Work Surface/Backsplash Detail*

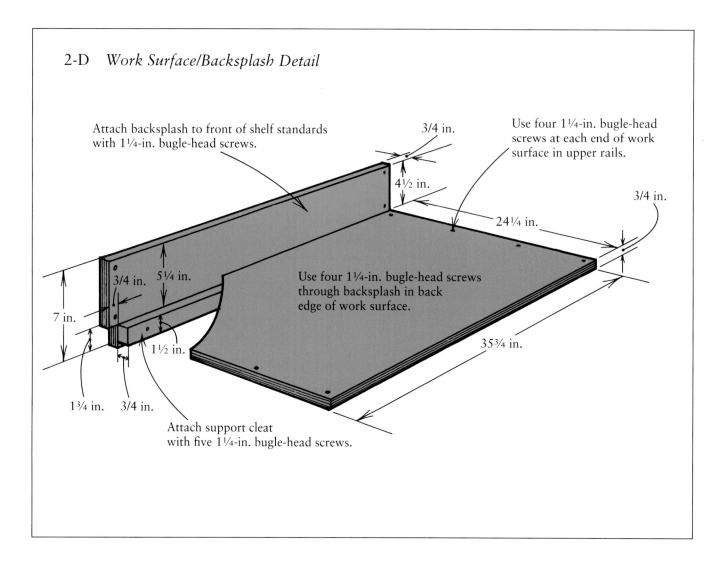

Attach backsplash to front of shelf standards with 1¼-in. bugle-head screws.

3/4 in.

Use four 1¼-in. bugle-head screws at each end of work surface in upper rails.

4½ in.

3/4 in.

24¼ in.

3/4 in.

5¼ in.

Use four 1¼-in. bugle-head screws through backsplash in back edge of work surface.

7 in.

1½ in.

35¾ in.

1¾ in.    3/4 in.

Attach support cleat with five 1¼-in. bugle-head screws.

Now I'm ready to install the work surface. Remember, I don't want to glue it to the rails, but I will run a bead of construction adhesive along the back edge to seal the joint between the work surface and the backsplash. This will keep water from rotting out the edge of the plywood. Now I place the work surface in position, pushing it tight against the backsplash. I fasten it to the side rails with 4 screws in each edge.

Crawling underneath the back of the workbench, I predrill through the backsplash into the back edge of the work surface and install four 1¼-in. screws. I'm careful to center the screws with respect to the thickness of the work surface.

To seal up the front edges of the work surface and tool shelf, I'm going to install a face frame of 3/4-in. by 1¼-in. redwood strips (*drawing 2-A*). I rip and joint 3 pieces to size and cut one piece 35¾ in. long for the top piece. I fasten this strip to the front edge of the work surface with adhesive and nails, keeping the top edge flush with the work surface.

## 2-E  Tool Storage Details

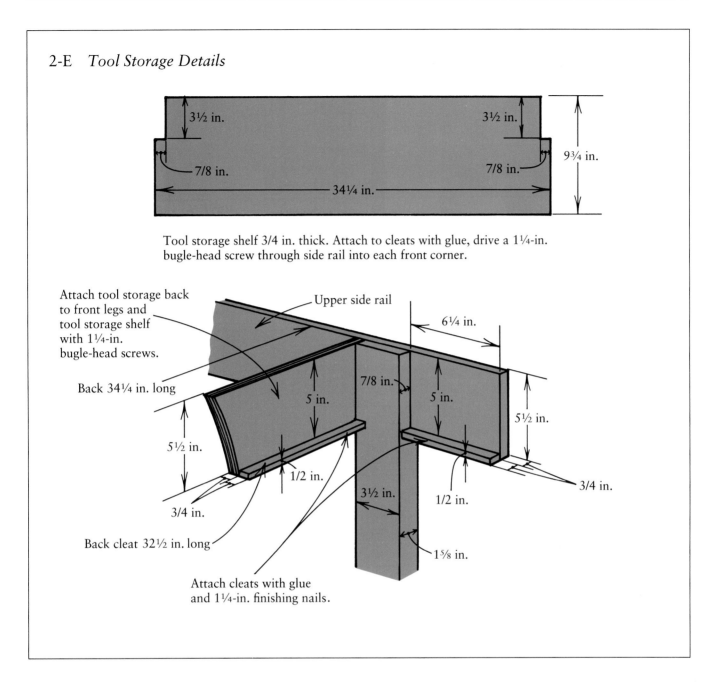

Tool storage shelf 3/4 in. thick. Attach to cleats with glue, drive a 1¼-in. bugle-head screw through side rail into each front corner.

Next, I cut two 5-in.-long pieces for the sides of the face frame. I glue and nail these pieces to the ends of the upper side rails. Then I cut and install the bottom piece of the face frame. This 33¼-in.-long piece gets fastened to the edge of the tool shelf.

To complete the work surface assembly, I need to make the 2 redwood side pieces (*drawing 2-A*). These sides are 5½ in. wide at the back end, tapering to 4 in. wide at the front. The taper starts 4 in. from the back end.

I cut these tapers on the table saw with a tapering jig I bought at my hardware store (*photo 2-6*). It works just like my shop-built wooden tapering jig (see Chapter 3, "Wooden Wheelbarrow").

**2-6** A tapering jig makes it easy to cut the tapered sides of the work surface. I adjust the angle of the jig until the layout line is parallel with the rip fence.

**2-7** After sawing the tapers on the side pieces, I smooth up the cuts on the jointer.

## 2-F   Bin Components

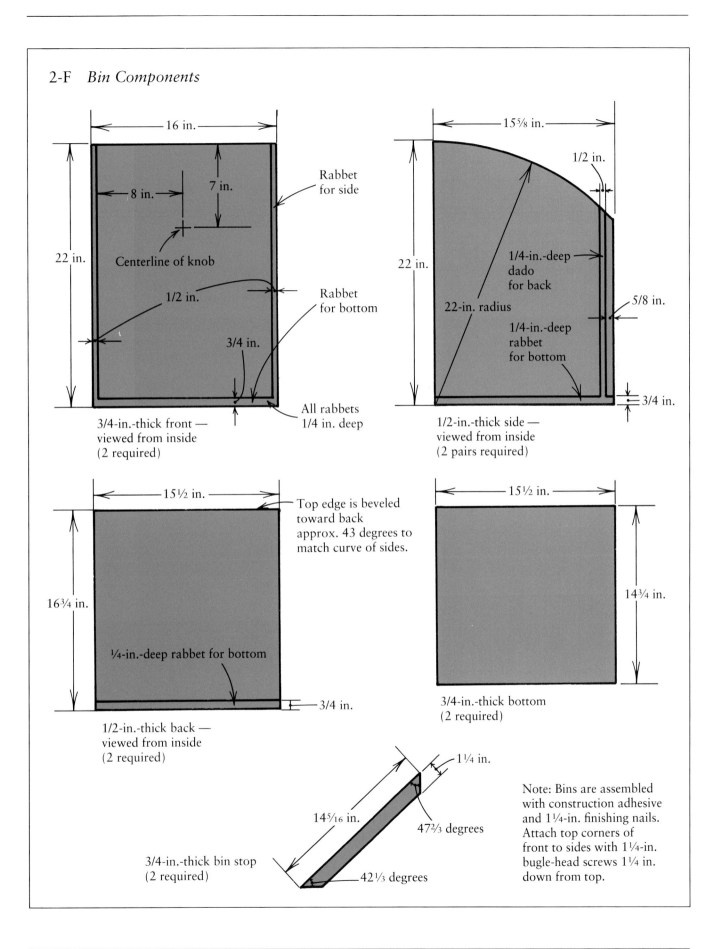

16 in.

8 in.

7 in.

Rabbet for side

Centerline of knob

22 in.

1/2 in.

Rabbet for bottom

3/4 in.

All rabbets 1/4 in. deep

3/4-in.-thick front — viewed from inside (2 required)

15⅝ in.

1/2 in.

1/4-in.-deep dado for back

22 in.

22-in. radius

5/8 in.

1/4-in.-deep rabbet for bottom

3/4 in.

1/2-in.-thick side — viewed from inside (2 pairs required)

15½ in.

Top edge is beveled toward back approx. 43 degrees to match curve of sides.

16¾ in.

¼-in.-deep rabbet for bottom

3/4 in.

1/2-in.-thick back — viewed from inside (2 required)

15½ in.

14¾ in.

3/4-in.-thick bottom (2 required)

1¼ in.

14⁵⁄₁₆ in.

47⅔ degrees

3/4-in.-thick bin stop (2 required)

42⅓ degrees

Note: Bins are assembled with construction adhesive and 1¼-in. finishing nails. Attach top corners of front to sides with 1¼-in. bugle-head screws 1¼ in. down from top.

**2-8** All I need to draw the arc on the storage bin sides is my tape measure and a pencil. I hold the 22-in. mark of my tape measure on one corner and hold a pencil at the end. I swing the pencil to draw the 22-in.-radius arc.

**2-9** After laying out the arc, I saw out the curve with my jigsaw. Note that I've clamped 2 sides together and I am sawing through both at once. This makes a perfectly matched pair.

**2-10** I clamp all 4 bin sides together and sand them all at the same time. This provides a wide base, which makes it easy to hold the belt sander square.

To set up the jig, I lay out the taper on one of the side pieces. Then I place the workpiece in the jig with the front and (narrow end) against the tapering jig's stop. With the side of the jig against the rip fence, I adjust the angle of the jig until the layout line on the wood is parallel to the rip fence. I check by measuring from the layout line to the fence at both ends of the line. When the layout line is parallel to the fence, I lock the jig's adjustment nut. Then I position the rip fence so the blade will cut to the layout line. I use this setting to taper both sides. Then I make a single pass over the jointer, wide end first, to smooth up the saw cut (*photo 2-7*).

**2-11**  To cut the rabbets on the bottom of the bin sides, I clamp an auxiliary wooden fence to my rip fence. This allows me to position the fence up against the cutter without damaging the metal rip fence or the blade.

I attach the side pieces to the edge of the work surface and ends of the backsplash with some 1¼-in. bugle-head screws. The bottom edge of the work surface sides is positioned 5¼ in. up from the bottom edge of the upper side rails (*drawing 2-A*).

*Making the Bins*

The 2 storage bins at the bottom of the workbench are made from MDO board. The fronts and bottoms of the bins are made from 3/4-in. MDO board. The sides and backs are made from 1/2-in. MDO board. The bins pivot forward on standard 3-in. butt hinges screwed to the lower front crosspiece (*drawing 2-A*).

The sides of the bins must be curved at the top so they can clear the bottom of the face frame when the bins pivot out (*drawings 2-A and 2-F*). To make the sides, I cut 4 pieces 15⅝ × 22 in. from 1/2-in. MDO board (see Project Planner). Then I clamp 2 of the sides together on my bench.

To lay out the curve, all I need is my tape measure and a pencil. With my left hand, I hold the 22-in. mark on one corner of the MDO board. With the other hand, I hold a pencil against the end of the tape and swing it to draw a 22-in.-radius arc (*photo 2-8*). I cut along the pencil line with my jigsaw, sawing through both side pieces at once (*photo 2-9*). I mark these 2 bin sides as a matched pair and repeat the process to cut the other 2 sides.

When all 4 sides are cut, I clamp them all together and sand the curved edges with a belt sander (*photo 2-10*). The wider the base is for the sander, the easier it is to keep everything nice and square.

The bottom of each bin sits in 1/4-in. by 3/4-in. rabbets in the sides, front, and back. To mill these rabbets, I mount my stack dado

2-12 The bottom of the bin goes on last, with construction adhesive and screws to secure it in place.

head on the table-saw arbor and screw a wooden auxiliary fence to the rip fence (*photo 2-11*). This wooden fence protects the metal rip fence from the dado head and allows me to position the fence right up against the edge of the cutter. I raise the blade for a 1/4-in.-deep cut and mill a rabbet along the bottom edges of all the sides, backs, and fronts (*drawing 2-F*).

I adjust the fence to expose only 1/2 in. of the cutter. With this setup, I mill 1/2-in.-wide rabbets along the inside side edges of the bin fronts (*drawing 2-F*). The bin sides will fit into these rabbets.

Next, I reset my dado head for a 1/2-in.-wide cut and mill a 1/4-in. by 1/2-in. groove along the back edges of the side pieces (*drawing 2-F*). The back panel will fit into this groove. I set the rip fence 5/8 in. from the blade to make this cut.

There's one more cut I need to make before I can assemble the bins, and that's a bevel cut along the top edge of the back panels to match the curve of the sides (*drawing 2-F*). I tilt the table-saw blade 43 degrees and set the rip fence 16¾ in. from the blade (measured at the surface of the saw table). I bevel the top edge of each panel, making sure to hold the rabbets facedown against the table.

**2-13** A wooden cleat, screwed to the outer side of each bin, butts against the front leg to keep the bin from falling completely open.

Now I'm ready to put the bins together. I use construction adhesive and some 1¼-in. galvanized finishing nails. With the front facedown on the bench, I glue and nail on the sides, toeing the nails to get a good hold in the front panel. Then I put in the back of the bin. The bottom goes on last (*photo 2-12*). The upper front corners of the bin bear a lot of stress when the bin is opened. To reinforce these points, I measure down 1¼ in. from the top and predrill and install a 1¼-in. galvanized bugle-head screw through the bin front into the side.

Next, I drill a 1/4-in.-dia. hole in the front of each bin and install a knob. I locate the hole 7 in. from the top edge and 8 in. from the sides (*drawing 2-F*).

To mount the bins on the workbench, I have to attach the 3-in. butt hinges on which the bins pivot. The hinges are just surface mounted — there's no need to mortise them. I secure the hinges to the bottoms of the bins first, setting them in 1 in. from each side. To make sure that the pilot holes for the screws are centered in the hinge holes, I use a special drilling device called a vix bit. This consists of a drill bit inside a spring-loaded sleeve. You place the end of the sleeve into the hinge holes and push. The sleeve retracts and the bit drills a perfectly centered pilot hole.

I remove the hinge pins and secure the mating-hinge leaves to the lower front crosspiece. The outer 2 hinges must be set in 1³/₁₆ in. from the front legs to provide 3/16-in. clearance between the bin sides and the legs (*drawing 2-A*). With the hinges installed, I put the bins in position and tap the hinge pins in place.

Only one thing more: I install a 3/4-in. by 1¼-in. wooden stop on the outside of each bin (*drawings 2-A and 2-F*). When a bin is opened, this stop hits the back of the front leg to keep the bin from falling all the way out.

I cut the stops to length, making angled cuts on the ends as shown (*drawing 2-F*). To install the stops, I measure and mark the end points of the stop on the outer side of each bin (*drawing 2-A*). Then I open each bin to line up these marks with the back edge of the front leg and install a clamp to hold it open (*photo 2-13*). I position the stop against the back of the front leg and screw it to the side of the bin with 3 screws.

You know, judging from the enthusiastic response I've gotten from all the gardeners around here, I have a feeling I'll be building a couple more of these workbenches before too long.

# 3

# *Wooden Wheelbarrow*

THE humble wooden wheelbarrow was an important tool in New England history. Every farm, mill, and factory from Connecticut to Maine had a wheelbarrow of some sort or another. Wheelbarrows were so important, in fact, that specialized types evolved to carry different kinds of loads. Field workers used harvesting wheelbarrows with cradlelike beds to hold long sheaves of grain. Farmers had barrows with sides that lifted off for toting firewood and other large loads.

The wheelbarrow is descended from the hand barrow, a wide board with a pair of handles on either end. It took two people to carry a hand barrow and they had to bear the entire weight of the load on their arms — no small feat with a big load of stones or bricks. The wheelbarrow improved on the hand barrow concept by using the principle of leverage to reduce the amount of force it took to lift the load. One person with a wheelbarrow could move as much weight as two people could with a hand barrow. No doubt about it, the wheelbarrow was a definite improvement.

The wooden wheelbarrow shown here was inspired by a trip to the Sloane/Stanley Museum in Kent, Connecticut. There I had the chance to examine several old wooden wheelbarrows from the collection of Eric Sloane, famous artist, writer, and tool collector. I borrowed the best features of some of the antique wheelbarrows and added a modern pneumatic tire to come up with a practical and serviceable wheelbarrow that's made mostly of red oak. The sides are removable for carrying large items like a bale of hay or peat moss, and it will also hold a lot of firewood. But the thing that I really like about this wheelbarrow, compared to its commercial cousins, is that it's pretty to look at.

## PROJECT PLANNER

*Time:* 5 days

*Special hardware and tools:*

(1) 9¾-in. length of 5/8-in.-dia. smooth, zinc-plated steel rod for axle

(1) 3-ft. length of 1/4-in.-dia. zinc-plated threaded rod

Cut one piece 10 in. long for front frame connector. Cut 2 pieces 13 in. long for side retainer rods.

(1) 5-ft. length of 1/8-in. by 1¼-in. galvanized flat steel

Cut 2 pieces 16¼ in. long for front braces. Cut 2 pieces 4 in. long for axle straps. Cut 2 pieces 7 in. long for stake brackets.

(1) 4.80/4.00-8 tire and wheel (sold as replacement for a contractor's wheelbarrow)

(1) 8-in. length of 3/4 E.M.T. conduit

Cut 2 pieces to fit for wheel spacers.

(1) 1/4-in. by 1-in. zinc-plated carriage bolt

(6) 1/4-in. by 2-in. zinc-plated carriage bolts

(6) 1/4-in. by 2½-in. zinc-plated carriage bolts

(2) 1/4-in. by 3-in. zinc-plated carriage bolts

(2) 1/4-in. by 3½-in. zinc-plated carriage bolts

(4) 1/4-in. by 4-in. zinc-plated carriage bolts

(25) 1/4-in. zinc-plated flat washers

(27) 1/4-in. zinc-plated hex nuts

(8) 1/4-in. by 1½-in. zinc-plated lag screws

(34) 1¼-in. #8 stainless steel flathead wood screws

(2) 2-in. #8 stainless steel flathead wood screws

(1) tube of construction adhesive and caulking gun

*Wood:*

(1) 6-ft. 8/4 × 6 red oak

Plane to 1⅝ in. thickness. Then rip, joint, and crosscut 2 pieces 1⅝ in. thick × 2½ in. wide × 60 in. long for handles. Use remainder to make front of frame.

(1) 6-ft. 8/4 × 4 red oak

Plane to 1⅝ in. thickness. Cut one piece 18 in. long. Rip into 2 tapered legs as explained in text. Rip and joint remainder into 2 pieces 1⅝ in. wide and cut 2 pieces 25 in. long for bed side pieces. Cut 2 pieces 23 in. long for bed front and back pieces.

(1) 2-ft. 1 × 12 red oak

Rip and joint to 11⅛ in. wide for front panel.

(1) 5-ft. 1 × 10 red oak

Cut 2 pieces 30 in. long for side boards.

(1) 12-ft. 1 × 4 red oak

Cut one piece 51 in. long. Then rip and joint one piece 1¾ in. wide and one piece 1½ in. wide. From 1¾-in.-wide length cut 2 pieces 22 in. long for X-braces. From 1½-in.-wide piece cut 2 pieces 25 in. long for struts.

Cut one piece 2 in. long. Then rip and joint one piece 1⅝ in. wide and one piece 1¼ in. wide for wedges for front panel. From 1¼-in.-wide piece cut 2 pieces 9 in. long for side stiffeners.

Cut one piece 22 in. long. Then rip and joint 2 pieces 1¼ in. wide for upper and lower front channels.

Cut one piece 25 in. long. Then rip and joint one piece 2 in. wide and one piece 3/4 in. wide. Cut 2 pieces 12 in. long from each piece for side stakes and side retainers.

(1) 3/4-in. medium-density overlay (MDO) plywood

Cut to 20 in. × 22 in.

The wheelbarrow has a lot of compound angles, which make it somewhat tricky to build. But with a power miter box to cut accurate angles, the joinery isn't any trouble: it just takes a little thought.

To get started on this project, the first thing I do is cut all the pieces of oak I need for the wheelbarrow to the dimensions shown in the Project Planner. Later, I mill each part to fit as explained below.

## Building the Frame

With all the oak parts cut to size, I'm ready to start fine-tuning the pieces to make the frame. I start with the 2 long pieces for the handles (*drawings 3-A and 3-B*). The front end of each handle is cut to an 84-degree angle (*drawing 3-B*). This angled cut is best made on the power miter box. I set the pointer on the miter-box scale 6 degrees from the zero mark. The remaining angle between the blade and the fence is 84 degrees — just what I want. I cut the front end of each handle. That takes care of the handles for now. I'll shape the grips at the opposite ends later.

The next frame piece is the short front piece that connects the 2 handles at the front (*drawings 3-A and 3-B*). The ends of this piece need to be cut at a 96-degree angle, which is the complementary angle of 84 degrees. With the miter box still set for an 84-degree cut, I trim one end of this front piece.

Now, if I examine this angled cut for a minute, I find that one corner measures 84 degrees, but the other corner — the complementary angle — measures 96 degrees. Laying my measuring tape on the 96-degree corner, I measure off 9 in. and make a pencil mark to mark the location of my second cut. I draw an angled mark on the top of the piece to make sure I cut at the correct angle and cut the other end to 96 degrees on my miter box. The finished piece should measure 9 in. in length from short point to short point (*drawing 3-B*).

The next step to making the front piece is to lay out and cut an angled rabbet at each end to fit over the front ends of the handles (*drawings 3-A and 3-B*). Each rabbet requires 2 cuts on the table saw — a crosscut with the stock held flat on the saw, and a rip cut with the stock on end, supported by a tenoning jig.

To make the crosscut, I tilt my table-saw blade 6 degrees and raise the blade to a height of 1 in. Then I make a cut on each end of the front piece, supporting the stock against the miter gauge (*photo 3-1*).

For the rip cut, I tilt the blade back to 90 degrees and clamp the front piece on end in my tenoning jig (*photo 3-1*). The long point of the end touches the table. I raise the blade high enough to meet the first cut (the thickness of the handle stock) and make a cut on both ends.

While I'm at the table saw, I want to make a 5/16-in. by 5/16-in. groove centered on the inside face of the front piece for a threaded rod that will hold the front of the frame together (*drawing 3-B*). Because I

3-A  *Major Anatomy and Dimensions*

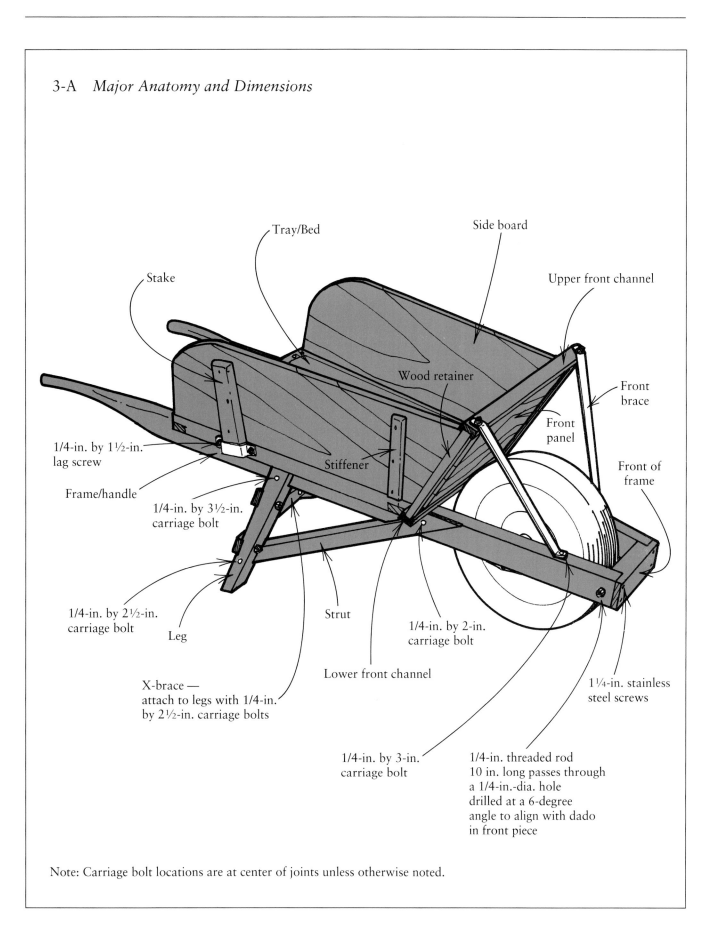

Tray/Bed

Side board

Stake

Upper front channel

Wood retainer

Front brace

Front panel

1/4-in. by 1½-in. lag screw

Front of frame

Frame/handle

Stiffener

1/4-in. by 3½-in. carriage bolt

1/4-in. by 2½-in. carriage bolt

Leg

Strut

1/4-in. by 2-in. carriage bolt

1¼-in. stainless steel screws

Lower front channel

X-brace — attach to legs with 1/4-in. by 2½-in. carriage bolts

1/4-in. by 3-in. carriage bolt

1/4-in. threaded rod 10 in. long passes through a 1/4-in.-dia. hole drilled at a 6-degree angle to align with dado in front piece

Note: Carriage bolt locations are at center of joints unless otherwise noted.

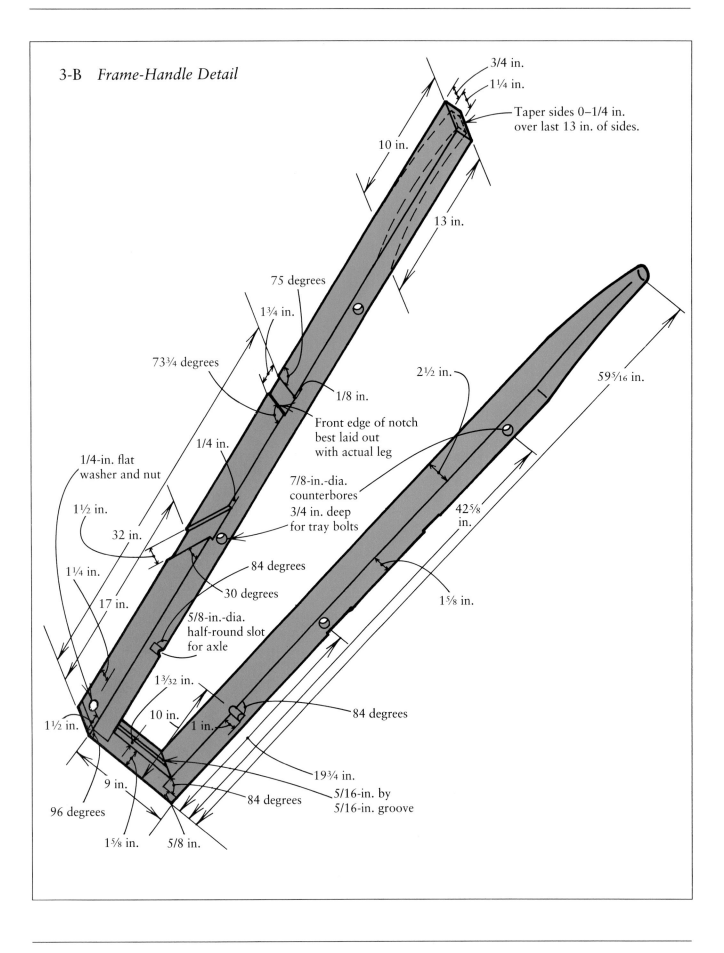

3-B *Frame-Handle Detail*

3/4 in.
1¼ in.

Taper sides 0–1/4 in.
over last 13 in. of sides.

10 in.

13 in.

75 degrees

1¾ in.

73¾ degrees

1/8 in.

2½ in.

59⁵⁄₁₆ in.

Front edge of notch
best laid out
with actual leg

1/4 in.

1/4-in. flat
washer and nut

7/8-in.-dia.
counterbores
3/4 in. deep
for tray bolts

42⁵⁄₈
in.

1½ in.

32 in.

84 degrees

30 degrees

1¼ in.

1⁵⁄₈ in.

17 in.

5/8-in.-dia.
half-round slot
for axle

1³⁄₃₂ in.

84 degrees

1½ in.

10 in.

1 in.

19¾ in.

9 in.

5/16-in. by
5/16-in. groove

96 degrees

84 degrees

1⁵⁄₈ in.

5/8 in.

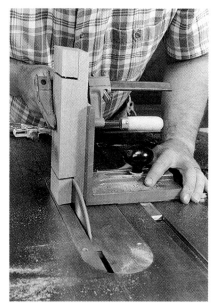

have only one groove to cut, I do it with my regular carbide saw blade. To keep the groove centered, I make one cut, then flip the stock end-for-end and make a second cut. I move the fence in or out as needed to get the finished width I need and repeat the process, cutting first from one end, then from the other.

## Making the Legs

Now for the legs. I cut both legs from a single piece of red oak 1⅝ in. thick × 4 in. wide × 18 in. long as explained in the Project Planner. The front edge of each leg is tapered — the legs are 1¾ in. wide at the top and 1¼ in. wide at the bottom (*drawing 3-C*). To cut this taper, I'll use my shop-made tapering jig on the table saw (*photo 3-2*).

My tapering jig consists of 2 long pieces of oak, about 30 in. long and 3⅛ in. wide. The pieces are hinged at one end like a capital letter V. At the other end, I've installed an adjustment bar that allows me to cut a variety of tapers by adjusting the spread of the V. The adjustment bar is just a piece of oak measuring 1½ in. × 9½ in., with a 1/4-in.-wide by 7-in.-long slot down the middle. One end of the adjustment bar is screwed permanently to one of the long pieces. A bolt in the other long piece sticks up through the slot. A wing nut on the bolt tightens down on the adjustment bar to lock the setting. A stop block is screwed to the side of the piece with the bolt.

To set up the jig, I first lay out the tapers of both legs on the top and ends of the stock as shown (*photo 3-4 and drawing 3-C*). Then I place the leg blank in the jig with the bottom end of one leg against the tapering jig's stop. With the side of the jig positioned against the rip fence, I adjust the opening of the jig until the taper line on the leg nearest the fence is parallel to the rip fence. I check by measuring from the layout line to the fence at both ends of the leg (*photo 3-3*). When

**3-2** The front edge of each leg is tapered, so I use my shop-made tapering jig to cut both legs from a single piece of red oak.

**3-3** To set up the jig, I lay out the tapers on the top and ends of the stock. Then I measure from the layout line to the fence at both ends of the leg and adjust the opening of the jig until the layout line is parallel to the blade.

**3-4** With the side of the tapering jig against the rip fence, I move the fence until the taper line on the end lines up with the blade. I cut one leg, then turn the stock around and cut the other.

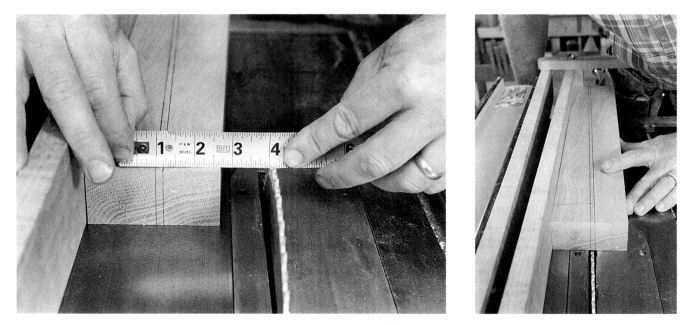

the layout line is parallel to the fence, I lock the jig's adjustment nut. Then I position the rip fence so the blade will cut to the layout line (*photo 3-4*).

When the setting is right, I cut the taper on one leg. Then I turn the stock around and taper the other leg. I clean up the saw cuts with a light cut on the jointer.

With the tapers complete, the next thing to do is make an angled cut at the top end of each leg where the leg will join with the handle (*drawings 3-A and 3-C*). I make these cuts on my power miter box, pivoting the blade to the right, 15 degrees from the zero mark. I place the straight, untapered edge of the leg against the fence to the left of the blade and cut off the top at an angle. The angle at the *back* edge of the leg (the untapered edge) should measure 105 degrees (*drawing 3-C*). I repeat the procedure to cut the top of the second leg.

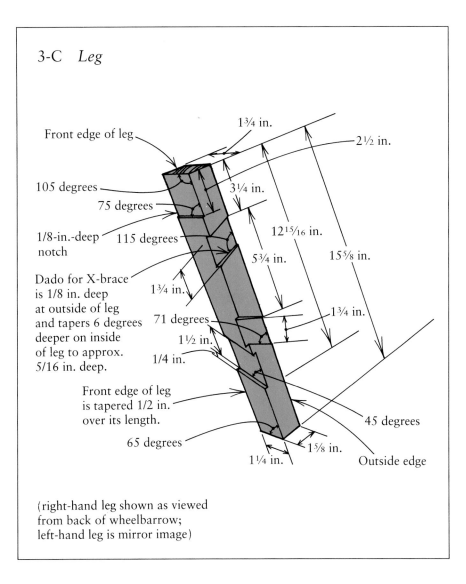

3-C  *Leg*

Front edge of leg

1¾ in.

2½ in.

105 degrees

3¼ in.

75 degrees

12¹⁵/₁₆ in.

1/8-in.-deep notch

115 degrees

15⅝ in.

5¾ in.

Dado for X-brace is 1/8 in. deep at outside of leg and tapers 6 degrees deeper on inside of leg to approx. 5/16 in. deep.

1¾ in.

1¾ in.

71 degrees

1½ in.

1/4 in.

Front edge of leg is tapered 1/2 in. over its length.

45 degrees

65 degrees

1⅝ in.

1¼ in.

Outside edge

(right-hand leg shown as viewed from back of wheelbarrow; left-hand leg is mirror image)

To cut the bottom ends, I measure 15⅝ in. along the back edge of the leg to mark the cut (*drawing 3-C*). Then I swing my miter box 25 degrees to the left and, with the leg to the left of the blade, cut a 65-degree angle on the bottom of each leg. I make sure to hold the untapered rear edge of the leg against the saw fence.

## Lap Joints

Before I complete the legs, let's talk about some of the connections in the understructure of the wheelbarrow.

Most of the joints are some form of angled lap joint: where the leg meets the handle (*drawings 3-A, 3-B, and 3-C*), where the strut meets the handle (*drawings 3-A, 3-B, and 3-D*), where the strut meets the leg (*drawings 3-A, 3-C, and 3-D*), where the X-shaped crossbrace laps over itself (*drawing 3-E*), where the X-brace joins with the leg (*drawings 3-A, 3-C, and 3-E*), and where the wheelbarrow bed members join at the corners (*drawings 3-A and 3-G*).

The best way to cut these lap joints is with a radial-arm saw fitted with a stack dado head. By changing the angle and the height of the blade I can easily make all the cuts I need for these lap joints.

## Completing the Frame

Getting back to the legs, I start by milling a 1/8-in.-deep angled rabbet where the leg joins the handle (*drawing 3-C*). At the top of each leg,

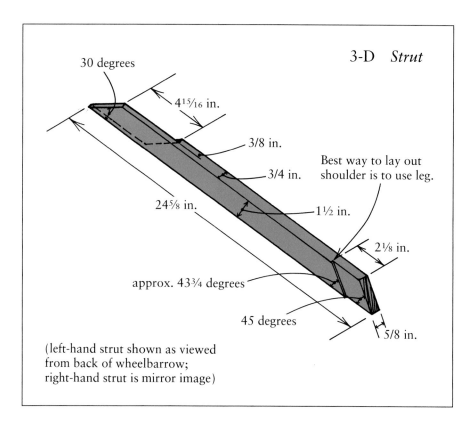

3-D  *Strut*

30 degrees

4¹⁵/₁₆ in.

3/8 in.

3/4 in.

Best way to lay out shoulder is to use leg.

24⅝ in.

1½ in.

2⅛ in.

approx. 43¾ degrees

45 degrees

5/8 in.

(left-hand strut shown as viewed from back of wheelbarrow; right-hand strut is mirror image)

on the *inside* face, I lay out the 2½-in.-wide rabbet. I swing the radial-arm saw 15 degrees to the right and adjust the height for a 1/8-in.-deep cut. With the untapered *back* edge of the left-hand leg against the fence, I make multiple cuts to complete the rabbet. The bottom edge of the rabbet should be parallel to the top of the leg. For the right-hand leg, I swing the saw 15 degrees to the left and repeat the procedure.

Next, I mill the 45-degree-angled dadoes in the legs that house the 1½-in.-wide struts (*drawings 3-A and 3-C*). These dadoes are located on the inside face of each leg near the bottom.

To cut the left leg (left as you're pushing the wheelbarrow), I swing the radial-arm saw 45 degrees to the right and set the blade to make a 1/4-in.-deep cut. With the untapered back edge of the leg against the fence, I cut the dado. To cut the right leg, I swing the saw 45 degrees to the left and make the cut, again keeping the untapered back edge of the leg against the fence (*photo 3-5*). The legs should be mirror images of each other.

The two struts come next (*drawings 3-A and 3-D*). I cut one end of each strut to a 45-degree angle on the miter box (*drawing 3-D*). This end will be the bottom of the strut, where it connects with the leg (*drawing 3-A*). Then I measure 24⅝ in. from the long point of the 45-degree cut to mark the long point of a 30-degree cut that I make at the other end.

The struts need to have angled rabbets at each end (*drawing 3-D*). In order to lay out these joints (plus a few others), I have to assemble the frame pieces temporarily. But first, to position the legs, I measure 32 in. from the front end of each handle and make a mark on the top outside corner. This mark locates the top rear corner of the leg (*drawing 3-B*). To mark for the struts, I measure in 17 in. from the front of each handle to locate the top rear corner of the strut (*drawing 3-B*).

I lay the 2 handles upside down on my bench and clamp the front piece in between. Next, I fit the 45-degree ends of the struts into the dadoes I cut in the legs. Holding the leg-and-strut assembly upside down, I line up the back corner of the leg with the pencil mark on the handle and clamp the leg to the outside of the handle (*photo 3-6*). The rear corners of the struts should line up with the pencil marks 17 in. from the front of the handle.

When everything's lined up, I run a sharp pencil along the *front* tapered edge of each leg to draw a line on each strut (*photo 3-7*). This line marks the edge of a 1/8-in.-deep rabbet that will fit into the dado in the leg to form a lap joint (*drawing 3-D*). At the other end of the strut, I trace along the handle to mark the shoulder of the other rabbet, which is 3/8 in. deep (*photo 3-8*). I also mark the handle, along the edges of the strut, for a 1/4-in.-deep dado.

Moving to the wide end of the leg (where it meets the handle), I run my pencil along the front and back of the leg to draw lines on the

**3-5** The struts fit into 45-degree-angled rabbets in the legs. The untapered rear edge of the leg must be against the radial-arm saw fence.

**3-6** In order to lay out some of the angled joints for the struts and the legs, I temporarily clamp the wheelbarrow frame together on my workbench.

handle. These lines mark the edges of the 1/8-in.-deep dado I'll cut in the handle (*drawing 3-B*).

Now, with the joints marked out, I can disassemble the frame and get back to the radial saw. First, I mill the 3/8-in.-deep angled rabbet on the top end of each strut, setting my saw to the angle I scribed (*drawing 3-D*). Then I mill the 1/8-in.-deep rabbet at the bottom of each strut where it connects with the leg.

Next, I cut the dadoes in the handles for the legs and struts. I set the depth of cut for 1/8 in. and I pivot the radial-arm saw to cut to the pencil lines I just scribed. The rear edge of the leg dado is a 75-degree angle. To cut the front edge, I have to reset the angle to match the pencil line — approximately 73¾ degrees (*drawing 3-B*). For the strut dadoes, I set the saw for a 30-degree angle and change the depth of the cut to 1/4 in.

## Fitting the X-Brace

The angles make things a little complicated where the X-brace joins the legs. Because the handles of the wheelbarrow flare outward at the back and because the legs of the wheelbarrow tip back slightly, the X-brace can't sit flush against the backs of the legs. That complicates things a bit because I can't cut straight dadoes in the legs to receive the X-brace. The dadoes have to be cut at a compound angle. In other words, the dadoes are *deeper* on the inside corner of the leg (*drawing 3-C*).

To cut these compound-angle dadoes, I've made a couple of simple jigs to help me on the radial-arm saw (*photo 3-9*).

The first jig is a piece of scrap wood, as long as the leg, with one face beveled at a 6-degree angle. This angle corresponds to the flare of the handles. The second jig is a long wedge that tapers from 1/2 in. at the wide end to a point.

3-7  With the frame clamped together, I run a sharp pencil along the *front* tapered edge of each leg to mark the edge of a 1/8-in.-deep rabbet in the strut.

3-8  At the opposite end of the strut, I trace along the handle to mark the shoulder of a 3/8-in.-deep rabbet in the strut.

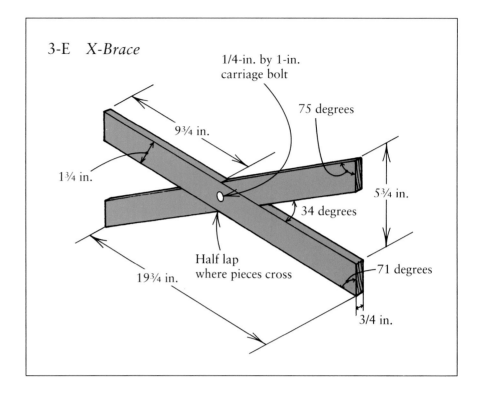

3-E  *X-Brace*

1/4-in. by 1-in. carriage bolt

75 degrees

9¾ in.

1¾ in.

5¾ in.

34 degrees

Half lap where pieces cross

71 degrees

19¾ in.

3/4 in.

To cut the X-brace dadoes, I place the 6-degree jig on the radial-arm saw table, tapered side up, with the wide edge against the fence (*photo 3-9*). I place the leg on top of this jig with the back (untapered) edge of the leg facing up and the inside edge of the leg against the fence. Then I slip the wedge under the narrow end of the leg (the bottom end) to make the top of the leg parallel with the saw table from end to end (*photo 3-9*). When the setup is correct, the leg will tilt forward sightly away from the fence. When I cut the dadoes, they'll be a little bit deeper on the fence side of the cut — just what I want. The bottom dado is cut at 71 degrees and the top dado is cut at 115 degrees (*drawing 3-C*). Note that the dadoes angle in opposite directions.

Where the pieces of the X-brace overlap, I make a half-lap joint. I swing the radial-arm saw 54 degrees (for a 34-degree-angle cut) and cut a 1¾-in.-wide notch, 3/8 in. deep, in each of the X-brace pieces. Now I can trim the ends of the X-brace according to the drawing (*drawing 3-E*).

## Completing the Handles

Before I can do any assembly there are a few more things to do to the handles.

The axle fits into half-round holes near the fronts of the handles (*drawing 3-B*). I measure back 9⅜ in. from the front of each handle and mark the center for the hole. Before I can drill these holes, I screw a small pine block on the underside of each handle where the hole will

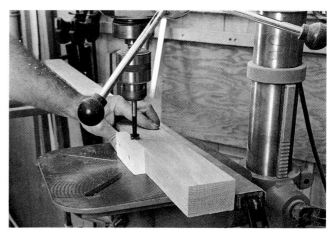

be located (*photo 3-10*). The blocks will give me something to drill into. I also mark the centers for the 1/4-in.-dia. holes that the threaded rod will pass through at the front ends of the handles (*drawing 3-B*).

On the drill press, I tilt the table 6 degrees to the left and install a straightedge clamp across the rear of the table as a guide (*photo 3-10*). Now, with a 5/8-in.-dia. forstner bit, I bore a 1-in.-deep hole in the left-hand handle for the axle. When I remove the pine block, I have a perfect half hole in the handle. I move the straightedge clamp to the front of the table to drill the right-hand handle.

While the drill-press table is tilted to 6 degrees, I drill the two 1/4-in.-dia. holes near the front of the handles for the threaded rod.

To lay out the grips at the ends of the handles, I make a little template from a piece of poster board and trace the grip profile onto the wood (*drawing 3-B and photo 3-11*). Then I saw out the grips on the band saw.

With the profile of the grips cut, I taper the sides of the grips on the band saw, taking off 1/4 in. of wood at the very end (*drawing 3-B*).

I sand the grips with a drum sander on the drill press and round the edges with a 3/4-in.-radius roundover bit in my router (*photo 3-12*). A block plane finishes up the shaping, and a little bit of sanding with my random-orbit sander removes all the tool marks.

## Assembling the Frame

Now I'm ready to start assembling the frame. To ensure that the frame doesn't loosen in use, I secure all the joints with a little construction adhesive and either screws or carriage bolts.

First, I assemble the front piece to the ends of the handles. I drill and countersink for 4 square-drive 1¼-in. #8 stainless steel screws. Then I apply some adhesive and screw the joints together. Next, I install the threaded rod that holds the front assembly together.

The legs go on next. I clamp the legs to the handles and drill a 1/4-in.-dia. hole through each leg and handle (*photo 3-13*). Then I apply

**3-9** To cut the compound-angle dadoes in the legs for the X-brace, I slip 2 scrap-wood jigs underneath the workpiece. The bottom jig (light color) is a piece of scrap wood, with one face beveled to a 6-degree angle. The top jig (dark color) is a long wedge tapering from 1/2 in. to a point. The wedge makes the top of the leg parallel to the table from end to end. The beveled jig tilts the leg forward away from the fence 6 degrees. This makes the dadoes a little deeper on the fence side of the cut.

**3-10** The axle fits into 5/8-in.-dia. half-round holes in the handles. Before I can drill these holes, I screw a small pine block on the underside of each handle. The blocks give me something to drill into. When I remove the block, I have a half-round hole. A straightedge clamp positions the workpiece under the bit.

**3-11** To lay out the grips at the ends of the handles, I make a template from a piece of poster board and trace the profile onto the wood.

**3-12** To round over the edges of the handle grips, I use a 3/4-in.-radius roundover bit in my router.

**3-13** I clamp the legs to the handles and drill a 1/4-in.-dia. hole. Then I apply adhesive and install a 1/4-in. by 3½-in. carriage bolt to secure the leg to the handle.

adhesive and install a 1/4-in. by 3½-in. carriage bolt through each hole.

The struts go on next, with adhesive and carriage bolts. I use a 1/4-in. by 2½-in. carriage bolt through the leg and a 1/4-in. by 2-in. carriage bolt through the handle (*drawing 3-A*).

Now for the X-brace. I place the brace into its dadoes in the legs and drill for the 1/4-in. by 2½-in. carriage bolts that hold the brace to the legs. Once the brace is glued and bolted to the legs, I drill through the center of the X-brace and install a 1/4-in. by 1-in. carriage bolt (*drawing 3-E*).

That takes care of the frame. All that's left are the wheel and the axle.

## The Wheel Assembly

I got all the parts for my wheel mechanism (*drawing 3-F*) right at my local hardware store. The tire is sold as a replacement for a contractor's wheelbarrow. For an axle I bought some 5/8-in.-dia. solid-steel bar stock, which is a perfect fit in the wheel. The axle and wheel just drop right into the half-round holes I drilled in the handles.

To keep the wheel from moving from side to side, I cut 2 spacers from a piece of 3/4-in.-dia. electrical conduit (*photo 3-14 and drawing 3-F*). These spacers slip onto the axle on either side of the wheel and are notched to fit over the handles and keep them from spinning.

I drop the whole assembly into the holes in the handles and secure the axle with two 4-in.-long strips of 1/8-in. by 1¼-in. galvanized steel. I center-punch and drill two 1/4-in.-dia. holes through the steel strips and fasten the strips down with two 1/4-in. by 1½-in. lag screws (*drawing 3-F and photo 3-15*).

## Making the Bed

The bed of the wheelbarrow is made of 4 pieces of oak with a piece of 3/4 MDO plywood set into rabbets (*drawing 3-G*). The corners of the bed frame are joined with a simple half-lap joint, which I cut on the radial-arm saw. These joints are angled as shown (*drawing 3-G*).

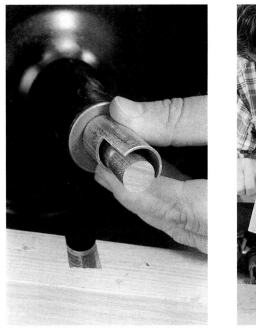

**3-14** To keep the wheel from moving from side to side, I cut 2 spacers from a piece of 3/4-in.-dia. electrical conduit. These spacers slip onto the axle on either side of the wheel and are notched to fit over the handles and keep them from spinning.

**3-15** I drop the axle assembly into the holes in the handles and secure the axle with two 4-in.-long strips of 1/8-in. by 1¼-in. galvanized steel and two 1/4-in. by 1½-in. lag screws.

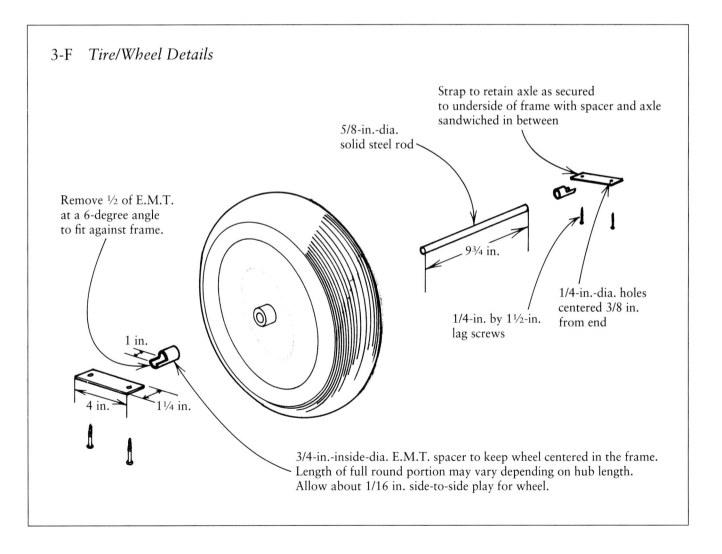

**3-F   Tire/Wheel Details**

Strap to retain axle as secured
to underside of frame with spacer and axle
sandwiched in between

5/8-in.-dia.
solid steel rod

Remove ½ of E.M.T.
at a 6-degree angle
to fit against frame.

9¾ in.

1/4-in. by 1½-in.
lag screws

1/4-in.-dia. holes
centered 3/8 in.
from end

1 in.

4 in.      1¼ in.

3/4-in.-inside-dia. E.M.T. spacer to keep wheel centered in the frame.
Length of full round portion may vary depending on hub length.
Allow about 1/16 in. side-to-side play for wheel.

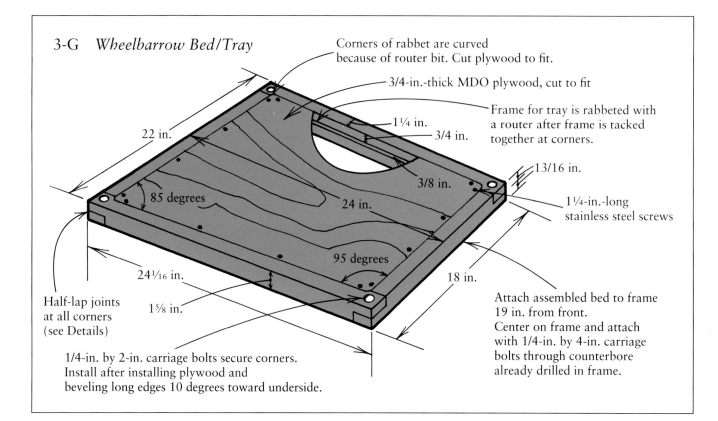

3-G  *Wheelbarrow Bed/Tray*

Corners of rabbet are curved
because of router bit. Cut plywood to fit.

3/4-in.-thick MDO plywood, cut to fit

Frame for tray is rabbeted with
a router after frame is tacked
together at corners.

1¼ in.

3/4 in.

13/16 in.

22 in.

85 degrees

1¼-in.-long
stainless steel screws

3/8 in.

24 in.

95 degrees

18 in.

24¹⁄₁₆ in.

1⁵⁄₈ in.

Half-lap joints
at all corners
(see Details)

Attach assembled bed to frame
19 in. from front.
Center on frame and attach
with 1/4-in. by 4-in. carriage
bolts through counterbore
already drilled in frame.

1/4-in. by 2-in. carriage bolts secure corners.
Install after installing plywood and
beveling long edges 10 degrees toward underside.

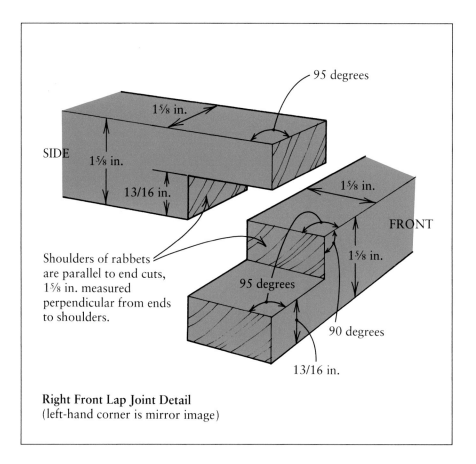

95 degrees

1⁵⁄₈ in.

SIDE

1⁵⁄₈ in.

13/16 in.

1⁵⁄₈ in.

FRONT

1⁵⁄₈ in.

95 degrees

Shoulders of rabbets
are parallel to end cuts,
1⁵⁄₈ in. measured
perpendicular from ends
to shoulders.

90 degrees

13/16 in.

**Right Front Lap Joint Detail**
(left-hand corner is mirror image)

To cut the half-lap joints for the back corners of the bed frame, I pivot the radial-arm saw 5 degrees and cut the rabbets (*drawing 3-G*). To cut the front corner joints, I swing the saw 5 degrees to the other side of zero. All cuts are 13/16 in. deep.

With the lap joints complete, I glue the joints together with construction adhesive and reinforce each joint with a couple of finishing nails. Because I'll drill holes later for carriage bolts, I make sure not to nail in the center of the joint.

Now I'm ready to mill the 3/8-in. by 3/4-in. rabbet for the MDO plywood deck. I use a 3/8-in. rabbeting bit in my router and make a couple of passes to get it to the 3/4-in. depth (*drawing 3-G*).

I place the frame upside down on a sheet of 3/4-in. MDO plywood and trace around the inside of the bed frame with a pencil where I made the rabbet (*photo 3-16*). I cut out the plywood with my circular saw and round the corners with my drum sander so they fit the rounded corners of the rabbet.

I install the plywood deck into the bed frame by running a bead of construction adhesive around the rabbet and screwing the plywood down with some 1¼-in. stainless steel screws.

I want the sides of the wheelbarrow to flare out. That means that the side edges of the bed frame have to flare out as well. The easiest way to do that is on the jointer. I tilt the jointer fence 10 degrees away

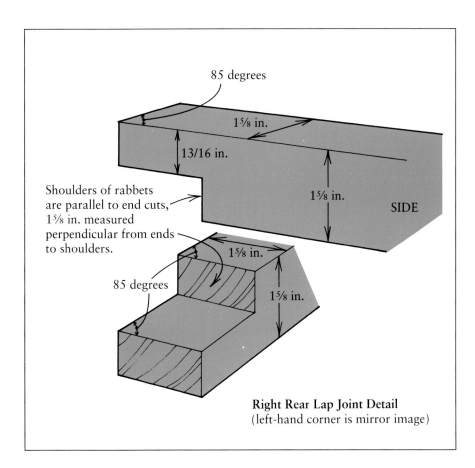

85 degrees

1⅝ in.

13/16 in.

1⅝ in.

SIDE

Shoulders of rabbets are parallel to end cuts, 1⅝ in. measured perpendicular from ends to shoulders.

85 degrees

1⅝ in.

1⅝ in.

**Right Rear Lap Joint Detail**
(left-hand corner is mirror image)

**3-16** To lay out the plywood deck, I place the frame upside down on the plywood and trace around the inside of the rabbet.

from the bed and make enough passes to bevel the sides of the bed frame (*photo 3-17*). I hold the bottom of the frame against the fence.

On the drill press, I drill 1/4-in.-dia. holes through the 4 lap joints of the bed frame for the carriage bolts that will secure the frame together. I'll install these later, after the bed frame is mounted on the wheelbarrow frame.

To install the bed on the frame assembly, I measure back 19 in. from the front piece. Then I place the bed frame in position with the front edge on the mark, center it from side to side, and clamp it to the handles.

Carriage bolts hold the bed frame to the handles. With a long 1/4-in.-dia. bit, I drill through the bed frame, boring clear through the handles underneath. Removing the bed frame for a minute, I drill a 7/8-in.-dia. counterbore 3/4 in. deep in the underside of holes in the handles for the washers and nuts on the carriage bolts. Now I can re-install the bed frame and fasten it to the frame assembly underneath with four 1/4-in. by 4-in. carriage bolts.

Now I install four 1/4-in. by 2-in. carriage bolts, nuts, and washers through the holes in the corners of the bed frame.

*Front Panel Assembly*

The front panel assembly has 7 wooden parts: the front panel, an upper and lower channel, 2 wedges, and 2 retainers at the sides (*drawings 3-A and 3-H*). There are also 4 metal parts: two 1/4-in.-dia. threaded rods and 2 front braces.

The first piece to make is the 18-in.-long wedge that attaches to the front of the bed frame (*drawing 3-H*). This wedge establishes the

## 3-H  Front and Sideboard Details

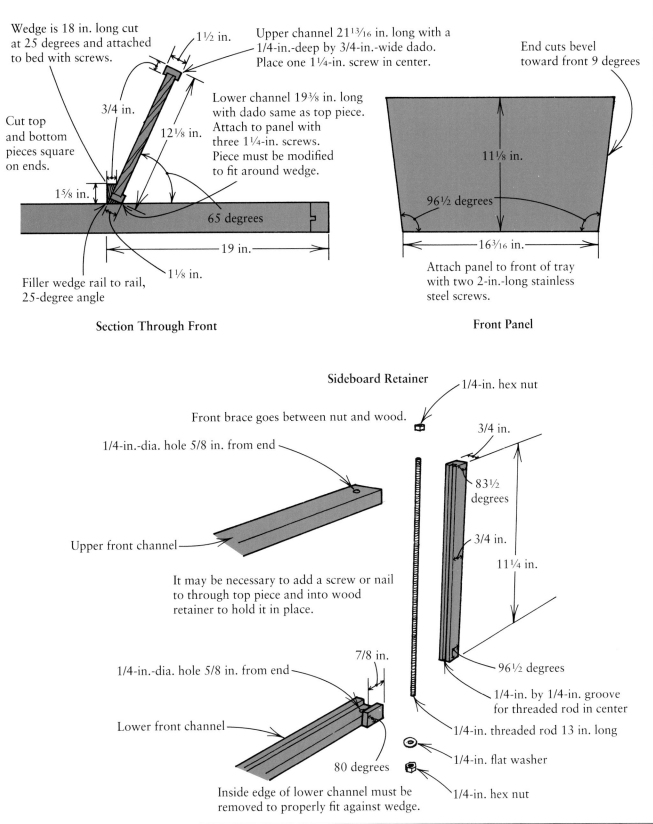

Wedge is 18 in. long cut at 25 degrees and attached to bed with screws.

Cut top and bottom pieces square on ends.

1 1/2 in.

3/4 in.

12 1/8 in.

1 5/8 in.

Upper channel 21 13/16 in. long with a 1/4-in.-deep by 3/4-in.-wide dado. Place one 1 1/4-in. screw in center.

Lower channel 19 3/8 in. long with dado same as top piece. Attach to panel with three 1 1/4-in. screws. Piece must be modified to fit around wedge.

65 degrees

19 in.

1 1/8 in.

Filler wedge rail to rail, 25-degree angle

**Section Through Front**

End cuts bevel toward front 9 degrees

11 1/8 in.

96 1/2 degrees

16 3/16 in.

Attach panel to front of tray with two 2-in.-long stainless steel screws.

**Front Panel**

**Sideboard Retainer**

1/4-in. hex nut

Front brace goes between nut and wood.

1/4-in.-dia. hole 5/8 in. from end

Upper front channel

It may be necessary to add a screw or nail to through top piece and into wood retainer to hold it in place.

3/4 in.

83 1/2 degrees

3/4 in.

11 1/4 in.

96 1/2 degrees

1/4-in. by 1/4-in. groove for threaded rod in center

1/4-in. threaded rod 13 in. long

1/4-in. flat washer

1/4-in. hex nut

1/4-in.-dia. hole 5/8 in. from end

Lower front channel

7/8 in.

80 degrees

Inside edge of lower channel must be removed to properly fit against wedge.

angle of the front panel. I cut this wedge from a 3/4-in. by 1⅝-in. by 20-in. piece of oak (see Project Planner). I tilt my table-saw blade 25 degrees and rip the wedge. Then I attach it, thick end up, to the front of the bed frame with construction adhesive and screws. The top of the wedge should be flush with the top of the bed frame.

The upper and lower channels come next. These channels hold the front panel in place (*drawing 3-A*). I have to mill a 1/4-in. by 3/4-in. groove down the center of each channel to fit over the front panel (*drawing 3-H*). I set up a dado head on the table saw for a 3/4-in.-wide cut. I set the blade for a 1/4-in.-deep cut and mill the groove in each channel.

After milling the grooves, I crosscut the channels to finished length — 19⅜ in. for the lower channel and 21¹³⁄₁₆ in. for the upper channel (*drawing 3-H*).

I have to remove some more wood from the lower channel to allow the panel to fit tight against the wedge. I need to remove 3/8 in. of wood from an 18-in.-long section in the middle of the channel. I place the channel in position against the wedge and make a pencil mark at each side of the bed frame to mark the ends of the area I have to remove (*photo 3-18*). I set the dado head on the table saw for a 3/8-in.-deep cut and make repeated cuts with the miter gauge to "nibble away" the wood. This creates an 18-in.-long notch that fits over the front of the bed frame.

Both the top and bottom channels get holes for the threaded rods that strengthen the front and hold the side boards (*drawing 3-H*). I measure in 5/8 in. from the ends and drill a 1/4-in. hole in each end.

A "filler" wedge goes underneath the lower channel to tilt it forward 25 degrees. To make this wedge, I start with a 3/4-in. by 1¼-in. by 20-in. piece of oak (see Project Planner). I set my table-saw blade to 25 degrees and rip a wedge that is 1⅛ in. wide and 1/2 in. thick at the thickest end.

The front panel has angled sides that are cut at a compound angle (*drawing 3-H*). I cut these angled sides on the radial-arm saw. To make the first cut, I tilt the blade 9 degrees to the right (counterclockwise) and swing the blade 6½ degrees to the left. I place the front panel on the table to the left of the blade with the top edge against the fence and the front facing up. Now I cut the right end of the panel.

Measuring from the long point of the angled cut I just made, I mark off 16³⁄₁₆ in. along the bottom edge of the panel (*drawing 3-H*). I'll cut the left end to this line. To make this left-end cut, I turn the panel around so the bottom edge is against the fence and facedown.

Next come the 2 side retainers that fit between the upper and lower channels (*drawings 3-A and 3-H*). Starting with the 3/4-in. by 3/4-in. by 12-in. stock I prepared when I cut out all the parts (see Project Planner), I mill a 1/4-in. by 1/4-in. groove down the middle of each piece for a 1/4-in-dia. threaded rod (*drawing 3-H*). I do this on the

**3-17**  So the sides of the wheelbarrow will flare out, I have to bevel the
sides of the bed frame. I tilt the
jointer fence 10 degrees and make as
many passes as necessary to bevel the
full width of the side. I hold the bottom of the frame against the fence.

table saw with a regular blade, cutting from each end to make sure the
groove is centered.

After milling the groove, I trim the ends to length on my power miter box. I trim the top end to an 83½-degree angle. Measuring from
this cut along the outer, ungrooved edge, I mark off 11¼ in. and trim
the bottom end to a 96½-degree angle (*drawing 3-H*).

Now I'm ready for a little assembly. First, I spread some adhesive
on the top and bottom of the filler wedge. Then I clamp the lower
channel in place with the filler wedge underneath. Next, I place the
front panel in the lower panel groove and make sure it's centered in

**3-18** I have to remove 3/8 in. of wood from an 18-in.-long section in the middle of the channel to allow the panel to fit tight against the wedge. With the channel against the wedge, I make a pencil mark at each side of the bed frame to mark the ends of the area I have to remove.

**3-19** I slip the side retainer between the upper and lower channels and flush it up with the ends of the channels. Then I drill through the upper channel into the end of the retainer for a screw to hold the retainer in place.

the lower channel. When it is, I drill and install a couple of 2-in. #8 screws through the panel into the wedge and bed frame behind it. Then, from underneath, I drill through the lower channel and install three 1¼-in. screws into the bottom edge of the front panel.

The upper channel goes on next. I drill and screw it to the top of the panel with a single screw through the center.

The side retainers are the next parts to install. I slip them in between the upper and lower channels and flush them up with the ends of the channels. Then I drill through the upper channel into the end of each retainer for a screw to hold the retainer in place (*photo 3-19 and drawing 3-H*).

The 13-in.-long threaded rods go in next. I tap them through the holes in the upper and lower channels. I'll add the nuts and washers later, after I've installed the 2 metal braces that support the front of the wheelbarrow.

*Bending the Braces*

Now I'm ready to do a little "blacksmithing." Well, not really. I don't need a forge or an anvil to bend the steel for the braces. What I *do* need to make the braces are a hacksaw, a centerpunch, a compass, a big machinist's vise, and a heavy hammer. My 20-oz. framing hammer packs enough of a punch.

With the hacksaw, or a jigsaw with a metal-cutting blade, I cut two 16¼-in. lengths of 1/8-in. by 1¼-in. galvanized steel (see Project Planner). At one end of each piece, I center-punch for a 1/4-in-dia. hole. With the point of my compass on the punch mark, I scribe a 5/8-in. radius on the end of each piece (*drawing 3-I*). Now I drill the hole and round off the end of the brace on my grinder. The rounded end will be

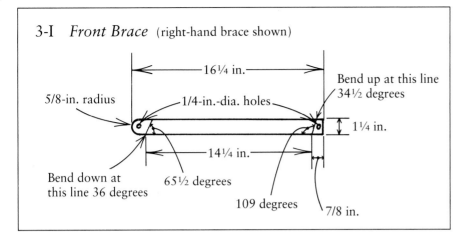

3-I  *Front Brace* (right-hand brace shown)

5/8-in. radius

16¼ in.

Bend up at this line
34½ degrees

1/4-in.-dia. holes

1¼ in.

Bend down at
this line 36 degrees

65½ degrees

14¼ in.

109 degrees

7/8 in.

the top of the brace. The hole slips over the threaded rod that sticks up from the upper channel in the front assembly.

Now I have to make compound-angled bends at the top and bottom of each brace (*drawings 3-A and 3-I*). I clamp the stock in the vise and bend it with the hammer. Getting the angles right is a hammer-and-fit process. Once I have the angles right, I punch and drill a 1/4-in.-dia. hole at the bottom end of each brace and grind off the sharp corners.

To install the braces, I slip the top ends over the threaded rods and put on washers and nuts at both ends of the rods. At the bottom end of each brace, I drill a 1/4-in.-dia. hole through the handle and install the 3-in. carriage bolt that holds the brace to the handle (*drawing 3-A*).

## Side Boards and Cleats

The sides of the wheelbarrow are made from pieces of 1 × 10 oak, 30 in. long (see Project Planner). The bottom edges must be beveled to 10 degrees in order to sit flush against the bed frame.

I rip the pieces to an 8⁷/₁₆-in. width. Then, with my jointer fence tilted 10 degrees, I bevel the edge, keeping the outer face of the side against the fence. I make enough passes until the side is 8⅜ in. wide, measured along the outer face (from the short point of the bevel).

I have to cut the fronts of the sides at an angle to match the angle of the front panel. I slip the side in between the front panel and the side retainer and use my sliding bevel gauge to measure the angle between the top edge of the side and the side retainer — about 22½ degrees. I use the bevel gauge to set my radial-arm saw to make the cut.

Now I can lay out the curve at the back ends of the sides (*drawing 3-J*). I measure back 26¼ in. along the bottom edge to establish the back end of the side.

With my compass, I lay out a 5-in. radius at the back end and cut out the curve on the band saw. Then I sand the curve smooth with the

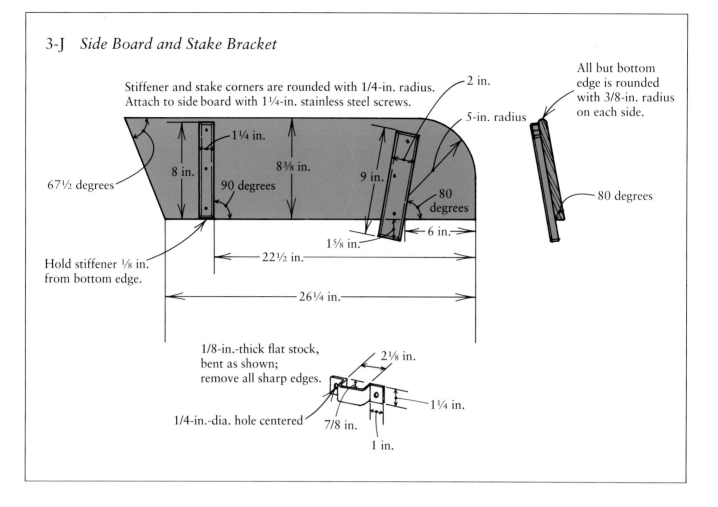

3-J  *Side Board and Stake Bracket*

Stiffener and stake corners are rounded with 1/4-in. radius.
Attach to side board with 1¼-in. stainless steel screws.

2 in.

All but bottom edge is rounded with 3/8-in. radius on each side.

5-in. radius

1¼ in.

8 in.

8⅜ in.

9 in.

67½ degrees

90 degrees

80 degrees

80 degrees

Hold stiffener ⅛ in. from bottom edge.

1⅝ in.

6 in.

22½ in.

26¼ in.

1/8-in.-thick flat stock, bent as shown; remove all sharp edges.

2⅛ in.

1¼ in.

1/4-in.-dia. hole centered

7/8 in.

1 in.

drum-sander attachment on my drill press and round over the top, front, and back edges with a 3/8-in.-radius roundover bit in my router.

Each side board has a stiffener and a stake (*drawings 3-A and 3-J*). The stake projects 1⅝ in. below the side board. It fits into a metal bracket on the bed frame to keep the side in place.

Working with the 1 × 4 oak I milled to size earlier (see Project Planner), I cut two 8-in. lengths of 1¼-in.-wide stock for the 2 stiffeners. I cut two 9-in. lengths of 2-in.-wide stock for the stakes (*drawing 3-J*). I round the corners with a 1/4-in.-radius roundover bit and screw the cleats to the sides with 3 screws through each.

*Making the Stake Brackets*

I make the steel brackets for the stakes from the same galvanized material I used for the front braces. Each bracket requires 4 right-angle bends (*drawing 3-J*). I bend one end, then place the bracket against the stake. With a pencil, I trace along the side of the stake to mark the length of the opening I need in the bracket — about 2⅛ in. Then I complete the bend in the vise.

When the brackets are bent, I center-punch and drill two 1/4-in.-dia. holes in each bracket and grind off any sharp edges. Then I install the brackets to the bed frame sides with 1/4-in. by 1½-in. lag screws.

That wraps up the woodworking part of the wheelbarrow. All that's left are a few licks of sanding here and there and a coat of appropriate finish.

## An Old-Fashioned Finish

It took me a long time to decide on a finish for my wheelbarrow. I was afraid that if I used a polyurethane or a varnish, the finish might chip in use. The same would be true for paint. Finally I recalled that old wooden ladders were often finished with boiled linseed oil, and decided that would make a good finish for my wheelbarrow too. It's important to use *boiled*, not raw, linseed oil. Raw linseed oil will never dry.

Linseed oil doesn't offer much protection against moisture but it makes the wood look nice. What's more important, it's an easy finish to renew in the future — just slap on another coat right over the dings and dents I know this wheelbarrow's going to get.

I apply a couple of coats of boiled linseed oil with a brush, letting each coat dry overnight. You know, this wheelbarrow's almost too pretty to use.

# 4

# *Picnic Table*

## PROJECT PLANNER

*Time:* 2 days
*Special hardware and tools:*
(16) 3/8-in.-dia. by 3½-in. zinc-plated carriage bolts with flat washers and nuts
(2) 3/8-in.-dia. by 4-in. zinc-plated lag screws with flat washers
55 (approx.) 2½-in. #8 galvanized bugle-head screws
(2) 3½-in. #8 galvanized bugle-head screws
(1) tube of construction adhesive and caulking gun
*Wood:*
(1) 12-ft. 4 × 4 fir
Cut in half to make seat support crossmembers.
(1) 12-ft. 2 × 6 pressure-treated pine
Cut into 4 pieces 36 in. long for legs.
(1) 10-ft. 2 × 4 spruce
Cut 3 pieces 36 in. long for top cleats.
(3) 2 × 8 spruce
Cut 5 pieces 71 in. long for top planks. From remaining piece, cut center braces to fit.
(1) 12-ft. 2 × 10 spruce
Cut 2 pieces 71 in. long for seat planks.

OVER the years I've had the opportunity to sit at and study many different styles of picnic tables. This one takes into account some of the best features I've seen. The size is just right. Its top is about 6 ft. long and 3 ft. wide and it will seat six people comfortably. Any bigger and the table would be too heavy to move around. It's also the right height — about 30 in. off the ground. The benches, or seats, are 16½ in. off the ground to give just the right relationship between top and seat. And the table's designed so that it won't tip over even if a couple of people sit on one side with no one on the other side.

A picnic table usually stays outdoors all year long, so it has to stand up to the weather. I've seen picnic tables built out of redwood, which is lightweight and weatherproof but very expensive if you live on the east coast, as I do. Red or white cedar will also hold up pretty well but these woods aren't always easy to find in the sizes I need.

So down at my local home center I bought what I think is the best material package for a picnic table (see Project Planner). I learned the hard way on my first picnic table that the bottoms of the legs are the first part to rot because of their contact with the ground. So I decided to make the legs from pressure-treated 2 × 6 pine. Pressure-treated wood is perfect for ground-contact applications. I don't want to use the pressure-treated lumber for the top and seats because I don't like the idea of food coming in contact with treated lumber. So for the top and the seats, I chose kiln-dried spruce — regular framing lumber. Spruce isn't especially weather-resistant but it's inexpensive and lightweight. The 4 × 4 that supports the seats and reinforces the legs is Douglas fir (*drawing 4-A*). With a couple of coats of stain (and a new coat every four or five years), the table will last for at least twenty years.

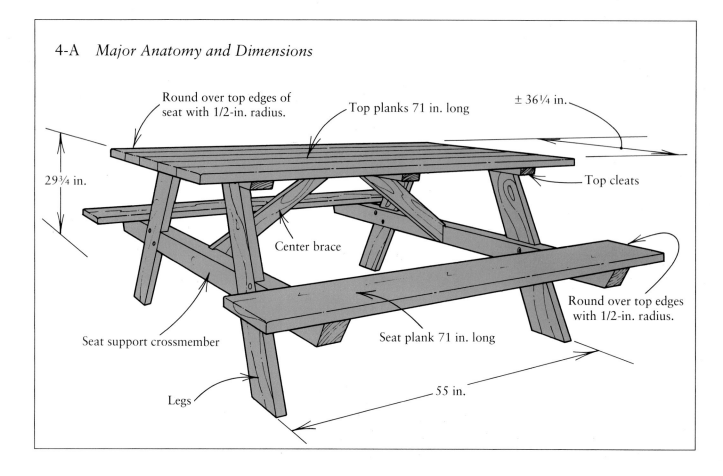

4-A   *Major Anatomy and Dimensions*

Round over top edges of seat with 1/2-in. radius.

Top planks 71 in. long

± 36¼ in.

Top cleats

29¾ in.

Center brace

Round over top edges with 1/2-in. radius.

Seat support crossmember

Seat plank 71 in. long

Legs

55 in.

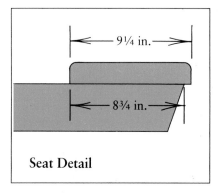

9¼ in.

8¾ in.

**Seat Detail**

## Legs, Crossmembers, and Cleats

I'll start by cutting the legs. Pressure-treated lumber varies in width, so the first thing I do after cutting the 4 legs to rough length (see Project Planner) is to rip the pieces to a 5½-in. width. Then I cut the ends of the legs to a 70-degree angle at both the bottom and the top. The measurement from the short point to the long point is 30 in. (*drawing 4-B*).

I make these angled cuts on the radial-arm saw. I swing the saw blade 20 degrees to the right and cut one end of the pressure-treated 2 × 6. Then I measure 30 in. from long point to short point and mark and cut the other end of the leg at the same angle. Now I use the first leg I cut as a pattern to mark and cut the other 3 legs.

The next pieces to cut are the two 4 × 4 crossmembers that reinforce the legs and support the seats (*drawings 4-A, 4-B, and 4-C*). On most picnic tables this crossmember is a 2 × 6 or 2 × 8 just bolted to the inside of the leg. The problem with this type of construction is that the strength of the joint comes from the bolts alone. A 4 × 4 is thick enough that I can let the leg into the crossmember, creating an interlocking joint that's really strong (*drawing 4-B*).

First I cut the 12-ft. 4 × 4 in half on my radial-arm saw (see Project Planner). Next, I bevel the ends of each piece at a 70-degree angle so I

## 4-B Support System Details

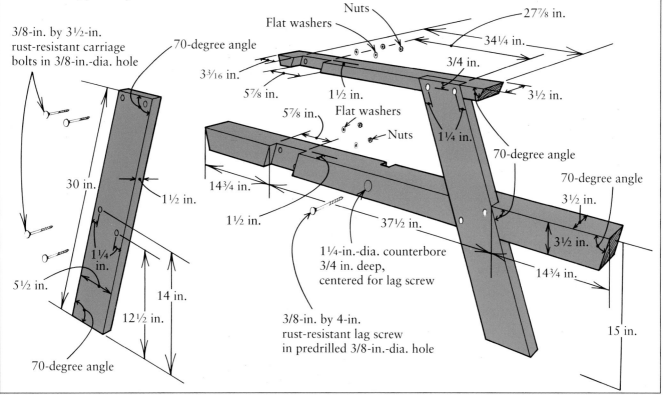

3/8-in. by 3½-in. rust-resistant carriage bolts in 3/8-in.-dia. hole

70-degree angle

Nuts

Flat washers

27⅞ in.

34¼ in.

3⅜₁₆ in.

3/4 in.

5⅞ in.

1½ in.

3½ in.

5⅞ in.

Flat washers

Nuts

1¼ in.

70-degree angle

30 in.

1½ in.

14¾ in.

70-degree angle

3½ in.

1½ in.

3½ in.

1¼ in.

37½ in.

3½ in.

5½ in.

1¼ in.

14 in.

1¼-in.-dia. counterbore 3/4 in. deep, centered for lag screw

14¾ in.

12½ in.

3/8-in. by 4-in. rust-resistant lag screw in predrilled 3/8-in.-dia. hole

15 in.

70-degree angle

won't catch myself on the ends under the seats (*drawings 4-A, 4-B, and 4-C*). I swing the radial-arm saw blade 20 degrees to the right and bevel one end to 70 degrees. Placing my tape on the long point of this angled cut, I measure off 67 in. along what will be the top of the crossmember and mark the long point of the angled cut I need to make on the opposite end. After making this cut, I bevel the ends of the second crossmember.

Before I make any changes to the radial-arm saw setup, I want to cut 3 pieces of 2 × 4 for the top cleats that join the legs and connect the boards for the top (*drawings 4-A, 4-B, and 4-C*). The ends of these cleats are beveled and the overall length is 34¼ in. from long point to long point (*drawing 4-B*). To bevel the ends, I install a high fence on the saw and hold the 2 × 4 on edge against the radial-arm saw fence (*photo 4-1*). Once I've cut one cleat, I use it as a template to mark the other 2 cleats.

The next step is to cut the leg dadoes in the crossmembers and the 2 end cleats (*drawings 4-A and 4-B*). For a good solid joint, the leg must be a tight fit in the dado. If the dado's even a little too wide, the leg will wobble and the joint will be weak.

I lay out the dadoes on the crossmembers by making a mark 14¾ in. from the long point on each end (*drawing 4-B*). Then I set my slid-

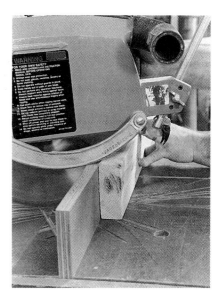

**4-1** With the radial-arm saw blade set for a 70-degree angle, I bevel the ends of the 2 × 4 cleats under the table. I install a high wooden fence so I can hold the stock on edge for the cut.

**4-2** To cut the leg dadoes in the 4 × 4 crossmembers, I use a stack dado head set for a 5/8-in.-wide cut. I swing the radial-arm saw 20 degrees to the right and make a series of multiple cuts. Because the dadoes are deep, I cut them in 2 passes, removing 3/4 in. of wood with each pass. Here I'm making the second pass.

**4-3** The center braces fit into 1-in. by 1½-in. dadoes in the centers of the 4 × 4 crossmembers. I make a few cuts with the stack dado head to complete the cut.

ing bevel to 70 degrees and draw a line to mark the outer edge of the dado. Next, I place one edge of the leg along this layout line and run a pencil down the opposite side of the leg to mark the width of the dado. I use the same procedure to lay out the dadoes on the 2 cleats (*drawing 4-B*).

To cut the dadoes for the legs, I set up my radial-arm saw with a stack dado head set for a 5/8-in.-wide cut. Then I swing the blade 20 degrees to the right. The dadoes are too deep to cut in one pass — it would be dangerous. So I'll cut the dadoes in 2 passes, removing 3/4 in. of wood with each pass (*photo 4-2*).

For the first pass, I set the height of the blade for a 3/4-in.-deep cut. With this setup, I make a series of cuts to "nibble away" one dado in each crossmember and one dado in each cleat. I'll come back and deepen these dadoes later after I cut the dadoes at the opposite ends.

With the saw still set for a 3/4-in.-deep cut, I swing the blade 20 degrees to the left of the 90-degree mark and cut the second dado in each piece. Then I lower the blade for a 1½-in.-deep cut to remove the balance of the material from the second dadoes. To finish up the first dadoes, I swing the saw back 20 degrees to the right of center and deepen the dadoes to 1½ in.

It may seem simpler just to cut the first dadoes full depth and *then* swing the saw for the second dadoes. The reason I do it this way instead is that it's easier to repeat an angle setting on the radial-arm saw than it is to repeat a depth setting. This method gives me a consistent depth of cut for all the dadoes.

Before I remove the dado head cutter from the radial-arm saw I want to cut one more dado in each 4 × 4. That's the 1-in. by 1½-in. dado that receives the 2 × 4 center brace (*drawings 4-A and 4-C*). I measure in 32¾ in. from one end of each 4 × 4 and mark a 1½-in.-wide dado (*drawing 4-C*). Then I set the blade height for a 1-in. depth of cut and make a few passes to complete each dado (*photo 4-3*).

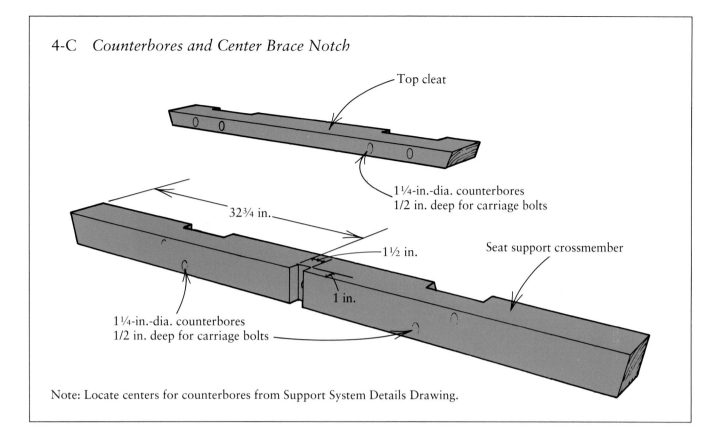

**4-C   Counterbores and Center Brace Notch**

Top cleat

1¼-in.-dia. counterbores
1/2 in. deep for carriage bolts

32¾ in.

1½ in.

1 in.

Seat support crossmember

1¼-in.-dia. counterbores
1/2 in. deep for carriage bolts

Note: Locate centers for counterbores from Support System Details Drawing.

## Leg Subassemblies

Now I'm ready to put the two leg subassemblies together. I place one
of the 4 × 4 crossmembers and one of the end cleats on the bench and
fit the legs into the dadoes with a little construction adhesive to
strengthen the joint. I position the legs so that the vertical distance
from the top of the crossmember to the bottom of the legs is 15 in.
(*drawing 4-B*). The cleat is set flush to the top of the leg. Then I secure
each joint with a single 8d finishing nail through the center of the joint
(*photo 4-4*). The nails will hold everything in position while I drill for
the carriage bolts that hold the joints together permanently.

One thing about carriage bolts: I've sat at too many picnic tables
where the ends of the bolts stick out and scrape your legs. To elimi-
nate this problem, I recess the nut, washer, and end of the bolt by
counterboring the bolt holes in the crossmembers and cleats (*photo
4-5*). Counterbores are best made with a forstner bit because it makes
a nice flat-bottomed hole. Each joint gets 2 holes, spaced as shown in
the drawing (*drawing 4-B*). After drilling the counterbores, I switch to
a 3/8-in.-dia. bit and drill all the way through for the bolts (*photo
4-6*).

With the holes drilled, I tap in the carriage bolts, washers, and
nuts, and torque them down with my socket wrench (*photo 4-7*).
Then I complete the other leg subassembly in the same way.

**4-4** After assembling the leg subassembly on my bench, I secure each joint with an 8d finishing nail through the center. The nails hold things in place while I counterbore and drill for the carriage bolts.

**4-5** I recess the nut, washer, and end of each carriage bolt by counterboring the holes with a forstner bit. Each joint gets 2 holes.

**4-6** After drilling the counterbores, I switch to a 3/8-in.-dia. bit, and drill all the way through for the bolts.

**4-7** With the carriage bolts, washers, and nuts installed, I tighten them up with a socket wrench.

**4-8**  I like to smooth up the face of the spruce top boards and seat boards by running them through the thickness planer. I remove only about 1/32 in.

## Top Boards and Seat Boards

The top boards and seat boards are the next thing to deal with. On my radial-arm saw, I crosscut the 5 top boards from 2 × 8 spruce and the 2 seat boards from 2 × 10 spruce (see Project Planner).

I could use these boards just as they came from the mill, but instead I run them through my planer to smooth up the top surface a little bit (*photo 4-8*). I just plane the face side, taking off about 1/32 in. or so. If I didn't have a planer I'd probably just belt-sand the top and seats after I assembled the table.

I place all the boards for the top facedown on a pair of sawhorses and squeeze the boards together with a couple of pipe clamps in preparation for installing the leg assemblies.

To locate the leg assemblies on the top, I measure in 8 in. from each end of the top and square a line across the top (*drawing 4-D*). Then I spread some construction adhesive where the top cleat will go and place the leg assembly in position on the top (*photo 4-9*). The idea is that the construction adhesive will minimize the tendency of the top boards to warp.

With the leg assembly in position, centered on the width of the top, I predrill and countersink for the galvanized screws that will secure the leg assembly to the top. I want to install 3 screws in each board. With the holes drilled, I screw the assembly in place (*photo 4-10*). The other leg assembly goes on in the same way.

Next, I put the center cleat in place with construction adhesive and screws. This cleat is spaced 22¼ in. from the end cleat as shown (*drawing 4-D*).

**4-9** Before I screw the leg assemblies to the underside of the top, I spread some construction adhesive where the top cleat will go.

**4-10** I place the leg assembly in position over the adhesive, center it on the width of the top, and predrill and countersink for the galvanized screws that secure the leg assembly to the top. I install 3 screws in each board.

*Center Braces*

Underneath the table there are 2 center braces that run from the center cleat down to the legs (*drawings 4-A and 4-D*). These braces have 2 angled cuts at each end. After cutting these braces to length and width (see Project Planner and *drawing 4-D*) I lay out the angled cuts as shown (*drawing 4-D*).

With the angles laid out, I'm ready to cut them on the radial-arm saw. First, I cut the angle that meets the 4 × 4 crossmember (*drawing 4-D*). I swing the saw to 35½ degrees and make the cut on each brace (*photo 4-11*).

**4-11** The center braces require 2 cuts at each end. First, I make a 35½-degree-angle cut. Then, I place this angled end against the radial-arm saw fence to make a second cut at right angles to the first.

## 4-D  *Center Brace and Cleat Details*

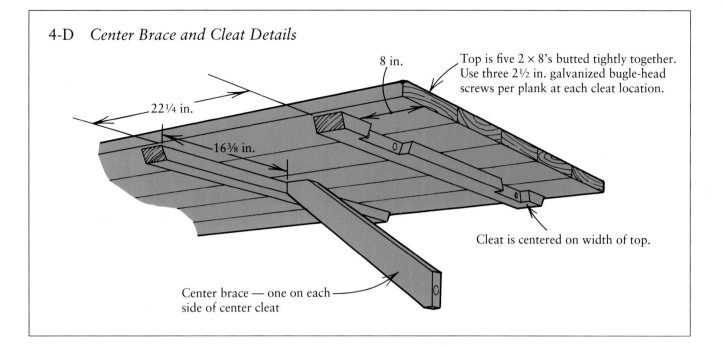

22¼ in.

8 in.

16⅜ in.

Top is five 2 × 8's butted tightly together. Use three 2½ in. galvanized bugle-head screws per plank at each cleat location.

Cleat is centered on width of top.

Center brace — one on each side of center cleat

**Center Brace Detail**

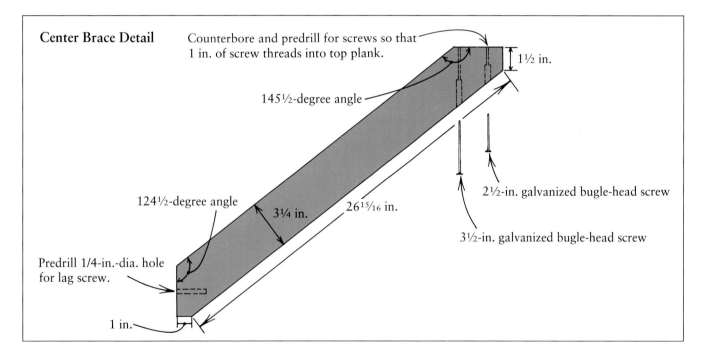

Counterbore and predrill for screws so that 1 in. of screw threads into top plank.

145½-degree angle

1½ in.

124½-degree angle

3¼ in.

26¹⁵⁄₁₆ in.

2½-in. galvanized bugle-head screw

3½-in. galvanized bugle-head screw

Predrill 1/4-in.-dia. hole for lag screw.

1 in.

At the other end of each brace, I make the angled cut that meets the 2 × 4 center cleat. This angle is also 35½ degrees, so I don't need to reset the saw for this cut.

After making the angled cuts at both ends of each cleat, I turn the saw back to 90 degrees and make a second cut on each end at right angles to the cuts I just made (*drawing 4-D*). I place the angled end of the cleat against the radial-arm saw fence to make these right-angled cuts.

**4-12** Construction adhesive and screws hold the seats to the cross-members. I countersink for the screws to keep the heads well below the surface.

**4-13** With the table assembled, I round off the top edges of the top and seats with a 1/2-in. roundover bit in my router.

One end of each center brace fits into the dado in the crossmember. The other end butts against the side of the center cleat (*drawings 4-A and 4-D*). I tap the braces into position with a mallet. To secure the braces to the 4 × 4, I use 3/8-in.-dia. 4-in. lag screws.

To recess the lag-screw heads and washers, I drill a 3/4-in.-deep counterbore with a 1¼-in.-dia. forstner bit in the center of each crossmember (*drawing 4-B*). Next, with a 3/8-in.-dia. bit, I drill a hole for the unthreaded portion of the lag bolt. Finally, with a 1/4-in. bit, I drill a pilot hole for the threaded portion. I install the lag bolts and washers and tighten them up.

At the other ends of the center braces, I counterbore and drill for a couple of galvanized screws that secure the brace to the top (*drawing 4-D*). I drill deep enough that 1 in. of the screw thread penetrates into the top. With the holes drilled, I install one 2½-in. #8 screw and one 3½-in. #8 screw in each brace.

*Installing the Seat Boards*

Now for the seats, which I've already cut to length and run through the planer. I draw a line on each crossmember, 8¾ in. from the end (*Seat Detail*). Next I spread a little construction adhesive on the ends of the crossmembers. Then I put the seat boards into position — with 8 in. overhanging the crossmembers on each end — and tack them in

place with an 8d finishing nail at each end. Then I drill and install 3 screws in each end to secure the seat to the crossmember (*photo 4-12*).

To relieve the sharp edges of the top and the seats, I round over the top edges with a 1/2-in. roundover bit in my router (*photo 4-13*).

## A No-Hassle Finish

To weatherproof my picnic table and even out the color of the different woods I used, I apply a good-quality, brown oil stain. I just brush on a heavy coat with a bristle brush, allowing the stain to soak into the wood. There's no need even to wipe it off.

Now, that's not a bad-looking picnic table. I'm sure it will see plenty of use in the next few years at our family get-togethers. One thing's for sure, this table will last for a long, long time.

# 5

# *Garden Swing*

## PROJECT PLANNER

*Time:* 6 to 10 days
*Special hardware and tools:*
  3/8-in.-dia. auger bit 7 in. to 8 in. long
  (4) 3/8-in. by 8-in. zinc-plated eyebolts
  (4) 3/8-in. by 6-in. zinc-plated eyebolts
  (4) 3/8-in. by 4-in. zinc-plated eyescrews
  (8) 3/8-in. by 3½-in. zinc-plated carriage bolts
  (20) 3/8-in. by 2½.-in. zinc-plated carriage bolts
  (14) 3/8-in. by 2-in. zinc-plated carriage bolts
  (62) 3/8-in. zinc-plated washers
  (50) 3/8-in. zinc-plated nuts
  (1) 36-in. length of 10-24 zinc-plated threaded rod
  (16) 10-24 zinc-plated nuts
  (16) 10 zinc-plated washers
  (1) 10-ft. length of 3/4-in. E.M.T. conduit
  (1) 10-ft. length of 1/2-in. E.M.T. conduit
  (8) 3/4-in. zinc-plated flat washers
  (1) 6-ft. length of 1/8-in. by 1½-in. flat aluminum bar stock
  (4) half-post connectors
  (8) 2½-in. #8 galvanized bugle-head screws
  (14) 1¼-in. #8 galvanized bugle-head screws
  (1) tube of construction adhesive and caulking gun
  *Wood:*
  (4) 8-ft. 2 × 4 redwood
  Cut each piece according to plan (*drawing 5-B*) with compound cuts on each end to make 2 pairs of swing-frame standards.
  (1) 14-ft. 2 × 4 redwood
  Cut 2 pieces 37¼ in. long for platform frame. From remainder cut swing frame crosspieces.
  (1) 10-ft. 2 × 4 redwood
  Cut according to plan for frame angle braces.
  (1) 14-ft. 2 × 6 redwood
  Cut in half, then rip and joint

AROUND the turn of the century, garden swings like this one were a common sight in the backyards of America. In those quieter times before television, people would while away a summer evening just swinging and talking for hours on end. Garden swings were so popular that in 1900 you could even order one by mail for the princely sum of $4.50!

My garden swing is built much like the old ones — using a tried-and-true design. In fact, I based it on an antique garden swing that must be at least 75 years old. The proportions of that old swing were just about perfect, but it was built out of pine — a poor choice of wood for outdoor furniture. The ends of the legs had rotted out badly and the joints were all falling apart.

I decided to build my swing from redwood, one of the most rot-resistant species you can find. Redwood, which grows in the western states, is expensive in New England but it never needs paint and will hold up forever outdoors. What's more, it's a beautiful wood to look at.

## *Building the Frames*

Let's get started by building the 2 frames that support the seats (*drawing 5-A and 5-B*). Each frame is a trapezoid consisting of two 2 × 4 standards connected at the top by a 2 × 4 crosspiece and at the bottom by a thinner crosspiece cut from a piece of 1 × 6. Crossbraces on either side of the swing hold the two frames together near the top (*drawing 5-A and 5-C*).

The first pieces to cut are the 2 × 4 standards that form the legs of each frame. The bottom ends of these standards will rest on the ground. So I can get a maximum amount of bearing surface, I cut the

each piece into 2⅝-in.-wide pieces for vertical seat hangers.

(2) 12-ft. 1 × 6 redwood

From one board, cut one piece 84 in. Then rip and joint into 2 strips 2⅝ in. wide for bottom crosspieces of swing frame. Rip and joint remainder into 2 strips 2⅝ in. wide, and then cut one piece 37 in. long for center platform cleat and 4 pieces 17 in. long for armrests.

Rip and joint remaining 12-ft. board into 2 strips 2⅝ in. wide. From each strip cut: 2 pieces 50 in. long for X-braces and one piece 38 in. long to make 2 seat back slats.

(7) 10-ft. 1 × 6 redwood

Cut 21 pieces 38 in. long. Rip and joint 19 pieces into 2⅝-in.-wide slats to make 14 seat back slats, 14 platform slats, and 10 seat slats. Rip and joint remaining 2 pieces into 2 pieces 1¾ in. wide for front seat slats and one piece 1⅝ in. wide for rear seat slats (drawing 5-G).

(2) 8-ft. 1 × 6 redwood

Rip and joint boards into 4 strips 2⅝ in. wide. From each of 2 strips cut 2 pieces 22½ in. long for armrest support (4 required) and 2 pieces 25 in. long for seat braces (4 required). From each of the remaining 2 strips cut one piece 38 in. long for remaining seat back slats (total of 18 required) and one piece 37 in. long for seat-hanger spacer (2 required).

(2) 10-ft. 1 × 4 redwood

From each board cut 2 pieces 24 in. long for seat supports (4 required) and 2 pieces 32 in. long for seat back supports (4 required.)

ends at a compound angle. The radial-arm saw is just the tool for the job (photo 5-1). Make sure to double-check the angles before you make these cuts so you end up with 2 pairs of standards.

I tilt the blade counterclockwise, 12 degrees from vertical. Then, I swing the saw's arm to the right 13½ degrees from zero. With this setup, I cut the bottom of 2 standards, trimming off as little as possible. Then I swing the saw's arm 13½ degrees to the left of zero and cut the bottoms of the other 2 standards. Then I lay out the 94⅝-in. length of the standards, measuring along the outer inside edge (drawing 5-B). I make an identical parallel cut at the top of each standard — for looks more than anything else.

The next pieces to make are the 2 bottom crosspieces for the frames (drawings 5-A and 5-B). From an 84-in.-long piece of 1 × 6 redwood I rip and joint 2 pieces 2⅝ in. wide (see Project Planner). The ends of the crosspieces must be cut to a 78-degree angle to match the splay of the standards (drawing 5-B). I swing my power miter-box blade 12 degrees to the left to make the cut. To save time, I stack one crosspiece on top of the other and cut both at once. After cutting one end, I measure off 83 in. from long point to long point. Then I swing the saw blade 12 degrees to the other side of center to cut the opposite ends of the crosspieces.

The top crosspiece of each frame is cut from a 2 × 4, and the angle on the ends is also 78 degrees. I cut these pieces on the miter box, setting the blade to 12 degrees as before. To mark off the length of these crosspieces I measure 45 in. from short point to short point and swing the saw to the other side of center to cut the opposite ends.

On the antique swing, the crosspieces were just bolted to the surface of the upright standards. I think it's much stronger if the cross-

5-1  I cut the ends of the frame standards to a compound angle to get the maximum amount of bearing surface where they'll contact the ground.

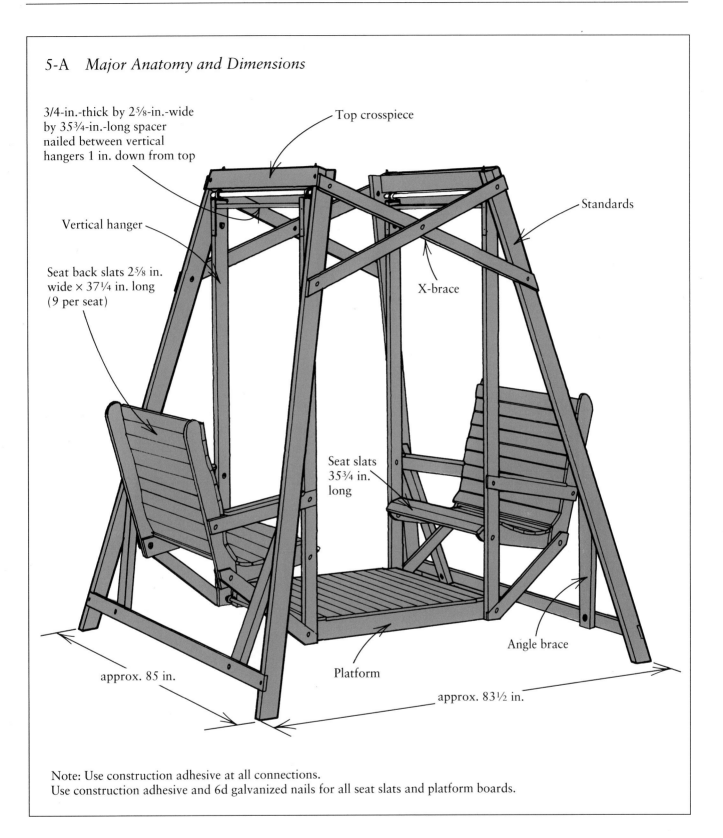

3/4-in.-thick by 2⅝-in.-wide by 35¾-in.-long spacer nailed between vertical hangers 1 in. down from top

Top crosspiece

Vertical hanger

Standards

Seat back slats 2⅝ in. wide × 37¼ in. long (9 per seat)

X-brace

Seat slats 35¾ in. long

Platform

Angle brace

approx. 85 in.

approx. 83½ in.

Note: Use construction adhesive at all connections.
Use construction adhesive and 6d galvanized nails for all seat slats and platform boards.

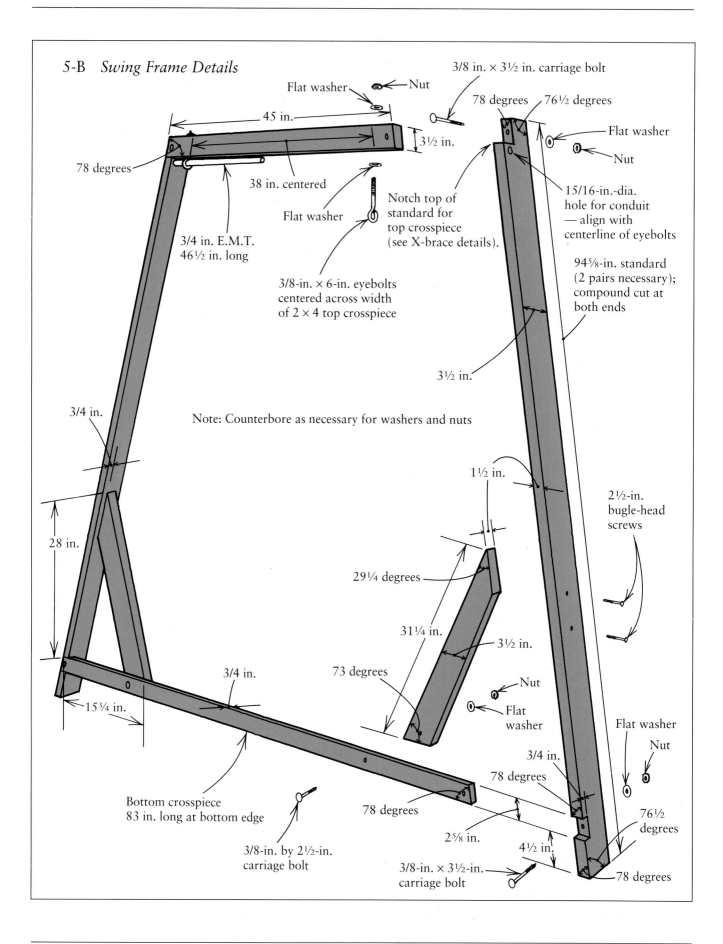

5-B  *Swing Frame Details*

3/8 in. × 3 1/2 in. carriage bolt

Flat washer — Nut

78 degrees    76 1/2 degrees

Flat washer

Nut

45 in.

3 1/2 in.

78 degrees

38 in. centered

Flat washer

Notch top of
standard for
top crosspiece
(see X-brace details).

15/16-in.-dia.
hole for conduit
— align with
centerline of eyebolts

3/4 in. E.M.T.
46 1/2 in. long

3/8-in. × 6-in. eyebolts
centered across width
of 2 × 4 top crosspiece

94 5/8-in. standard
(2 pairs necessary);
compound cut at
both ends

3/4 in.

Note: Counterbore as necessary for washers and nuts

3 1/2 in.

1 1/2 in.

2 1/2-in.
bugle-head
screws

28 in.

29 1/4 degrees

31 1/4 in.

3 1/2 in.

73 degrees

Nut

Flat
washer

15 3/4 in.

3/4 in.

3/4 in.

78 degrees

Flat washer

Nut

Bottom crosspiece
83 in. long at bottom edge

78 degrees

76 1/2
degrees

3/8-in. by 2 1/2-in.
carriage bolt

2 5/8 in.

4 1/2 in.

3/8-in. × 3 1/2-in.
carriage bolt

78 degrees

pieces are let into the standards. To do this, I have to cut angled dadoes for the bottom crosspieces and notches for the top ones (*drawings 5-A, 5-B, and 5-C*).

I lay out the dadoes and notches on the outer edge of each standard (*drawings 5-B and 5-C*), double-checking to make sure that the standards will splay in the proper direction and that I'll be making the cuts on the *outer* edges. These dadoes are angled 12 degrees so that the cuts will be parallel to the angled ends of the standards.

To lay out the dadoes and notches, I set my sliding bevel gauge to a 78-degree angle and draw an angled line across the edge of the standard — just to make sure that I angle the cuts in the proper direction. I'll make these cuts on the radial-arm saw with a stack dado head set for a 3/4-in.-wide dado.

I cut the dadoes for the bottom crosspieces first. This operation requires 2 separate saw settings — one for the left-hand standards and one for the right-hand standards.

First I install a high wooden fence on my radial-arm saw. Then, to dado the left-hand standards, I swing the radial-arm saw blade 12 degrees to the right and adjust the blade for a 3/4-in.-deep cut. Holding the 2 × 4 standard on edge with the inside face against the fence, I make a series of crosscuts to "nibble out" the 2⅝-in.-wide dado. I cut the other left-hand standard in the same way. To dado the right-hand standards, I simply swing the saw blade 12 degrees to the left of center.

The notches for the top crosspieces come next (*photo 5-2*). I lower the dado head for a 1½-in.-deep cut and use the same angle settings I used for the dadoes. That takes care of the standards for now.

The next pieces to make are the angled braces at the bottoms of the frames. Each frame has 2 of these braces to minimize racking (*draw-*

5-3  Because of their size, I assemble the frames on the floor. Construction adhesive, nails, and clamps hold the joints together while I drill holes for the carriage bolts that will secure the joint.

ings 5-A and 5-B). I cut the braces from a 2 × 4 (see Project Planner) and cut the top end of each brace to a 29¼-degree angle on my radial-arm saw. The bottom ends get cut to a 73-degree angle. From long point to long point the braces measure 31¼ inches.

Now I'm ready to cut the X-braces (drawings 5-A and 5-C). I rip and joint two 2⅝-in. pieces of 1 × 6 and cut them into 4 pieces 50 in. long (see Project Planner). On my power miter box, I cut one end of each piece to an angle of 53½ degrees. This end will become the bottom end of the brace when it's installed (drawing 5-C). Measuring along what will be the bottom edge of each X-brace, I mark off 49⁷⁄₁₆ in. and cut an 82-degree angle on the opposite end.

### Assembling the Frames

With all of the frame pieces cut I'm ready for a little assembly. Because of the size of the frames, I find it easiest to work on the floor of my shop (photo 5-3). To get ready, I need my pneumatic nail gun with some 6d finishing nails, a caulking gun with a tube of construction adhesive, eight 3½-in. carriage bolts, and four 2½-in. carriage bolts. I also need my socket wrench with a socket to fit the nuts.

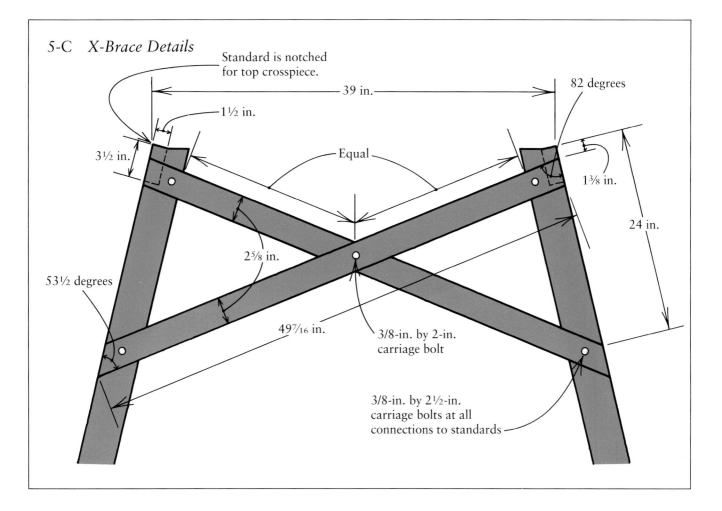

**5-C   X-Brace Details**

Standard is notched for top crosspiece.

39 in.

82 degrees

1½ in.

3½ in.

Equal

1³⁄₈ in.

24 in.

2⁵⁄₈ in.

53½ degrees

49⁷⁄₁₆ in.

3/8-in. by 2-in. carriage bolt

3/8-in. by 2½-in. carriage bolts at all connections to standards

I place a pair of standards on the floor with the dadoes and notches facing up. I spread a little construction adhesive in the dadoes and fit the bottom crosspiece in place. I flush up the ends with the sides of the standards and tack the joint with a couple of nails to hold things together when I drill for the carriage bolts.

The angled braces go on next. Locate the braces according to the measurements in *drawing 5-B*. The top end butts against the standard and gets a nail to hold it in place. I apply adhesive and clamp the bottom end to the crosspiece to hold it in place while I drill for the bolt. Next, I install the top crosspiece in its notches, gluing and nailing the joint as before.

With the frame pieces assembled, I'm ready to drill the holes for the carriage bolts. I chuck a 3/8-in. bit in my drill and bore one hole through each joint, holding a square next to the bit to act as a guide to keep it vertical. To secure the top end of each angled brace, I drill, countersink, and install two 2½-in. screws.

I counterbore the inside of each bolt hole to recess the nut and washer. I use a 1¼-in.-dia. forstner bit, drilling about 1/2 in. deep. Then I install the carriage bolts and torque the nuts down tight. If any adhesive squeezes out, I clean it up after it hardens with a utility knife. With one frame completed, I assemble the other one in the same way.

Now that both frames are assembled, I can install the X-braces that tie the 2 frames together (*drawings 5-A and 5-C*). To position these braces, I make 2 pencil marks near the top of each frame: one mark 1⅜ in. from the top edge of the crosspiece and a second mark 24 in. from the top (*drawing 5-C*).

With a frame on its side on the floor, I clamp 2 crosspieces to one standard, aligning the corners with the pencil marks as shown (*drawing 5-C*). Then I drill a 3/8-in. hole through the center of each brace for a 2½-in. carriage bolt. I clamp the other ends of the braces to a standard on the opposite frame, drilling a bolt hole through each piece. I counterbore the inside of each hole with my 1¼-in. forstner bit and install the bolts, nuts, and washers. No adhesive on these joints; I'll have to disassemble these joints later to get the frame through the shop door.

Now I can stand the swing frame upright and install the X-braces on the opposite side. Here, too, I clamp the braces on the pencil marks and then drill, counterbore, and bolt the braces in place. Where the braces cross, I install a 2-in. carriage bolt after making sure that the measurements across the top edge of each brace are equal (*drawing 5-C*).

### Installing the Eyebolts

The swing and platform assembly hangs from 2 pieces of 3/4-in.-dia. E.M.T. electrical conduit — one on each frame (*drawing 5-B*). The

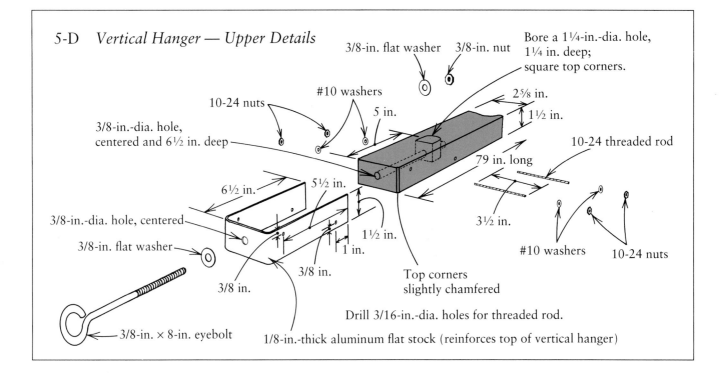

5-D  *Vertical Hanger — Upper Details*

Bore a 1¼-in.-dia. hole, 1¼ in. deep; square top corners.

3/8-in. flat washer    3/8-in. nut

#10 washers

10-24 nuts

5 in.

2⅝ in.

1½ in.

3/8-in.-dia. hole, centered and 6½ in. deep

10-24 threaded rod

79 in. long

6½ in.    5½ in.

3½ in.

3/8-in.-dia. hole, centered

1½ in.

#10 washers    10-24 nuts

3/8-in. flat washer

1 in.

3/8 in.

3/8 in.

Top corners slightly chamfered

3/8-in. × 8-in. eyebolt

Drill 3/16-in.-dia. holes for threaded rod.

1/8-in.-thick aluminum flat stock (reinforces top of vertical hanger)

conduit fits into two 3/8-in. by 6-in. eyebolts in each top crosspiece as shown in the drawing.

To locate the holes for these eyebolts, I mark the center of the crosspiece and measure out 19 inches to each side. Then I drill 3/8-in.-dia. holes up through the crosspiece, holding a square against the brace to help me keep the drill square and parallel (*photo 5-4*). When the holes are all drilled, I get up on a ladder and tap the eyebolts up through the holes, making sure to put on a washer between the eye and the brace. Another washer and nut go on top.

## Vertical Hangers

Next, I want to start working on the 4 vertical hangers from which the seats are suspended (*drawings 5-A and 5-F*). An eyebolt in the top

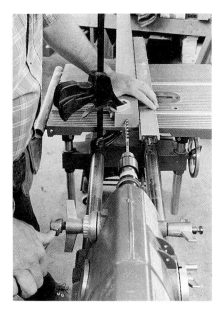

5-5 The horizontal boring function on my combination machine is ideal for drilling long, straight, perfectly centered holes. Here, I'm drilling one of the 3/8-in.-dia. eyebolt holes in the tops of the vertical hangers.

5-6 After drilling the 3/8-in.-dia. holes, I drill a 1¼-in.-dia. hole at right angles to the first one so I can install a nut and washer on the eyebolt. I use a forstner bit for a clean, flat-bottomed hole.

5-7 I square up the top end of the 1¼-in.-dia. hole with a chisel so the eyebolt's washer can sit on a flat surface.

end of each hanger fits over the conduit on the top crosspiece (*drawing 5-D*). These hangers are going to take a lot of stress and strain, so I want to make sure that they're properly reinforced.

After milling the hangers to width and length (see Project Planner), I bore a 3/8-in.-dia. hole in one end for the eyebolt (*drawing 5-D*). The holes have to be perfectly centered and straight. Fortunately, my 5-in-1 combination machine has a horizontal boring function — a handy device for accurately drilling long holes like this (*photo 5-5*). It's possible to drill these holes freehand, but it's tough to keep such a deep hole centered. If you drill the hanger hole freehand, here's a trick to keep the bit straight: on the drill press, drill a 3/8-in.-dia. hole through a 3-in. block. Use the block as a guide for boring the hole in the hanger.

I set up my 5-in-1 machine in the horizontal boring mode and install a 3/8-in.-dia. auger bit in the chuck. Next, I mark the center point on the top end of each hanger by drawing diagonals from corner to corner. I adjust the height of the machine's table so the bit is centered from top to bottom and clamp a straightedge clamp across the table to position the stock from side to side. When the bit's lined up on center, I drill a 6½-in.-deep hole.

In order to get the washer and nut on the eyebolt, I have to drill a second hole that intersects the first one at right angles (*drawing 5-D*). I do this on the drill press with a 1¼-in.-dia. forstner bit (*photo 5-6*). I center the hole on the width of the hanger, 5 in. down from the top end. I set the depth stop for a 1¼-in.-deep cut and drill a hole in each vertical hanger. In order for the washer to sit on a flat surface, I square up the top edge of each hole with a chisel (*photo 5-7*).

To reinforce the tops of the vertical hangers so they won't split right down the middle, I make a U-shaped bracket out of some 1/8-in.

by 1½-in. aluminum stock. This aluminum is very easy to bend by hand.

To make the brackets, I cut 4 pieces of aluminum 15¾ in. long. I draw a pencil line 6½ in. from one end to mark the location of the first bend I need to make. I clamp the metal in my vise so it's square to the bench top and bend it over 90 degrees with my hands. Then I flatten the bend with a hardwood block and a hammer to sharpen up the corner. With one bend finished, I clamp the other end in the vise and make the second bend so that the sides will be 2⅝ in. apart (*photo 5-8*).

The brackets should just slip over the tops of the hangers without any slop. In order to make the brackets fit snugly where the slightly rounded inside corners of the bracket touch the wood, I knock off the corners of the wood with a block plane.

Next, I have to drill a hole in each bracket for the eyebolt. I measure carefully to make sure that each hole will align with the hole in the hanger itself. I prick a center mark with a center punch and drill a 3/8-in.-dia. hole.

Now I'm ready to install the brackets on the hangers. I slip on a bracket and align the holes. Then I slip a washer on an eyebolt and tap the bolt in the hole (*drawing 5-D*). When the end of the eyebolt comes through into the forstner-bit hole, I slip on a washer and nut. I hold the nut with a screwdriver as I tighten the eyebolt with a second screwdriver. I snug up the eyebolt, but not so tight that I start to deform the eye.

To secure the brackets to the hangers, I install 2 threaded steel rods in each bracket (*drawing 5-D*). On the drill press I drill two 3/16-in-dia. holes clear through the bracket and hanger. To avoid hitting the eyebolt, I drill the holes off center: one on the left side of the rod, one on the right (*photo 5-9*). I cut eight 3½-in.-long pieces of 10-24 threaded rod with a hacksaw. I slip the rods into their holes and install a nut and washer on each end. Those brackets sure aren't going to go anywhere.

There are still 2 more operations to perform on the vertical hangers. I need to cut a 2⅝-in.-wide dado in each hanger for the arm supports and an angled notch at the bottom for the lower braces (*drawings 5-A, 5-E, and 5-F*). I make both of these cuts on the radial-arm saw with my stack dado head set for a 3/4-in.-wide cut.

These cuts go on the *outside* of the hanger — the side opposite the forstner-bit hole — and I also must make matching pairs. I lay out the joints with my sliding bevel gauge and a pencil. The armrest support dado is cut at an 80-degree angle (*drawing 5-E*). I swing the radial-arm saw 10 degrees and set the height for a 3/4-in.-deep cut. Then I make repeated crosscuts to mill each 2⅝-in.-wide dado.

To cut the notches, all I do is reset the radial-arm saw to 38 degrees (for a 52-degree angle) and cut a notch at the bottom of each hanger. The depth setting stays the same.

5-8   Here I'm making the second bend for one of the U-shaped brackets that reinforce the tops of the vertical hangers. I bend the 1/8-in.-thick aluminum with my hands, then sharpen up the corner with a hardwood block and a hammer.

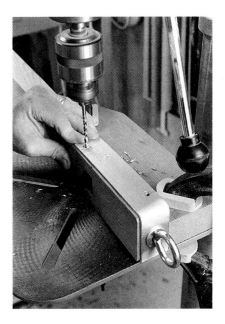

5-9   Two threaded steel rods secure the bracket to the hanger. I drill two 3/16-in.-dia. holes through each bracket. To avoid hitting the eyebolt, I offset one hole to the left and one hole to the right of center.

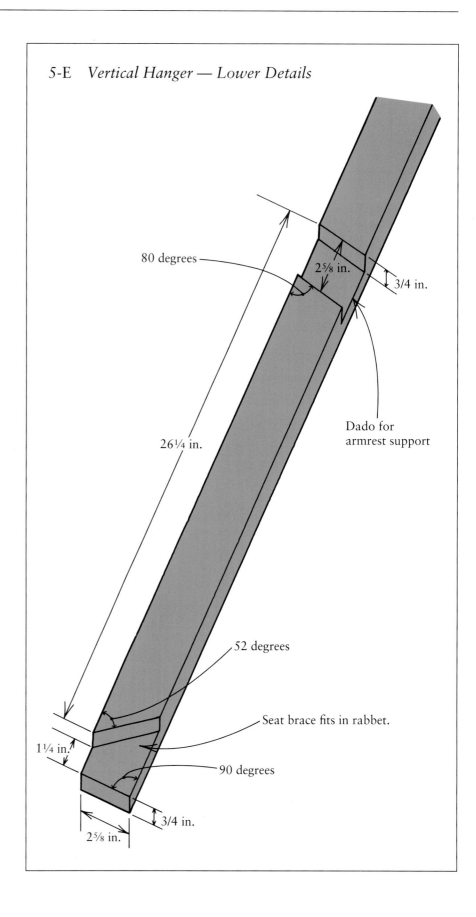

5-E  *Vertical Hanger — Lower Details*

80 degrees

2⅝ in.

3/4 in.

Dado for armrest support

26¼ in.

52 degrees

Seat brace fits in rabbet.

1¼ in.

90 degrees

3/4 in.

2⅝ in.

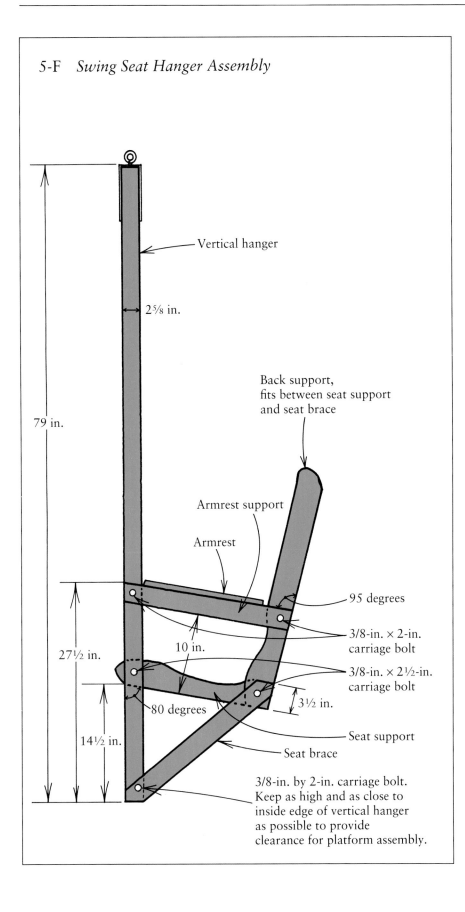

Vertical hanger

2⅝ in.

79 in.

Back support,
fits between seat support
and seat brace

Armrest support

Armrest

27½ in.

10 in.

95 degrees

3/8-in. × 2-in.
carriage bolt

3/8-in. × 2½-in.
carriage bolt

3½ in.

80 degrees

Seat support

14½ in.

Seat brace

3/8-in. by 2-in. carriage bolt.
Keep as high and as close to
inside edge of vertical hanger
as possible to provide
clearance for platform assembly.

One final bit of business on the vertical hangers: I need to draw a layout line for positioning the seat supports later. I set my sliding bevel gauge to 80 degrees, measure up 14½ degrees from the bottom end of each hanger, and draw a line on the inside face of each hanger (*drawing 5-F*). This line will locate the bottom edge of the seat support.

## Armrest Supports and Seat Braces

I mill the 4 armrest supports from 1 × 6 redwood, ripping and jointing them to a width of 2⅝ in. (see Project Planner). I cut the front end of each support at an 80-degree angle (*drawing 5-G*). Then I measure 22¼ in. from the long point of the cut to mark the long point of the back end. This back end gets an 85-degree-angle cut. I make both cuts on my power miter box.

The next parts to make are the angled seat braces that support the back ends of the seats (*drawings 5-A, 5-F, and 5-G*). After cutting these pieces from 1 × 6 stock (see Project Planner), I make 2 angled cuts on each end (*drawing 5-G*). I lay out these cuts with my sliding bevel gauge and a pencil and make the cuts on the radial-arm saw.

## Seat Supports and Back Supports

Now I'm ready to start working on the seat supports and the back supports (*drawings 5-F and 5-G*). Both of these parts are contoured so the seat will be comfortable (*drawing 5-G*). Instead of cutting a smooth curve, however, I cut a series of facets so that each seat slat will have a flat surface to bear on. I make a wooden pattern for each piece by plotting the midpoints between slats as shown in *drawing 5-G*. I need 2 measurements to locate each point.

After sawing out the patterns, I trace around them with a pencil to lay out the actual parts on the wood. Next, I have to mark a few layout lines. The first layout line is an angled line near the front of each seat support (*drawing 5-G*). I set my sliding bevel gauge to a 100-degree angle and draw a line 18¹³⁄₁₆ in. from the lower back corner. This line locates the position of the front edge of the vertical hanger.

On the outer face of each back support, I draw a pair of parallel layout lines to mark the position of the armrest support (*drawing 5-G*). I set my sliding bevel to 85 degrees and draw the first line 10 in. from the lower back corner. I draw the second line 2⅝ in. above the first.

Once the parts are laid out, I cut the back end of each seat support and back support to a 95-degree angle (*drawing 5-G*). Then I band-saw the faceted profile and clean up the cuts with a drum-sander attachment on my drill press.

Next, I group matching boards together and square lines across the 3/4-in. width with a square to mark the locations of the slats (*drawing 5-G*).

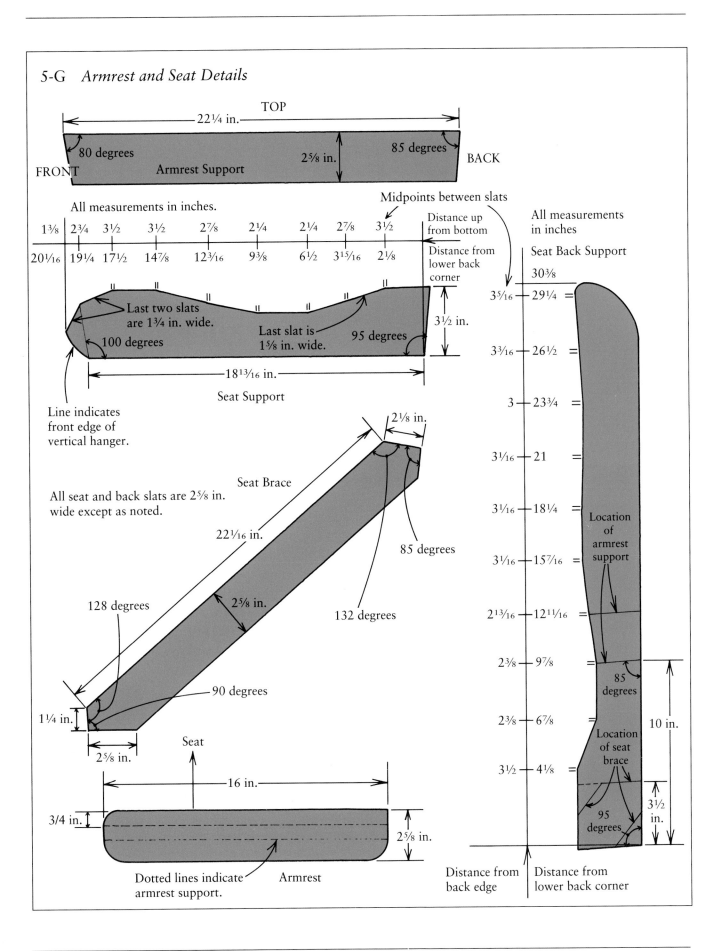

TOP

22¼ in.

80 degrees

FRONT

Armrest Support

2⅝ in.

85 degrees

BACK

All measurements in inches.

Midpoints between slats

Distance up from bottom

| 1⅜ | 2¾ | 3½ | 3½ | 2⅞ | 2¼ | 2¼ | 2⅞ | 3½ |
|---|---|---|---|---|---|---|---|---|

Distance from lower back corner

| 20 1/16 | 19¼ | 17½ | 14⅞ | 12 3/16 | 9⅜ | 6½ | 3 15/16 | 2⅛ |

All measurements in inches

Seat Back Support

30⅜

3 5/16 — 29¼ =

3 3/16 — 26½ =

3 — 23¾ =

3 1/16 — 21 =

3 1/16 — 18¼ =

Last two slats are 1¾ in. wide.

100 degrees

Last slat is 1⅝ in. wide.

95 degrees

3½ in.

18 13/16 in.

Seat Support

Line indicates front edge of vertical hanger.

3 1/16 — 15 7/16 =

Location of armrest support

All seat and back slats are 2⅝ in. wide except as noted.

2 13/16 — 12 11/16 =

2½ in.

Seat Brace

85 degrees

22 1/16 in.

2⅜ — 9⅞ =

85 degrees

128 degrees

2⅝ in.

132 degrees

10 in.

2⅜ — 6⅞ =

Location of seat brace

90 degrees

1¼ in.

2⅝ in.

Seat

3½ — 4⅛ =

3½ in.

95 degrees

16 in.

3/4 in.

2⅝ in.

Dotted lines indicate armrest support.

Armrest

Distance from back edge

Distance from lower back corner

**5-10** The seat frames go together with construction adhesive and galvanized finishing nails. Then I drill a 3/8-in.-dia. hole through each joint and install carriage bolts to permanently fasten the frame.

*Assembling the Seat Frames*

Now I'm ready to assemble all the parts. I assemble one side frame at a time. I place a vertical hanger on my bench and spread a little construction adhesive in the armrest-support dado. Then I place the front end (with the 80-degree cut) of an armrest support in the dado, flush up the front end, and tack it with a couple of 1¼-in. finishing nails. I'll install carriage bolts later to really hold the joints together.

I flip the hanger over to install the seat support. I spread some construction adhesive on the hanger, just above the layout line on the hanger that locates the seat support. I place the seat support on the hanger, lining up the bottom edge of the support with the layout line on the hanger. To position the seat support from front to back, I line up the vertical hanger's front edge with the layout line I drew on the seat support. When everything's properly aligned, I tack the joint with one nail.

The back support goes on next, at the rear end of the seat support (*drawings 5-A and 5-F*). I put on some adhesive and tack the support in place with one 1¼-in. nail. Then I line up the armrest support with the layout lines on the back support, and glue and tack that joint together.

The seat brace goes on next. I put some construction adhesive in the notch at the bottom of the hanger and a little more at the back end of the seat support. A couple of nails hold each joint together.

That about does it for assembling the frame. I drill a 3/8-in. hole through the center of each joint for a carriage bolt (*drawing 5-F*). I counterbore only for the head of the carriage bolt that holds the seat support to the vertical hanger. I drill the 1/4-in.-deep counterbore with my 1¼-in. forstner bit and install the bolts, nuts, and washers (*photo 5-10*).

One bolt hole isn't centered; I offset the hole at the bottom of the hanger to provide clearance for the platform assembly (*drawing 5-F*).

That's one frame down and only 3 more to go. When I put the others together I make sure I end up with 2 matching pairs of frames.

## Building the Platform

The platform hangs from 2 pieces of 1/2-in. E.M.T. conduit that passes through eyescrews mounted in the ends of the 2 platform frame members (*drawing 5-H*). The ends of this conduit fit into holes drilled in the bottom ends of the vertical hangers. These 11/16-in.-dia. holes are "blind" holes, that is, they don't go all the way through the wood. I want to drill them 7/8 in. deep, so I put a piece of tape on an 11/16-dia. speed bit to act as a depth gauge (*photo 5-11*). I lay out the hole centers 7/8 in. from the bottom of the hanger and 7/8 in. from the front edge (*drawing 5-H*) and drill a hole on the inside of each hanger.

The ends of the 2 × 4 platform frame members are reinforced with metal brackets similar to the ones I installed on the vertical hangers. The only difference is that I make these brackets from galvanized steel half-post caps — a standard item at most building-supply centers. I have to modify the post caps slightly by cutting off the unnecessary part with a metal-cutting blade in my jigsaw.

In the center of each bracket, I drill a 3/8-in.-dia. hole just as I did for the vertical hanger brackets. Then I slip a bracket over the end of each 2 × 4 frame member and nail it in place with some 4d galvanized box nails.

With the brackets in place, I drill a 1/4-in.-dia. pilot hole for the 4½-in. eyescrew that threads into the end of each frame member. I drill these holes on my 5-in-1 combination machine as I did for the vertical hangers. I put a washer on each eyescrew before I thread it into its hole. The handle of my socket wrench makes a handy lever for tightening the screws.

Next I mill my platform boards and the center cleat. I cut the center cleat 36¼ in. long. I cut twelve 35¾-in.-long platform boards and two 35¼-in.-long platform boards (see Project Planner). Now I'm ready to assemble the platform.

First I square a line across the top of each frame member 2²¹/₃₂ in. from each end. Then I space the 2 frame members 31¼ in. apart on my bench and put a little construction adhesive on the center side of

5-11   A piece of tape on my bit acts as a depth stop for drilling the 11/16-in.-deep conduit holes at the bottom ends of the vertical standards.

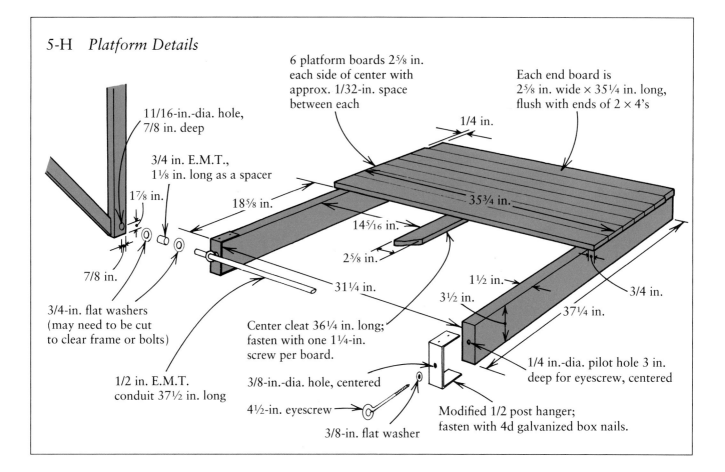

5-H  *Platform Details*

11/16-in.-dia. hole, 7/8 in. deep

3/4 in. E.M.T., 1⅛ in. long as a spacer

6 platform boards 2⅝ in. each side of center with approx. 1/32-in. space between each

Each end board is 2⅝ in. wide × 35¼ in. long, flush with ends of 2 × 4's

1/4 in.

1⅞ in.

18⅝ in.

35¾ in.

14⁵⁄₁₆ in.

2⅝ in.

7/8 in.

3/4-in. flat washers (may need to be cut to clear frame or bolts)

31¼ in.

1½ in.

3½ in.

3/4 in.

37¼ in.

1/2 in. E.M.T. conduit 37½ in. long

Center cleat 36¼ in. long; fasten with one 1¼-in. screw per board.

3/8-in.-dia. hole, centered

4½-in. eyescrew

3/8-in. flat washer

Modified 1/2 post hanger; fasten with 4d galvanized box nails.

1/4 in.-dia. pilot hole 3 in. deep for eyescrew, centered

the lines I just drew. I place 2 of the platform boards across the top, holding the boards to the insides of the lines. The ends of the boards overhang the 2 × 4 frame by 3/4 in. on each side. I use a piece of 3/4 scrap as a gauge block so I don't have to measure this overhang.

Once these 2 platform boards are in position, I nail them in place with some 6d galvanized finishing nails. Then I measure diagonally from corner to corner to make sure the platform is square. If the diagonals aren't equal, the frame isn't square. To correct this, I shift the frame until the diagonals are exactly equal. When everything's square, I lay a bead of construction adhesive along the tops of the frame members and nail on the rest of the platform boards. I start in the middle and work out to either end, spacing the boards about 1/32 in. apart. I shoot 2 nails into the end of each board.

The last board on each end of the platform goes over the metal brackets. I put some construction adhesive right on each bracket, but I have to predrill through the board and the bracket for the nails. These outer 2 boards are shorter than the others by 1/2 in. so that they'll overhang the frame members by only 1/2 in. on each side. This provides clearance for the vertical hangers.

I install a center cleat on the underside of the platform boards to stiffen the structure. With the platform upside down on my bench, I

5-12  To mark the holes in the standards for the conduit that supports the swings, I insert a scrap piece of conduit through one of the eyebolts. I line it up parallel with the crosspiece and tap the end hard enough to leave a mark in the wood.

predrill through the cleat for 1¼-in. #8 galvanized screws in each board. That takes care of the platform.

*Mounting the Swing Seats*

Now I'm ready to hang the swing seats from the frame. The first thing to do is drill a 15/16-in.-dia. hole in each frame standard for the 3/4-in. conduit that supports the seats (*drawings 5-A and 5-B*).

To mark the location of these holes, I slip a scrap length of conduit through one of the eyebolts in the crosspieces. I hold the conduit parallel to the crosspiece and place an end against one of the frame standards. I tap the opposite end of the conduit with a hammer hard enough to leave an impression in the wood (*photo 5-12*). I make a similar mark on all 4 standards to mark the locations of the holes.

On one side of the frame, I drill clear through the standards with a 15/16-in.-dia. speed bit, drilling from the inside of the frame (*photo 5-13*) and being careful not to drill through the X-brace when the bit breaks through. On the opposite side of the frame, I drill blind holes that are 1¼ in. deep.

With a hacksaw, I cut two 46½-in.-long pieces of the 3/4-in. conduit. Before I can install the conduit in the frame, I have to unbolt the two X-braces that partially cover the holes in the standards. I lift the X-braces up just enough to slide the conduit through the hole and through one of the eyebolts. Next, I slip on a pair of vertical hangers and guide the conduit through the other eyebolt and into the blind hole on the opposite side of the frame. I give the end a little tap with a hammer to drive the conduit home. After installing both pieces of conduit in this way, I bolt the X-braces back in place. These braces partially cover the holes and keep the conduit in place.

Now let's install the platform. But first, there's a little more metalwork to do. I cut two 37½-in.-long pieces of the 1/2-in. E.M.T. con-

5-13  Placing my drill on the mark, I bore a 15/16-in.-dia. hole clear through the standard, holding the bit parallel to the X-brace. The conduit slips through this hole, through the eyebolts, and into a blind hole drilled on the opposite side of the frame.

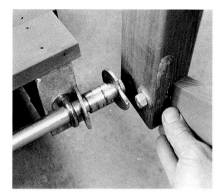

**5-14** The platform hangs from a piece of 1/2-in. conduit mounted in eyescrews in the platform frame. Two modified washers and a spacer made from 3/4-in. conduit fit over each end of the conduit. The conduit end fits into a hole in the vertical hanger. I notched the outside washer to clear the bolt in the hanger.

duit. Then I cut four 1⅛-in.-long pieces of 3/4-in. E.M.T. conduit to serve as spacers. These spacers will fit over the 1/2-in. conduit on the platform (*drawing 5-H*). Next, I have to modify eight 3/4-in. washers — 4 of which go on the 1/2-in. conduit at each end of the platform. I grind flat spots on the washers that will be against the eyescrews and grind notches on the others to clear the nuts of the carriage bolts at the bottoms of the hangers.

Here's how the whole thing goes together: I place the platform on the floor under the swings and slip a piece of 1/2-in. conduit through each set of eyescrews (*drawing 5-H*). On each end of the conduit, I slip on one of the 3/4-in. washers with the flat spot. The washer should fit flat against the eyebolt. The 3/4-in. conduit spacer goes on next. Finally, I slip on the 3/4-in. washer with the notch.

When all of the hardware's in place, I lift up one end of the platform and guide the ends of the conduit into the holes in the bottoms of the vertical hangers. I rotate each outer washer so the notch will fit over the bolt in the hanger (*photo 5-14*). The seat slats will keep the assembly from coming apart.

### Seat Slats and Back Slats

I rip and joint all the seat slats from 1 × 6 redwood and cut them all 35¾ in. long (see Project Planner). The back slats are longer — 37¼ in. long. The seat slats and back slats are all 2⅝ in. wide with 3 exceptions: the first 2 slats on the seat are 1¾ in. wide and the last seat slat is 1⅝ in. wide (*drawing 5-G*). Before I install the slats I knock off the sharp edges with a block plane.

I nail and glue the slats in place across the seat frames and seat back, holding the ends of the slats flush to the outside edge of the seat supports and back supports (*photo 5-15*). I line up the slats with the lines I drew earlier and shoot two 6d galvanized finishing nails into the end of each slat.

### Spacers and Armrests

I cut two 2⅝-in. by 35¾-in. spacers from 1 × 6 redwood and install one between each pair of vertical hangers at the top (*drawing 5-A*). I toenail the spacers into the hangers with 4d finishing nails, setting the heads with a nail set.

The armrests are the last parts to make and install. I cut them out of 1 × 6 stock (see Project Planner and *drawing 5-G*) and round the ends and clean up the cuts with the drum-sander attachment on the drill press.

To install the armrests, I run a bead of construction adhesive along the top edge of each armrest support and place the armrests in position. Using a 3/4-in. scrap as a spacer block, I adjust each armrest so it overhangs 3/4 in. on the inside of the support. Then I nail them in place with some 6d galvanized finishing nails.

Unfortunately, I have to take the swing apart to get it out of the

**5-15** I fasten the seat slats and back slats with 6d galvanized finishing nails. The slats hold the 2 seat frames together.

shop. I take off the X-braces and drop the seats from the 3/4-in. conduit. Once I get the thing reassembled outside — this time gluing the X-braces in place — I put a few dabs of grease on the moving metal parts and I'm ready to ride.

You know, I have a feeling that this project is going to be even more fun to use than it was to build. It rides like a dream.

*Postscript:* After a few weeks in the weather my swing started to squeak. The conduits at the top were turning in their holes in the hangers. I silenced the squeaking by drilling a 1/8-in.-dia. hole through each hanger and the conduit. Then I installed galvanized nails in the holes to keep the conduit from turning.

# 6

# *Outdoor Planters*

E VERY home can use a couple of good-looking outdoor planters. Here are two that will look great on a porch or a deck or
anywhere around the yard. I built them out of durable, rot-
resistant swamp cypress so they'll hold up outdoors, but they'd look
just as handsome indoors in a greenhouse or a sunroom.

The larger planter is the easier of the two to build. The joinery's
simple: the legs and the rails are joined with dadoes. The small, square
planter is a classic English design with frame-and-panel sides. The
frames are joined with mortise-and-tenon joints. Turned finials at the
tops of the posts provide a nice formal flourish and a great opportunity to have some fun on the lathe.

These planters will be filled with damp soil, so the wood must be
highly resistant to rot. I chose swamp cypress (also known as bald cypress) because it stands up so well to moisture. Pressure-treated southern yellow pine would be even more durable than cypress but I don't
think it would look as good. If cypress isn't available, either white or
red cedar would be a good second choice. Left unfinished, all three of
these woods will weather outdoors to a beautiful silver-gray color in a
couple of years.

## SMALL PLANTER

The first thing to do is mill the stock for the posts. I start with an 8-ft.
length of 2¼-in.-square cypress. First I cut 4 pieces 21¾ in. long (the
finished legs will be 20⅝ in. long). Next I square up 2 adjacent faces
of each piece on the jointer. Then I set my table-saw rip fence 2 in.
"strong" (that is, 2 in. plus an extra 1/32 in.) and rip the stock square.
Next, with the jointer set for a 1/32-in. cut, I joint each sawn face to

### SMALL PLANTER
*Time:* 1½ days
*Special hardware and tools:*
None
*Wood:*
(1) 8-ft. 2¼-in. by 2¼-in. cypress
Cut 4 pieces 21¾ in. long and
then rip and joint pieces to 2 in.
square for posts.

(1) 8-ft. 2 × 6 cypress
Rip and joint 2 pieces 2 in. wide
and then cut 8 pieces 16½ in. long
for rails.

(1) 8-ft. 1 × 8 cypress
Cut one piece 18 in. long. Rip and
joint into 3 pieces 2 in. wide and cut
17⅛ in. long for bottom slats. From
remaining piece, rip and joint one
piece 2 in. wide and cut into 4 pieces
17⅛ in. long for bottom slats.

Joint edges of remaining piece and
cut 4 pieces 16½ in. long for top
halves of side panels.

(1) 6-ft. 1 × 8 cypress
Cut 4 pieces 16½ in. long and
joint edges for lower halves of side
panels. Edge-glue these pieces to the
16½-in. pieces cut above to make 4
panels approximately 12¼ in. × 16½
in.

### LARGE PLANTER
*Time:* 1½ days
*Special hardware and tools:*
3/8-in.-dia. plug-cutter
(16) 3-in. #8 hot-dipped galvanized deck screws
*Wood:*
(1) 6½-ft. 2¼-in. by 2¼-in. cypress
Rip and joint to 2 in. square.
Then cut 4 pieces 18 in. long for corner posts.

(1) 8-ft 2 × 6 cypress
Rip and joint 2 pieces 2 in. wide.
Then cut 2 pieces 31 in. long and 2
pieces 16 in. long from each length
for rails.

(3) 10-ft. 1 × 6 cypress

Surface-plane 2 pieces to 1/2-in. thickness. Then rip and joint into 2 pieces 2¹⁷⁄₃₂ in. wide and crosscut into 36 pieces 12¾ in. long for side slats.

Rip and joint one piece into 2 pieces 2 in. wide and then cut 14 pieces 16⅝ in. long for bottom slats.

clean up the saw marks. After jointing, the piece measures exactly 2 in. square.

## Getting Ready to Turn

With the posts milled to size, the next thing to do is lay out the finials prior to turning (*drawings 6-A and 6-B*). First I draw a line to mark the end of the square section (*drawings 6-A and 6-B*). I place all 4 posts side by side on the bench top and square a line across the posts 18⅜ in. from one end. I continue this line around all 4 sides of each post with a square and a pencil.

Next I locate the center points on the ends of the posts. With a straightedge, I draw pencil lines from corner to corner. I'll locate the

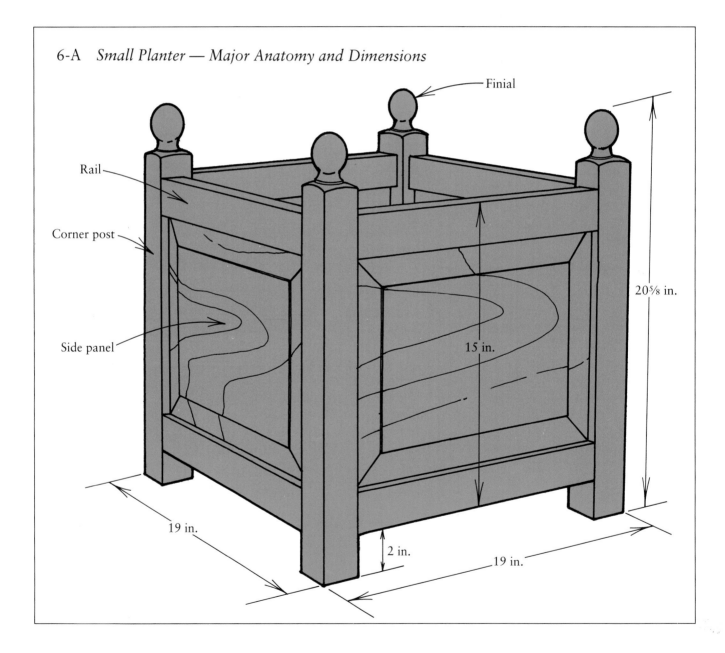

6-A  *Small Planter — Major Anatomy and Dimensions*

Finial

Rail

Corner post

Side panel

20⅝ in.

15 in.

19 in.

2 in.

19 in.

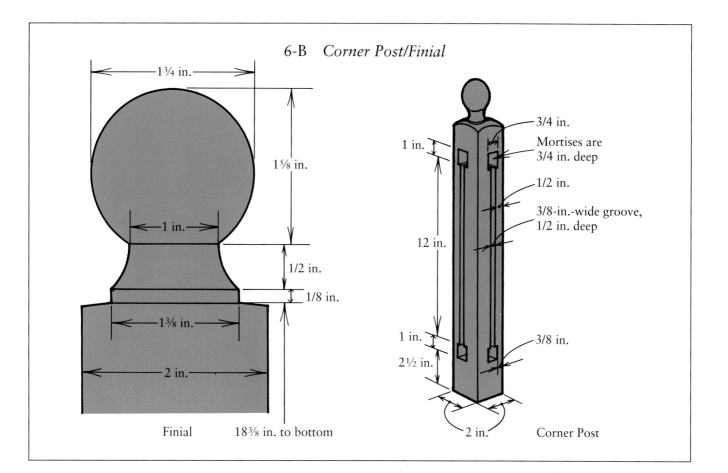

6-B   *Corner Post/Finial*

1¾ in.

1⅝ in.

1 in.

1/2 in.

1/8 in.

1⅜ in.

2 in.

Finial        18⅜ in. to bottom

3/4 in.

1 in.

Mortises are
3/4 in. deep

1/2 in.

3/8-in.-wide groove,
1/2 in. deep

12 in.

1 in.

2½ in.

3/8 in.

2 in.        Corner Post

tailstock and headstock centers where the 2 lines intersect. When turning dense hardwoods, I usually make shallow diagonal saw cuts along these lines at one end to give the spurs of the drive center a better "bite" in the wood. With softwood like cypress, however, it isn't necessary.

With the centers marked, I'm ready to mount a post in the lathe. I use a 4-spur drive center in the headstock spindle and a cup center (or a cone center) in the tailstock.

I use 4 different tools to turn the finials: a skew chisel, a parting tool, a roughing gouge (ground square across), and a shallow-flute spindle gouge with the end ground to a "fingernail" shape. Before getting started I sharpen my tools on the grinder, and hone the edges by hand. The gouges need only a lick or two with a slipstone to knock off the burr from the grinder, but the skew chisel requires more careful honing on an oilstone. A skew works best when the edge is keen enough to shave the hair from the back of your hand.

## Turning the Finials

It takes a little practice to turn a perfect ball. I like to warm up on a practice piece or two until I get the hang of it, especially if I haven't turned for a while.

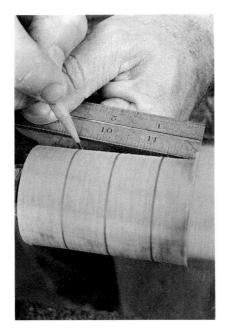
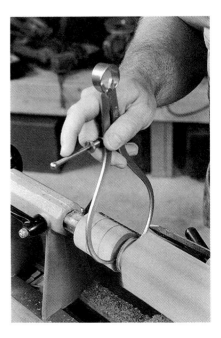

**6-1** To minimize chipping at the corners, I make a scoring cut at the shoulder at the top of the post's straight section. I make the cut with the skew's long point.

**6-2** With the lathe running at its slowest speed, I hold a rule next to the spinning wood and, measuring up from the shoulder, draw pencil lines to mark the bottom, the top, and the middle or "equator" of the ball.

**6-3** With a parting tool, I part down to a 1-in. dia. just under the ball, measuring with the calipers as I go.

The first thing to do is make a scoring cut at the pencil line that marks the shoulder at the top of the straight section (*photo 6-1 and drawing 6-B*). This will minimize chipping at the corners of the post. I make this cut with the long point of the skew chisel, setting the tool rest a little below center and gently pushing the skew point forward into the wood.

Next, with my roughing gouge, I round the entire finial section to an approximately $1^{13}/_{16}$-in.-dia. cylinder. I check my progress with a pair of outside calipers set to the proper diameter. The diameter's right when the calipers just slip over the cylinder. After rounding the cylinder, I switch to a parting tool and square up the shoulder at the scoring cut.

With the cylinder rounded, the next step is to mark 3 key diameters on the finial. With the lathe running at its slowest speed, I hold a rule next to the cylinder and, measuring up from the shoulder, draw pencil lines to mark the bottom, the top, and the middle or "equator" of the ball (*photo 6-2 and drawing 6-B*).

Now, with the parting tool, I reduce the diameter of the finial in 3 places, measuring with the calipers as I go. First, to the right of the scoring cut, I part down to a $1^3/_8$-in. diameter. This forms the 1/8-in.-wide flat at the bottom of the finial (*drawing 6-B*). Next I part down to a 1-in. dia. at the bottom and top of the ball (*photo 6-3*). Once these key diameters are established, I use my spindle gouge to remove some of the excess wood above and below the ball so I have some room to move with my gauge.

Now I'm ready to round the ball. The idea is to round one-half of the ball at a time by making a series of rolling cuts with the spindle gouge. I start by rounding the bottom half of the ball (to my left as I stand at the lathe). The first cut will round the sharp shoulder at the left-hand end of the cylinder. I hold the gouge with the groove facing up and let the bevel of the gouge rub on the spinning wood without cutting. I lift the handle slowly until the edge starts to cut, and then simultaneously roll the gouge to the left (counterclockwise) by rotating the handle with my right hand. It's a smooth, flowing movement that requires some practice.

I make several more cuts like this one, extending the curve a little more with each cut. The first cut rounds off the shoulder. The next cut rounds a little more, and so on. The last cut starts at the "equator" and ends with the gouge cutting practically upside down at the bottom end of the ball.

I round the top half of the ball with the same technique (*photo 6-4*), rolling the gouge to the right this time (clockwise). Now, with my parting tool, I reduce the diameter of the wood at the tailstock end to about a 3/8-in. dia. so I can round the top of the ball with the skew chisel (long point down) and sandpaper.

To make sure the ball is perfectly round, I find it helpful to use a concave template cut from a piece of cardboard. I place the template over the ball and refine the shape as necessary.

Once the ball is complete, I use my spindle gouge to cut the cove at the bottom of the ball. I start the cut with the gouge on its right side and roll it counterclockwise to make the cut, finishing up at the bottom of the ball (*drawing 6-B*). Then I finish sand the finial, taking care not to round the sharp edges of my turning.

After sanding, I part off the top of the finial. With the lathe on slow speed, I hold the skew in my right hand and slowly cut through the thin wood that remains at the top of the ball. As I cut through, I catch the post with my left hand to avoid marring the wood on the bed of the lathe.

A little hand-sanding on the top of the ball and the post is complete — only 3 more to go. I find it helpful to lay the first post behind the lathe bed where I can see it as I turn. This way, I can use it as a reference when I turn the other posts.

## Mortises and Tenons

Now that the posts are turned, I'm ready to cut the mortises for the rails (*drawing 6-B*). To lay out and cut the mortises, I place the posts side by side on my bench with the bottoms lined up. Then I square 2 pencil lines across all 4 posts. The first line is 2½ in. from the bottom of the post and the second line is 1 in. above the first. These lines mark the mortise for the bottom rail. To lay out the top mortise, I draw a line 15½ in. from the bottom of the post and a second line 16½ in. from the bottom.

I turn each post 90 degrees and extend all these lines across an adjacent side. Then I measure in 3/8 in. from the outer corner to position the mortises 3/8 in. from the edge. Now I can mark off the 3/4-in.

**6-4** I round each half of the ball by starting at the ball's midpoint and rolling the gouge away from the center. Here I'm rounding the top half of the ball, rolling the gouge clockwise to make the cut.

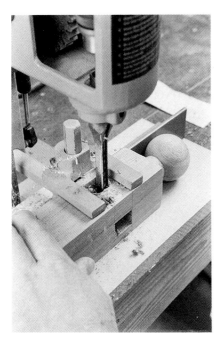

6-5 I mill the 3/4-in.-deep mortises in the posts on my hollow-chisel mortising machine.

6-6 To cut the tenons for the small planter, I set up a gauge block to give me a 3/4-in.-long tenon. I feed the stock with the miter gauge to cut the tenon shoulders.

width of the mortises (*drawing 6-B*) and mill the mortises on my hollow-chisel mortising machine (*photo 6-5*). I set the chisel for a 3/4-in.-deep cut. I use a 3/8-in. chisel and make several cuts to complete each mortise.

Now that the mortises are complete, I can make the tenons on the rails. First I rip, joint, and crosscut the rails to size (see Project Planner and *drawing 6-C*). Then I set up the table saw with a wooden gauge block clamped to the rip fence a couple of inches in front of the blade. I want to cut a 3/4-in.-long tenon, so I position the rip fence with the gauge block 3/4 in. away from the left side of the blade (*photo 6-6*).

With this setup I'll make the shoulder cuts for the tenons. I raise the blade 3/8 in. above the table. Next I place a rail against the miter gauge and butt the end against the gauge block. Now I feed the rail into the blade to cut the shoulder. I turn the rail over and make an identical cut on the other side (*photo 6-6*). These cuts form the shoulders at the cheeks of the tenon — the outside and inside faces of the rails. I repeat this process at both ends of all 8 rails.

The next cuts form the shoulders at the top and bottom of the tenon. Without moving the rip fence, I raise the blade to 1/2 in. and make 2 cuts at each end. That takes care of the shoulder cuts.

To complete the tenons, I need my tenoning jig (*photo 6-7*). First I raise the blade to a height of 3/4 in. Then I adjust the jig to cut the top and bottom of the tenon first (*drawing 6-C*). I cut one side and then turn the rail around to cut the other side. I repeat this procedure on all 8 rails to complete the 3/4-in.-long tenons.

To cut the tenon cheeks, I adjust the tenoning jig so it's 1/8 in. farther away from the blade. Without changing the blade height, I make one cut on each side to complete the tenon (*photo 6-7*). Every rail gets the same treatment.

### Routing Panel Grooves

Now that the mortises are complete I have to rout grooves in the posts and rails to receive the raised panels (*drawings 6-B and 6-C*). I do this with a hand-held router and a 3/8-in. spiral flute bit. I set the router fence 1/2 in. from the bit and set the bit for a 1/4-in.-deep cut. Then I clamp 2 rails together on my bench top, to provide adequate support for the router base (*photo 6-8*). With the fence riding along what will be the outside face of the rail, I mill a 3/8-in.-wide by 1/2-in.-deep groove in 2 passes. I do the same for all 8 rails. In the posts, I run the panel grooves from mortise to mortise, guiding the router fence against the outside face of the rail (*drawing 6-B*).

### Raising Panels

The panels come next. I edge-glue pieces of 1 × 8 cypress with biscuits and waterproof yellow glue to make 4 panels approximately 12¼ in. × 16½ in. (see Project Planner). When the glue is dry, I remove excess glue with my scraper and smooth up the panels with my random-orbit

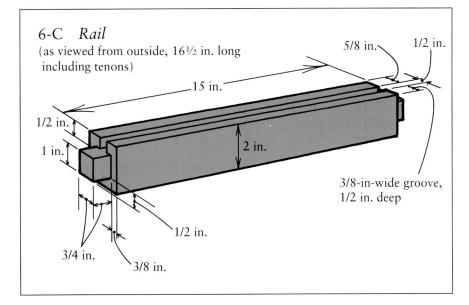

6-C *Rail*
(as viewed from outside, 16½ in. long
  including tenons)

15 in.

5/8 in.

1/2 in.

1/2 in.

1 in.

2 in.

3/8-in-wide groove,
1/2 in. deep

1/2 in.

3/4 in.

3/8 in.

6-7   I use my tenoning jig to cut the tenon cheeks. I make one cut on each side of the rail. The jig holds the stock securely on end for the cut.

6-8   To rout the 3/8-in. by 1/2-in. panel grooves in the rails, I clamp 2 rails together to provide adequate support for the router base. Then I make the cut in 2 passes with a 3/8-in. spiral flute bit.

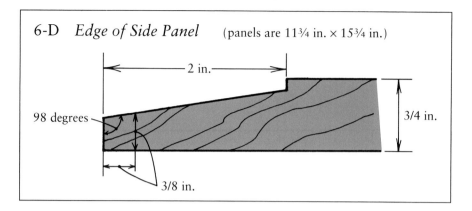

**6-D** *Edge of Side Panel*    (panels are 11¾ in. × 15¾ in.)

2 in.

98 degrees

3/4 in.

3/8 in.

**6-9**  I raise the panels on the table saw with a U-shaped plywood jig that fits over the rip fence to hold the panel perpendicular to the table. I tilt the blade 8 degrees and use a stick to hold the panel flat against the jig.

sander. Next, I square up the panels on my table saw with my panel cutter, trimming them to 11¾ in. wide and 15¾ in. long.

There are several ways to "raise" the panels, that is, to cut the bevel around the perimeter (*drawings 6-A and 6-D*). I could use a router or shaper, but the easiest way is on the table saw with a fine-tooth carbide-tipped blade (40–60 teeth). To support the panels on edge during the cut, I use a U-shaped plywood jig that fits over the rip fence to hold the panel perpendicular to the saw table (*photo 6-9*).

First, I position the rip fence to the left of the blade. Then I tilt the blade 8 degrees and raise it 2 in. above the table. I clamp a panel against the jig with a spring clamp. Then I adjust the rip fence so the face of the jig is 3/8 in. from the saw blade, measured at a point 3/8 in. above the saw table. This setup will give me a panel that's 3/8 in. thick where it fits into the grooves in the rails and posts (*drawing 6-D*). I cut the ends of the panel first to minimize tearout, then cut the long-grain sides. I like to use a stick to hold the panel flat against the jig as I make the cuts (*photo 6-9*). After raising the panels, I clean up the bevels with my sander to remove any saw marks.

6-E   *Bottom Detail*

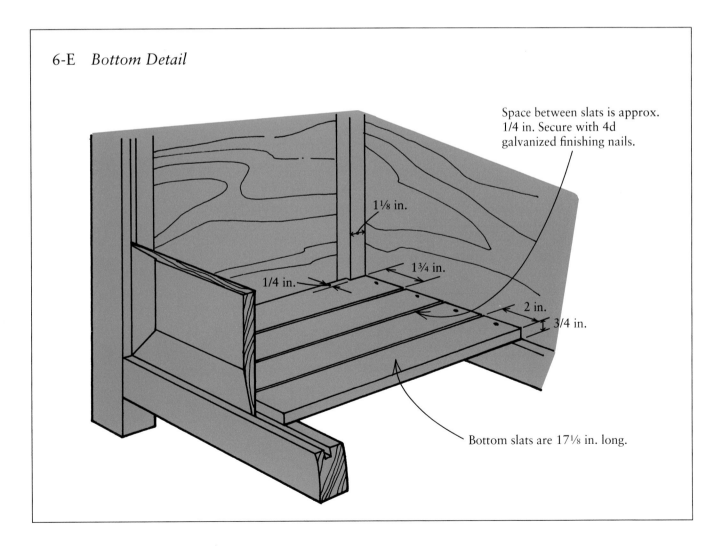

Space between slats is approx. 1/4 in. Secure with 4d galvanized finishing nails.

1⅛ in.

1¾ in.

1/4 in.

2 in.

3/4 in.

Bottom slats are 17⅛ in. long.

**6-10** I assemble the side frames with waterproof glue and clamps. I shoot a 1¼-in. nail through each mortise and tenon to secure the joint while the glue dries.

**6-11** I place one of the assembled sides inside up on my bench and install 4 more rails and 2 more panels. The other assembled side gets glued onto the rails.

*Assembling the Sides*

Now for some assembly. I brush some waterproof glue on the tenons of 2 rails and in the mortises of 2 posts. I insert the rails into one post, slide a panel into the grooves, and tap on the other post. The panel must be free to "float" in its grooves, so I don't glue the panel in place. I clamp the joints together and shoot one 1¼-in. nail through each mortise and tenon to secure the joint while the glue cures (*photo 6-10*).

Next I glue up a second side just like the first. After about 10 minutes, I can remove the clamps. Then I place one of the assembled sides inside up on my bench and install 4 more rails and 2 more panels. The other assembled side gets glued onto the rails to complete the 4 sides of the planter (*photo 6-11*).

*Bottom Slats*

All that's left is to cut and install the bottom slats (*drawing 6-E*). I cut seven 2-in. by 17⅛-in.-long slats from 1 × 8 cypress (see Project Planner). The outer 2 slats need to be notched to fit around the posts (*drawing 6-E*), and I cut these notches with my jigsaw. Then I nail in the slats, spacing them 1/4 in. apart for good drainage and securing them to the rails with 4d galvanized finishing nails.

## LARGE PLANTER

Compared to the small planter, this larger one is really easy to make. The first thing to do is mill the posts and rails to size (see Project Planner).

### Posts and Rails

With the posts and rails cut to size, I'm ready to mill dadoes in the posts for the rails (*drawings 6-F and 6-G*). I do this on the radial-arm saw with my stack dado head set for a 3/4-in.-wide cut. I clamp all 4 posts together with the ends evened up. Then I lay out the 1½-in.-wide dadoes at the top and bottom (*drawing 6-G*). I adjust the blade height for a 1/2-in.-deep dado. Now I can plow out the material, cutting a dado at each end.

Now I remove the clamp and turn each post 90 degrees so I can cut dadoes on a side adjacent to the dadoes I cut in the step above (*photo 6-12*). I take great care before I reclamp the posts to make sure all the dadoes will line up perfectly.

Next I have to mill grooves in the rails and posts for the slats that form the sides of the planter (*drawings 6-G and 6-H*). I use the same router technique I used for the small planter except that I use a 1/2-in. straight flute bit and set the guide fence 5/8 in. from the bit. The grooves for this planter are 1/2 in. wide and 3/8 in. deep and I cut them in 2 passes.

Next I mill 45-degree chamfers along the top and bottom edges of the upper rails, the top of the lower rails, and the inside edges of the post. I do this only on the sides that will show (there's no need to mill chamfers on the inside, where they won't be seen). The chamfers on the top of the upper rails are 5/16 in. wide and stop 1½ in. from the ends of the rails (*drawing 6-H*). The ones that face the panel are 3/16 in. wide and stop 2 in. from the ends of the rails (*drawing 6-F*). I mark the stopping points with a pencil and just rout to the line.

I install a chamfering bit in my router. Then I chamfer the rails and posts, guiding the bit's pilot bearing along the edge of the wood. I also chamfer the tops and bottoms of each post with a 1/4-in. chamfer, clamping the post vertically in my vise and routing around the end.

There's one more step to perform on the rails. I have to cut a 45-degree miter on the inside corner of each rail so the rails won't interfere with each other where they meet at the posts (*drawing 6-H*). I make this cut on my power miter box, setting the blade to 45 degrees.

Now I need to drill some holes in the posts for the screws that fasten the posts and the rails (*drawing 6-F*). Screws in adjacent sides of

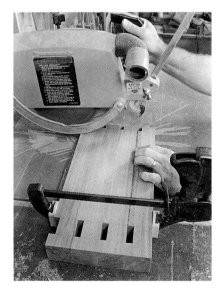

6-12 After cutting the dadoes in one face, I rotate each post 90 degrees and mill dadoes in an adjacent face.

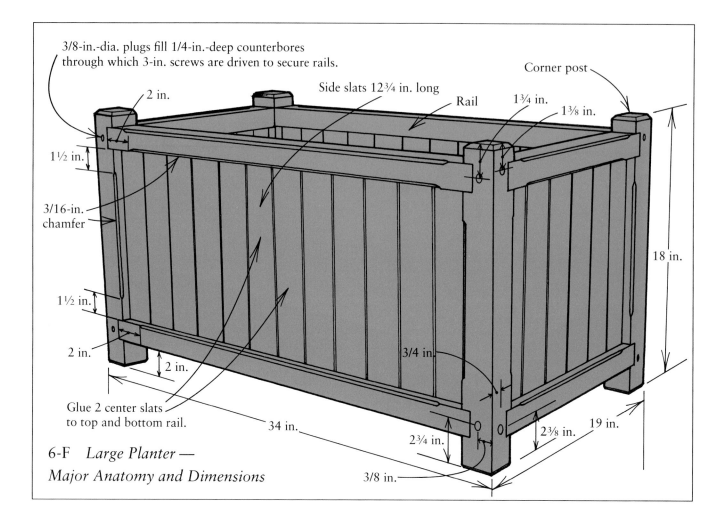

3/8-in.-dia. plugs fill 1/4-in.-deep counterbores through which 3-in. screws are driven to secure rails.

2 in.

Side slats 12¾ in. long

Rail

Corner post

1¾ in.

1⅜ in.

1½ in.

3/16-in. chamfer

18 in.

1½ in.

2 in.

3/4 in.

2 in.

Glue 2 center slats to top and bottom rail.

34 in.

2¾ in.

2⅜ in.

19 in.

3/8 in.

6-F   *Large Planter —*
*Major Anatomy and Dimensions*

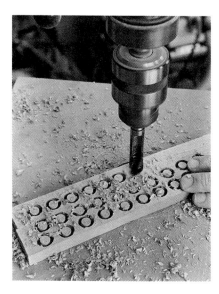

**6-13**   With a 3/8-in.-dia. plug-cutter, I cut cypress plugs to hide the screw heads in the posts.

the post must be offset 3/8 in. so they will miss each other inside the post. I drill the holes on my drill press with the hole-drilling accessory I normally use in my hand drill. This device drills a pilot hole and a 3/8-in.-dia. counterbore — about 1/4 in. deep — at the same time. I drill 4 holes and counterbores in each post according to the plan (*drawing 6-F*).

To cover the screw heads I'll need some cypress plugs to fill the counterbore holes. That's an easy operation with my 3/8-in.-dia. plug-cutter. I chuck the plug-cutter in my drill press and plunge the cutter into a piece of scrap cypress to make the plugs (*photo 6-13*). I need 16 plugs altogether.

### Side Slats

The side slats for the large planter are cut from 1 × 6 cypress. I surface-plane two 10-ft. boards to 1/2-in. thickness and then rip and joint each board into 2 pieces 2¹⁷⁄₃₂ in. wide. Then I cut these boards into 36 slats 12¾ in. long.

On the side that faces out, I want to slightly chamfer the corners of

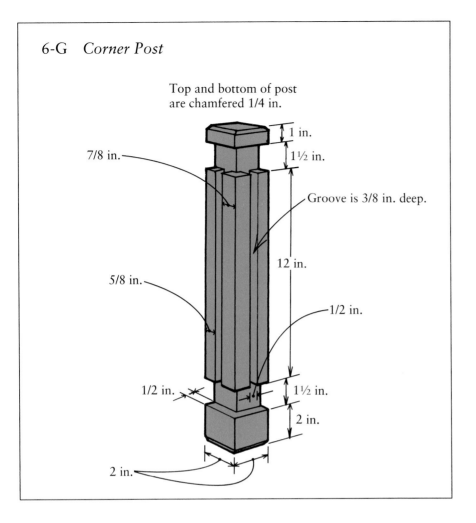

## 6-G   Corner Post

Top and bottom of post
are chamfered 1/4 in.

1 in.

7/8 in.

1½ in.

Groove is 3/8 in. deep.

12 in.

5/8 in.

1/2 in.

1/2 in.

1½ in.

2 in.

2 in.

the slats. To save time, I'm going to do this on the jointer instead of with a router. I tilt the jointer fence 45 degrees away from the cutter head and make one pass on each outside corner, cutting a chamfer about 1/8 in. wide. Eight of the slats get chamfered on only one edge — the unchamfered edge fits into the grooves in the posts.

### Assembling the Planter

To assemble all the joints on this planter I'm going to use waterproof yellow glue. First I assemble one of the 2 long sides. I spread glue in the dadoes of one post and on the ends of 2 long rails. I insert the rail ends into the dadoes and pull the joints tight with some clamps. Next I install one of the 3-in. #8 deck screws in the end of each rail. These rust-resistant screws need no pilot hole because the screw has little wings at the bottom that act like a drill.

Now I can slip the first side slat in place between the rails. I slide in a slat with an unchamfered edge and just tap the slat about 3/16 in. into the groove in the post. The rest of the groove depth will allow for expansion. Now I just slip the slats in one at a time without any glue

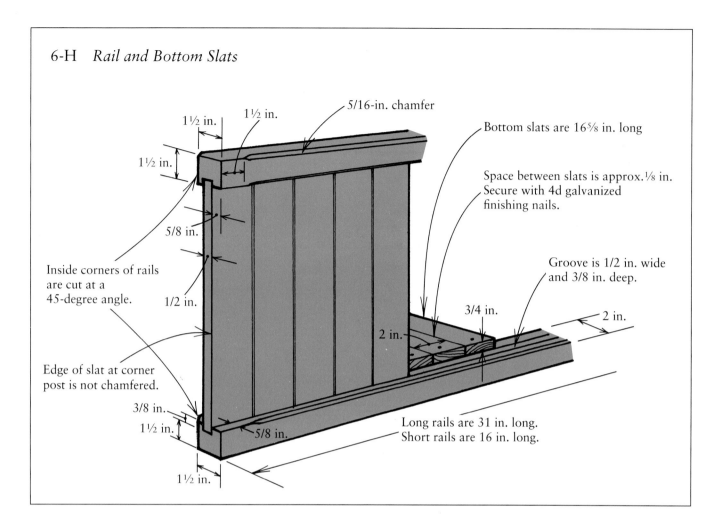

6-H   *Rail and Bottom Slats*

1½ in.

1½ in.

1½ in.

5/16-in. chamfer

Bottom slats are 16⅝ in. long

Space between slats is approx. ⅛ in. Secure with 4d galvanized finishing nails.

5/8 in.

Groove is 1/2 in. wide and 3/8 in. deep.

Inside corners of rails are cut at a 45-degree angle.

1/2 in.

3/4 in.

2 in.

2 in.

Edge of slat at corner post is not chamfered.

3/8 in.

1½ in.

5/8 in.

Long rails are 31 in. long.
Short rails are 16 in. long.

1½ in.

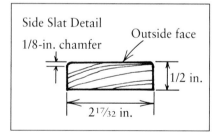

Side Slat Detail

1/8-in. chamfer

Outside face

1/2 in.

2¹⁷/₃₂ in.

or fasteners. I glue the 2 middle slats in place to tie the top and bottom rails together and add a little strength to the planter. With the center slats glued, the slats on either side are free to expand and contract. When the slats are all installed, I put on the other post with glue and screws. I assemble the other long side in the same way.

With one of the long sides inside up on my bench, I insert the 4 short rails into the posts with glue and screws. Now I can slip in the side slats (*photo 6-14*) and install the other long side.

To plug the screw holes, I use a small screwdriver to pop a plug out of the hole. I apply a little glue to the edges of the plug and tap it into the counterbore hole, lining up the grain to make the plug less conspicuous. After the glue dries I plane off any excess with a block plane (*photo 6-15*) and then sand it smooth with my random-orbit sander.

For the bottom slats I use some second-grade 1 × 6 cypress. I cut 14 pieces 2 in. wide and 16⅝ in. long. Then I space the bottom slats about 1/8 in. apart for drainage and fasten them to the rails with 4d galvanized finishing nails — one at each end.

**6-14** With the 4 short rails glued and screwed into one of the long sides, I slip in the side slats without any glue.

**6-15** After gluing plugs into the screw holes to cover the heads, I plane them off flush with a block plane and sander.

# 7

# *Child's Wagon*

*Time:* 5 days
*Special hardware and tools:*
(1) 3-ft. length of 1/2-in-dia. 13 TPI zinc-plated steel threaded rod.
  Cut 2 pieces 16¾ in. long for axles.
  (1) 3-ft. length of 10-24 zinc-plated steel threaded rod
  Cut 2 pieces 16 in. long for front and back of wagon bed.
  (1) 1½-in. 10-24 machine bolt for handle shaft
  (5) 10-24 nuts
  (5) #10 zinc-plated washers
  (8) 1/2-in. zinc-plated washers
  (4) 1/2-in. nuts
  (4) 1/2-in. nylon lock nuts for axles
  (3) 3/8-in. by 2-in.-dia. fender washers
  (1) 3/8-in. by 7-in. carriage bolt
  (1) 3/8-in. by 4-in. carriage bolt
  (4) 3/8-in. flat washers
  (3) 3/8-in. nuts
  (4) 1/4-in. by 3-in. carriage bolts
  (4) 1/4-in. by 1-in. carriage bolts
  (4) 1/4-in. flat washers
  (8) 1/4-in. lock washers
  (10) 1⅝-in. #8 F.H. screws
  (4) 1/2-in. #6 F.H. screws
  (50) 3/4-in. #6 F.H. plated screws
  (1) 2-ft. length of 1/8-in. by 3/4-in. by 3/4-in. aluminum angle
  Cut according to plan for rear wheel–assembly braces.
  (1) 6-ft. length of 1/16-in. by 9/16-in. by 57/64-in. aluminum channel
  Cut according to plan for edging for rear axle support and steering yoke.
  (1) 3/8-in. by 3-in. iron dowel screw
  (4) 8-in. by 1.75 offset rib wheel/tire with ball bearings; hub length=1⅜ in., bore=1/2 in.
  (1) 3-in. length of 1-in. I.D. copper tubing
  Metal-cutting blade for jigsaw
  Metal countersink bit

WOODEN wagons like this one can jog a few memories. Perhaps you pulled one behind you on your paper route rounds or ran daredevil races down some hill long ago. Seems like only yesterday. Well, times may have changed but kids are still kids, and this little wagon is guaranteed to put a grin on any young face.

I got the idea from a 1920s vintage wagon I saw at the Margaret Woodbury Strong Museum in Rochester, New York. I made a few improvements to the original design and worked in some modern materials. But on the whole, my wooden wagon still has the feel of those old-time originals.

The bed is made from red oak and medium-density overlay (MDO) plywood. It has removable "stake body" sides made of oak that slip into mortises in the sides of the bed. The ball bearing wheels are standard hardware store items, as are all the rest of the hardware items I used. There's a little bit of metalwork involved in making the running gear, but the only special tool required is a metal-cutting blade for the jigsaw (a hacksaw will work just as well).

## *Building the Bed*

The bed of the wagon is the first thing to make. It's really quite simple — 2 sides and 2 ends all made of oak with a bottom made of 1/2-in.-thick MDO board. The sides are joined to the ends with a dado joint reinforced with lengths of 10-24 threaded rod (*drawing 7-B*). The bottom fits into grooves milled in the sides and ends.

I'll start with the bottom. On the table saw, I cut a 15¼-in. by 33¾-in. piece of 1/2-in. MDO board. First I rip the piece to width and then I square up the ends with my homemade panel cutter.

1/2-in.-dia. by 7-in. to 8-in. auger bit

(1) Tube of construction adhesive and caulking gun

*Wood:*

(1) 14-ft. 1 × 4 red oak

Cut one piece 104 in. long. Rip and joint to 3½ in. wide. Then cut it into 2 pieces 36 in. long for sides and 2 pieces 15 in. long for front and rear ends of wagon bed. Rip and joint remaining piece into 2 strips 1¼ in. wide and then cut into 10 pieces 8½ in. long for stakes.

(1) 4-ft. 1 × 8 red oak

Rip and joint into 2 pieces 2½ in. wide and one piece 1⅜ in. wide. Rip all pieces in half along 3/4-in. thickness (see text for resawing procedure) and surface sawn face through a thickness planer to 5/16-in. thickness. From each length, cut one piece 32⅛ in. long and one piece 14½ in. long for side slats (12 required).

(1) 1-ft. 5/4 × 8 red oak

Plane to 1-in. thickness and then cut one piece 5½ in. long for handle and one piece 3 in. long. Cut 3-in. piece according to text for blocks on steering yoke.

(1) 1-ft. 8/4 × 6 red oak

Rip and joint one piece 2⅝ in. wide and plane to 1⅝-in. thickness. Cut 2 pieces 2⅝ in. square for steering post. Rip and joint remainder to 1¾ in. wide and plane to 1½-in. thickness for front axle support.

(1) 12-in. by 18-in. piece of 3/4-in. medium-density overlay (MDO) plywood

Cut one piece 5⅛ in. × 11⅛ in. for rear axle support. Cut remaining piece according to plan for steering yoke.

(1) 16-in. by 36-in. piece of 1/2-in. medium-density overlay (MDO) plywood

Trim to 15¼ in. × 33¾ in. for bottom of wagon bed.

(1) 3-ft. length of 1-in.-dia. oak dowel

Cut one piece 27½ in. long for handle shaft.

The sides come next. From a length of 1 × 4 red oak, I cut 2 pieces 36 in. long for the sides of the bed and 2 pieces 15 in. long for the front and rear ends (see Project Planner).

The 2 long side pieces need a dado 1/4 in. deep and 3/4 in. wide in each end to receive the front and rear side pieces (*drawing 7-B*). I mill these dadoes on the table saw with a stack dado head set for a 3/4-in.-wide cut.

To locate the dadoes, I clamp a gauge block to my table-saw rip fence (*photo 7-1*). I position the fence and gauge block so the dadoes will be 3/4 in. from the ends of the stock. I set the blade height for a 1/4-in.-deep cut and then mill a dado on both ends of each side piece — 4 dadoes in all.

With the dadoes complete, I'm ready to mill a 3/8-in.-deep by 1/2-in.-wide groove in each piece for the MDO bottom. The grooves in the short end pieces can run full length (the ends will be hidden in the dadoes). I can't run full-length grooves on the side pieces, though, because the grooves will show on the ends. Stop grooves are the answer, and it's hard to beat the router table for making this type of cut.

I set up my router table with a 1/2-in. straight bit and adjust the height for a 3/16-in.-deep cut. Because oak is pretty hard, I'll cut the groove in 2 passes. Then I adjust the fence so it's 3/8 in. away from the bit. So I know where to start and stop the grooves, I draw 2 pencil lines on the router-table fence to serve as indicator marks. I draw a line 3/4 in. away from the bit on either side (*photo 7-2*).

To start the cut, I hold the workpiece against the router-table fence and above the cutter with its left-hand end aligned with the left-hand indicator mark on the fence. With the power on, I make a "plunge cut" by lowering the wood onto the spinning bit (*photo 7-2*). Then I feed the stock from right to left, carefully lifting the workpiece up off the bit when the right-hand end lines up with the right-hand indicator mark (*photo 7-2*). I mill a 3/16-in.-deep groove in both sides and then raise the bit to 3/8 in. and make a second pass. I use the same setup to rout grooves in the ends of the bed as well, but I run these grooves the entire length.

This wagon will probably end up outside, where it will take a lot of abuse. To hold the sides firmly together I install a zinc-plated threaded rod at each end of the bed to hold the sides tightly to the ends (*drawing 7-B*). The rods are recessed into 3/16-in. by 3/16-in. grooves in the front and rear of the bed.

I mill these grooves on the table saw with a regular saw blade set for a 3/16-in.-deep cut. My blade cuts a kerf that's 1/8 in. wide, so I set the rip fence 1¾ in. from the blade and make a cut on each piece with the top edge of the side against the fence. Then I move the fence 1/16 in. farther away from the blade and make a second cut.

For safety's sake, the washers and the nuts for the threaded rods must be recessed in the sides. On the drill press, I drill a 1/4-in.-deep counterbore with a 5/8-in. dia. forstner bit, centering the hole 1²⁷/₃₂ in.

## 7-A  *Major Anatomy and Dimensions*

Note: All corners should be rounded over and any pointed pieces should be made blunt for safety.

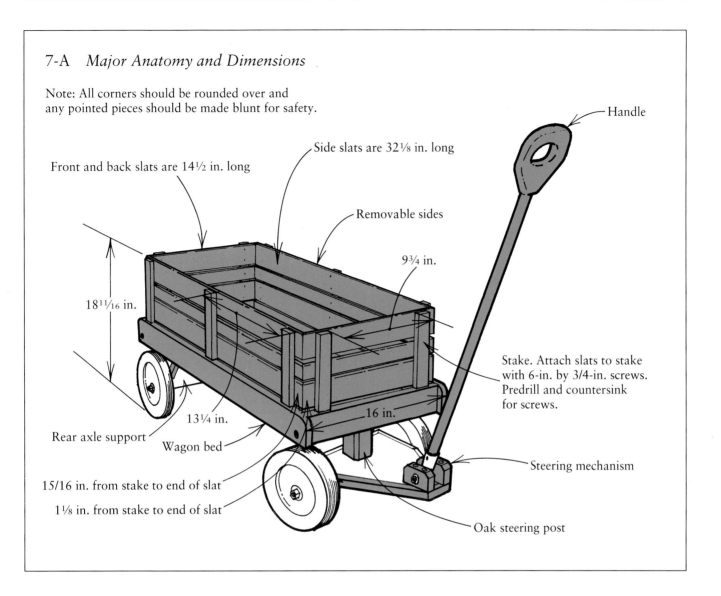

Front and back slats are 14½ in. long

Side slats are 32⅛ in. long

Removable sides

Handle

9¾ in.

18¹¹⁄₁₆ in.

Stake. Attach slats to stake with 6-in. by 3/4-in. screws. Predrill and countersink for screws.

13¼ in.

16 in.

Rear axle support

Wagon bed

Steering mechanism

15/16 in. from stake to end of slat

1⅛ in. from stake to end of slat

Oak steering post

**7-1** I cut the dadoes in the bed sides with a dado head, clamping a gauge block on the table-saw rip fence to set the length of the tenon. I butt the end of the stock against the block, then use the miter gauge to move it into the blade.

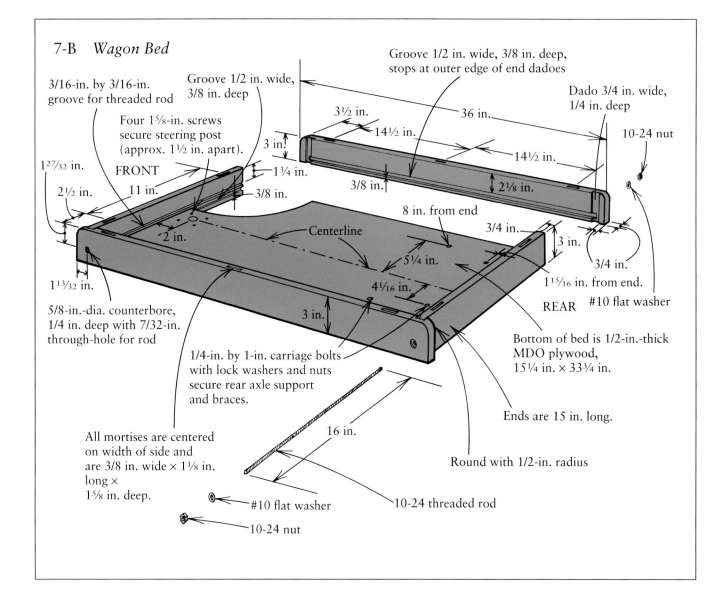

**7-B  Wagon Bed**

3/16-in. by 3/16-in. groove for threaded rod

Groove 1/2 in. wide, 3/8 in. deep

Groove 1/2 in. wide, 3/8 in. deep, stops at outer edge of end dadoes

Dado 3/4 in. wide, 1/4 in. deep

10-24 nut

Four 1⅝-in. screws secure steering post (approx. 1½ in. apart).

3½ in.

14½ in.

36 in.

14½ in.

1²⁷⁄₃₂ in.

FRONT

11 in.

3 in.

1¾ in.

3/8 in.

3/8 in.

2⅛ in.

2½ in.

8 in. from end

3/4 in.

Centerline

1¹³⁄₃₂ in.

−2 in.

5¼ in.

3 in.

4¹⁄₁₆ in.

3 in.

REAR

3/4 in.

1¹⁵⁄₁₆ in. from end.

#10 flat washer

5/8-in.-dia. counterbore, 1/4 in. deep with 7/32-in. through-hole for rod

1/4-in. by 1-in. carriage bolts with lock washers and nuts secure rear axle support and braces.

Bottom of bed is 1/2-in.-thick MDO plywood, 15¼ in. × 33¾ in.

16 in.

Ends are 15 in. long.

All mortises are centered on width of side and are 3/8 in. wide × 1⅛ in. long × 1⅝ in. deep.

Round with 1/2-in. radius

#10 flat washer

10-24 threaded rod

10-24 nut

down from the top edge of the side piece and 1¹³⁄₃₂ in. from the end (*drawing 7-B*). Then I drill a 7/32-in.-dia. through-hole for the rod.

The removable sides of the wagon have stakes that fit into mortises in the sides of the bed (*drawings 7-A and 7-B*). These mortises are the next thing to tackle. The long sides get 3 and the short sides get 2. I set up the drill press with my mortising attachment and a 3/8-in. hollow-chisel mortising bit (*photo 7-3*). I mark the locations of the 1⅛-in.-long mortises on the side- and end pieces (*drawing 7-B*) and mill the mortises 1⅝ in. deep, centered on the 3/4-in. thickness.

I don't want any sharp corners on this project, so I soften the edges of the sides with a small radius plane (a block plane will work just as well). Then I set up the drum-sander attachment on my drill press and round off the top corners to a 1/2-in. radius and slightly round the bottom corners of the long sides (*drawing 7-A*).

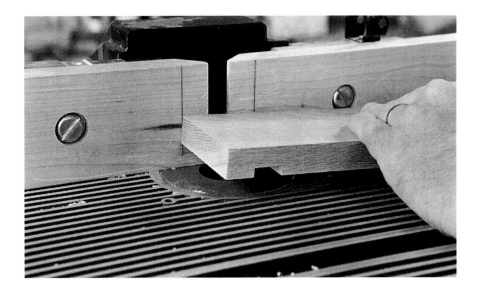

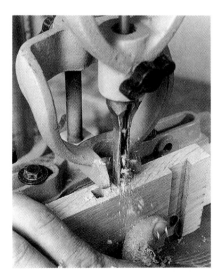

7-2 So I know where to start and stop the grooves for the wagon bottom, I draw 2 indicator marks on the router-table fence, 3/4 in. away from the bit on either side. To start the cut, I hold the workpiece against the fence with its left-hand end aligned with the left-hand indicator mark and lower the wood onto the spinning bit (TOP LEFT). Then I feed the stock from right to left, carefully lifting the workpiece up off the bit when the right-hand end lines up with the right-hand indicator mark (TOP RIGHT).

Now for a little assembly. I put the side pieces together, slipping the bottom piece into its grooves. Then I slide the threaded rods through their holes, put on the washers and nuts, and tighten them up. Make sure there are no sharp edges at the end of the threaded rod. That's all there is to it — the bed is complete.

## Rear Wheel Assembly

With the bed of the wagon completed, I'm ready to start working on the rear wheel assembly (*drawing* 7-C). This assembly consists of a rear axle support made of MDO plywood and aluminum channel, which is mitered and bent around the plywood. The axle, a piece of 1/2-in.-dia. threaded rod, fits into a groove in the bottom edge of the MDO board. The axle support is bolted to the wagon bed with carriage bolts and reinforced with 2 braces made of aluminum angle.

First I cut out the 5⅛-in. by 11⅛-in. piece of 3/4-in. MDO board. Next I rip a 1/2-in. by 1/2-in. groove in one edge for the axle. I raise my table-saw blade 1/2 in. above the table, set the rip fence 1/8 in. from the blade, and make a cut along one edge. Then I flip the piece around and make a matching cut on the other side (same edge). I continue to move the fence and run the piece through until the wood between the first 2 cuts is removed.

To make the aluminum edging for the rear axle support, I cut a piece of aluminum channel 23 in. long (see Project Planner). I measure in 5¹³⁄₁₆ in. from one end and square a line across. With my square, I lay out a 90-degree notch on the sides of the channel, centered on the line. I saw out the notch with a metal-cutting blade in my jigsaw (*photo* 7-4). Now I place the MDO plywood in the channel and bend one end of the channel around the plywood. With the support in the channel, I mark the location for the second bend, cut another notch like the first, and make a second 90-degree bend.

7-3 The stakes on the removable sides of the wagon fit into 1⅝-in.-deep mortises in the bed sides. I mill these with a 3/8-in. hollow-chisel mortising attachment on the drill press.

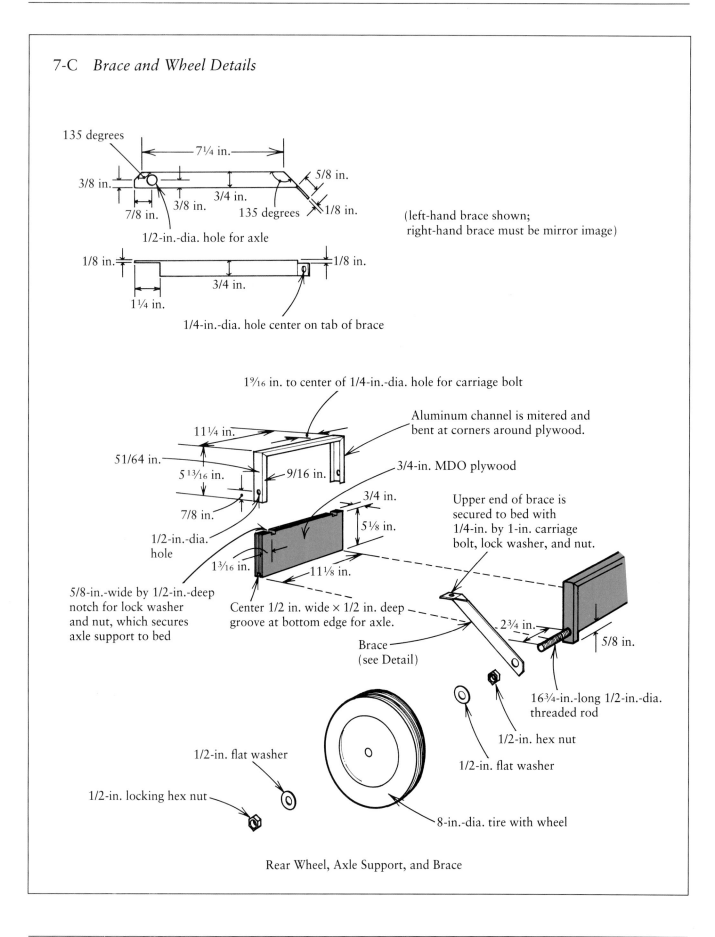

135 degrees

3/8 in.

7/8 in.

3/8 in.

7¼ in.

3/4 in.

5/8 in.

135 degrees

1/8 in.

1/2-in.-dia. hole for axle

(left-hand brace shown;
right-hand brace must be mirror image)

1/8 in.

1/8 in.

3/4 in.

1¼ in.

1/4-in.-dia. hole center on tab of brace

1⁹⁄₁₆ in. to center of 1/4-in.-dia. hole for carriage bolt

Aluminum channel is mitered and
bent at corners around plywood.

11¼ in.

51/64 in.

5 ¹³⁄₁₆ in.

9/16 in.

7/8 in.

3/4-in. MDO plywood

3/4 in.

5⅛ in.

Upper end of brace is
secured to bed with
1/4-in. by 1-in. carriage
bolt, lock washer, and nut.

1/2-in.-dia.
hole

1³⁄₁₆ in.

11⅛ in.

5/8-in.-wide by 1/2-in.-deep
notch for lock washer
and nut, which secures
axle support to bed

Center 1/2 in. wide × 1/2 in. deep
groove at bottom edge for axle.

2¾ in.

5/8 in.

16¾-in.-long 1/2-in.-dia.
threaded rod

Brace
(see Detail)

1/2-in. hex nut

1/2-in. flat washer

1/2-in. flat washer

1/2-in. locking hex nut

8-in.-dia. tire with wheel

Rear Wheel, Axle Support, and Brace

I'm not finished with the channel just yet. I still have to drill a couple of holes. First I drill two 1/2-in.-dia. holes for the axle. I want the holes to be centered on the axle groove, so I mark the location of the groove on the inside of the channel. On my wagon, the centers of the holes ended up being 7/8 in. from the ends of the channel (*drawing 7-C*). I drill these holes on the drill press with a special bit called a step drill (*photo 7-5*). This cone-shaped gadget is designed for drilling metal and other thin materials. Each step on the drill is 1/16 in. larger than the one preceding. Step drills aren't found in every hardware store, but they're sold by most industrial supply houses. One nice thing about them is you don't need a center punch to get the hole started.

On the top of the channel, I drill two 1/4-in.-dia. holes for the carriage bolts that will fasten the axle support to the bottom of the bed. These holes are centered 1⁹⁄₁₆ in. from the bend on either side (*drawing 7-C*).

Now I'm ready to mount the axle support to the bed. With the bed upside down on my bench, I mark the location of the rear axle support. The back edge of the aluminum channel should be 1½ in. from the rear end of the wagon (measured from the inside face of the rear end piece). I place the channel in position and center it from side to side. Then, with a 1/4-in. bit in a hand-held drill, I drill through the 1/4-in. holes in the channel clear through the plywood bed. Now I can bolt the channel to the bed with 1/4-in. by 1-in. carriage bolts with lock washers and nuts.

In order for the plywood to seat completely inside the channel, I cut some notches to accommodate the bolts. I place the plywood in the channel and mark where the notches need to go. Then I cut them on the table saw, holding the plywood against the miter gauge and "nibbling out" the notches. Now the rear axle MDO plywood fits nicely into the channel.

The axle support would be pretty flimsy without some front-to-back support, so I reinforce it with 2 braces made from aluminum angle (*drawing 7-C*). The braces are mirror images of each other. To make them, I lay out one according to the plan (*drawing 7-C*) on the length of aluminum channel and cut it out with my jigsaw or a hacksaw. Then I lay out and cut the second brace, double-checking to make sure it's a mirror image of the first.

I clean up the edges of the metal with a file and then clamp the end that attaches to the bed in my vise and bend it to 45 degrees. I hold a speed square against the bench as a guide for the proper angle (*photo 7-6*). Then, on my drill press, I drill a 1/2-in.-dia. hole for the axle. The other end gets a 1/4-in.-dia. hole for bolting the brace to the bed.

Now I can put the rear axle assembly together. With the bed still upside down on my bench, I put a clamp across the sides of the rear axle support to hold the metal edging in place. I slip the axle through the hole in one brace and then through the hole in the aluminum edg-

7-4   To make the aluminum edging for the rear axle support, I saw out a 90-degree notch on each side of the channel with a metal-cutting jigsaw blade.

7-5   I drill the axle holes on the drill press with a special bit called a step drill. Each step on the drill is 1/16 in. larger in diameter.

7-6   I bend the end of the brace that attaches to the wagon bed to 45 degrees. I hold a square against the bench as a guide for the proper angle.

ing (*drawing 7-C*). I slide it across the axle support, push it through the second hole in the edging, and put on the second brace. I thread a nut on each end of the axle to hold the braces in place, keeping an equal length of axle on each end. Now I can mark for the holes that fasten the braces to the bed. I line up the braces parallel to the sides of the bed and square up the axle support to the bottom of the bed. Then I drill 1/4-in. holes through the bed to secure the braces. Now I can install the 1/4-in. by 1-in. carriage bolts, with lock washers and nuts, which fasten the braces to the bed.

Now for the wheels. I slip a 1/2-in. washer on each end of the axle and put on the wheels. Another washer goes on after the wheel. After making sure there are no sharp ends on the axles, I install locking nuts with a nylon insert that keeps them on tight. Not too tight or the bearings will bind.

*Front Steering Mechanism*

The front wheels and axle are bolted to the bottom of a plywood steering yoke (*drawing 7-D*). This assembly is fastened to the bottom of the wagon with a single 7-in. carriage bolt, which passes through an oak steering post. The yoke assembly pivots on this bolt so the wagon can be steered.

The first piece to make is the oak steering post. The post is 2⅝ in. square. Since I don't have any oak that thick, I glue up the post from 2 thinner pieces of wood. I start with a 6-in. by 12-in. piece of 8/4 (2-in.-thick) red oak (see Project Planner). I rip and joint a piece 2⅝ in. wide and plane it down to 1⅝ in. with my thickness planer. Next, on the power miter box, I cut 2 pieces 2⅝ in. square. I glue these pieces together — one on top of the other — to make a 3¼-in.-long post. I

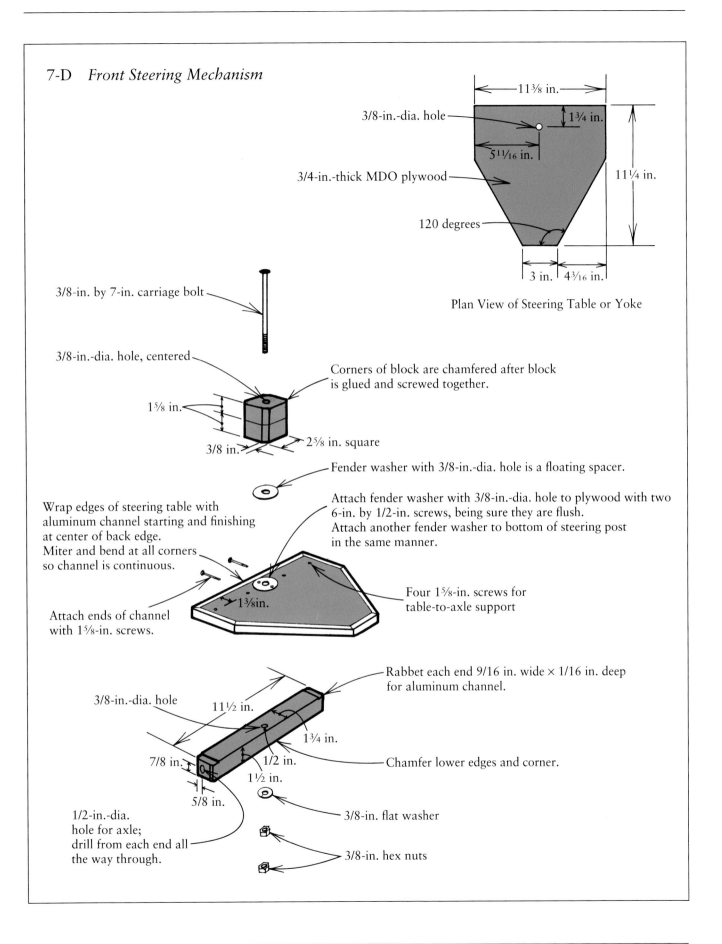

7-D  *Front Steering Mechanism*

11³⁄₈ in.

3/8-in.-dia. hole

1³⁄₄ in.

5¹¹⁄₁₆ in.

3/4-in.-thick MDO plywood

11¼ in.

120 degrees

3 in.   4³⁄₁₆ in.

Plan View of Steering Table or Yoke

3/8-in. by 7-in. carriage bolt

3/8-in.-dia. hole, centered

Corners of block are chamfered after block is glued and screwed together.

1⁵⁄₈ in.

3/8 in.   2⁵⁄₈ in. square

Fender washer with 3/8-in.-dia. hole is a floating spacer.

Wrap edges of steering table with aluminum channel starting and finishing at center of back edge. Miter and bend at all corners so channel is continuous.

Attach fender washer with 3/8-in.-dia. hole to plywood with two 6-in. by 1/2-in. screws, being sure they are flush.
Attach another fender washer to bottom of steering post in the same manner.

1³⁄₈in.

Four 1⁵⁄₈-in. screws for table-to-axle support

Attach ends of channel with 1⁵⁄₈-in. screws.

Rabbet each end 9/16 in. wide × 1/16 in. deep for aluminum channel.

3/8-in.-dia. hole

11½ in.

1³⁄₄ in.

7/8 in.   1/2 in.

1½ in.

Chamfer lower edges and corner.

5/8 in.

1/2-in.-dia. hole for axle; drill from each end all the way through.

3/8-in. flat washer

3/8-in. hex nuts

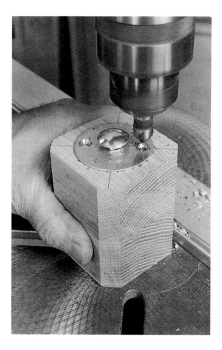

7-7 To prevent the fender washers from wearing into the wood, I screw one to the steering post. The carriage bolt keeps the washer centered on the hole in the post while I drill and countersink for 2 screws.

predrill and install two 2½-in. #8 screws through one face to reinforce the glue joint.

I need to drill a 3/8-in.-dia. hole through the center of the block for the carriage bolt on which the steering assembly turns (*drawing 7-D*). To mark the center, I draw diagonal lines from corner to corner on both ends of the block. Then I chamfer the long edges of the post on the table saw, positioning the rip fence to the left of the blade and tilting the blade 45 degrees. Ripping short pieces like this can be dangerous, so it's important to use a push stick.

Now I can drill through the post. I install a 3/8-in. brad-point bit in the drill press and clamp a straightedge clamp to the table, positioned so the center point of the post is right under the bit. I drill as deep as I can from one side, then turn the block around and complete the hole from the other side.

Three fender washers will go on the steering bolt as spacers between the post and yoke (*drawing 7-D*). If the washers are loose, they'll eventually wear their way into the oak and the plywood. To prevent this, I drill through 2 of the washers and screw one to the steering post and one to the yoke. The third washer just floats as a spacer between these other 2. To center the washer on the block, I slip a 3/8-in. carriage bolt through the washer and block. Then I make 2 dimples with a center punch and drill 1/8-in.-dia. holes on the drill press, drilling through the washer only. I countersink for the screw heads with a metal countersink (*photo 7-7*). Then I drill 1/16-in. pilot holes for the screws and install the screws.

Now I can screw the steering post to the bottom of the wagon. I drill a 3/8-in. hole centered across the width of the bend and 2 in. from the inside edge of the oak end piece. Using a 3/8-in. bolt to position the post, I predrill through the bed and install four 1⅝-in. screws to secure the post to the bed. Next, I insert a 3/8-in. drill through the hole in the post to drill through the plywood bed of the wagon.

The yoke is the next piece to make (*drawing 7-D*). I cut an 11¼-in. by 11⅜-in. piece of 3/4-in. MDO board. I mark the midpoint of each 11⅜-in. side and draw a centerline to connect these 2 points. Then I mark off a 30-degree angle on each side, as shown in the plan view (*drawing 7-D*) and make these 2 angled cuts on the table saw, setting my miter gauge to 30 degrees.

The edges of the yoke get wrapped with the same aluminum channel I used for the rear axle support. I start with a piece of channel 42 in. long. From the midpoint, I measure out 1½ in. on either side to mark the first 2 bends. I lay out and cut a 60-degree notch at each mark. Now I can place the channel over the 3-in. end of the yoke and bend the metal around the angled sides. I mark the locations of the next 2 bends, cut a 30-degree notch at each point, and make 2 more bends, holding the channel in place with a clamp as I bend. The 90-degree corners get 90-degree notches. When I bend the channel around the plywood, I trim the 2 ends so they meet at the middle. I

7-8 I predrill, countersink, and screw the ends of the channel to the plywood with two 1⅝-in. screws.

predrill, countersink, and screw the ends of the channel to the plywood with some 1⅝-in. screws (*photo 7-8*).

Next I want to install the fender washer on the top of the yoke. I drill a 3/8-in.-dia. hole on the yoke's centerline, 1⅜ in. from the back edge (*drawing 7-D*). I put the carriage bolt through a fender washer, then into the hole in the yoke. I drill and countersink through this washer as I did for the washer on the steering post, and screw it to the yoke.

## Front Wheel Assembly

The front axle support comes next. The axle, a length of 1/2-in.-dia. threaded rod, passes through a hole in an oak axle support (*drawings 7-D and 7-E*). I cut the front axle support from the remainder of the 8/4 oak I used for the steering post (see Project Planner). I rip and joint a piece 1¾ in. wide and plane it to a 1½-in. thickness with my planer. I square up one end on the miter box and trim the support to a

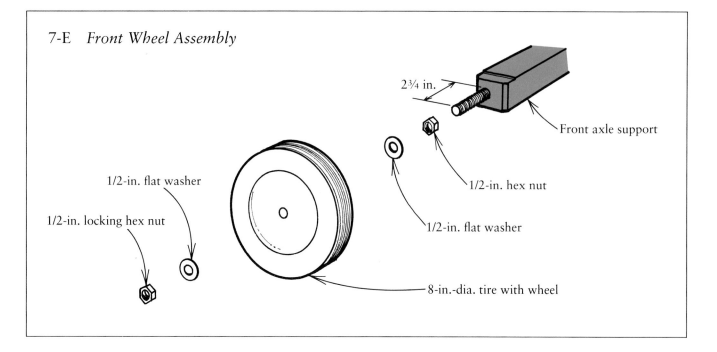

7-E   *Front Wheel Assembly*

2¾ in.

Front axle support

1/2-in. hex nut

1/2-in. flat washer

1/2-in. flat washer

1/2-in. locking hex nut

8-in.-dia. tire with wheel

length of 11½ in. (*drawing 7-D*). On each end, I lay out the axle support according to the plan (*drawing 7-D*).

Now comes the tricky part — drilling a 1/2-in.-dia. hole nearly 12 in. long. Long holes like this tend to drift off center. To secure the wood in a vertical position, perpendicular to the drill-press table, I clamp the piece in 2 wooden carriage clamps, one on top of the other (*photo 7-9*). I clamp the bottom carriage clamp to the drill-press table with 2 bar clamps.

With a 1/2-in.-dia. auger bit in the drill press, I drill into one end as far as the travel of the quill will allow — about 3 in. on my drill press. When the quill hits bottom, I raise the table and drill another 3 in. When I've gone as deep as I can with the bit, I turn the axle support upside down and drill in from the other end until the 2 holes meet.

There's one more hole to drill in the axle support and that's a 3/8-in.-dia. hole for the carriage bolt that holds the steering assembly in place (*drawing 7-D*). I measure in 1/2 in. from the front edge to mark the center point. I don't want this hole to interfere with the axle.

Now, with a chamfering bit in my router, I chamfer the bottom ends and edges of the axle support. There's one more bit of work to do to complete the axle support. The aluminum edging on the yoke interferes with the axle support seating flush on the yoke, so I have to cut a tiny rabbet (1/16 in. deep and 9/16 in. wide) at each end of the support to clear the metal. I "nibble away" these rabbets on the table saw.

Now for some assembly. First I fasten the axle support to the bottom of the yoke with some construction adhesive and four 1⅝-in. screws (*drawing 7-D*), using a bolt to align the holes. Next, with the

7-9 To secure the front axle support in a vertical position for drilling, I clamp it between 2 wooden carriage clamps, one on top of the other. I clamp the bottom carriage clamp to the drill-press table with 2 bar clamps.

wagon upside down on my bench, I slip the 7-in. carriage bolt through the bed and the steering post. A fender washer goes on the bolt next, followed by the yoke assembly. A 3/8-in. washer goes on top of the axle support, followed by a 3/8-in. nut to hold the whole thing together. Not too tight or the yoke won't turn. I thread a second nut on top of the first to act as a lock nut. I use 2 wrenches to tighten one nut against the other (*photo 7-10*).

The axle goes in next, with a nut on either end. Then I install the washers, wheels, and nylon lock nuts just as I did with the rear wheels (*drawing 7-E*). Remember, no sharp metal on the ends of the axle.

7-10 Two nuts go on the steering bolt, one on top of the other. I use 2 wrenches to tighten one against the other and lock them firmly so they won't come loose.

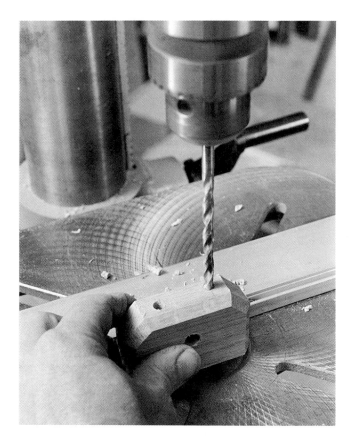

**7-11** I cut the 2 oak blocks that secure the handle shaft to the yoke from a single piece of wood. First I knock off all 4 corners. A stop block clamped to the miter-saw fence provides sideways support so I can keep fingers well away from the blade.

**7-12** I drill two 1/4-in. holes through each block, spaced 5/8 in. on each side of center, for the 1/4-in. by 3-in. carriage bolts that fasten the blocks to the steering yoke.

*Handle Shaft Assembly*

The handle shaft is attached to the steering yoke with a carriage bolt through 2 oak blocks. The blocks in turn are bolted to the yoke (*drawings 7-A and 7-F*). I want the grain of these blocks to run horizontally because that will give them the most strength. To make the blocks, I crosscut a 3-in.-long piece off the end of a 5/4-in. by 8-in. oak board. I'll cut both blocks from this piece.

First I want to knock off the corners on my miter saw. I swing the blade 45 degrees to the right and clamp a stop block to the left of the blade (*photo 7-11*). I position the workpiece securely against the stop block so I can keep my hands well away from the blade. I cut all 4 corners with this setup, holding the end of the block against the fence.

On one end of the block, I measure in 15/16 in. and make a mark to locate the center for the bolt holes. Then I measure in 1⅞ in. from each end and square a line across. These lines mark the height of each block. Next, with a chamfering bit in my router, I chamfer all the edges. Then I saw along the lines to cut two 1⅞-in. by 3-in. blocks. Finally, on the drill press, I place one block on top of the other and drill a 3/8-in.-dia. hole through both blocks at once.

Next I drill two 1/4-in. holes through each block, spaced 5/8 in. on each side of center (*drawing 7-F and photo 7-12*). These holes are for the 1/4-in. by 3-in. carriage bolts that fasten the blocks to the steering yoke.

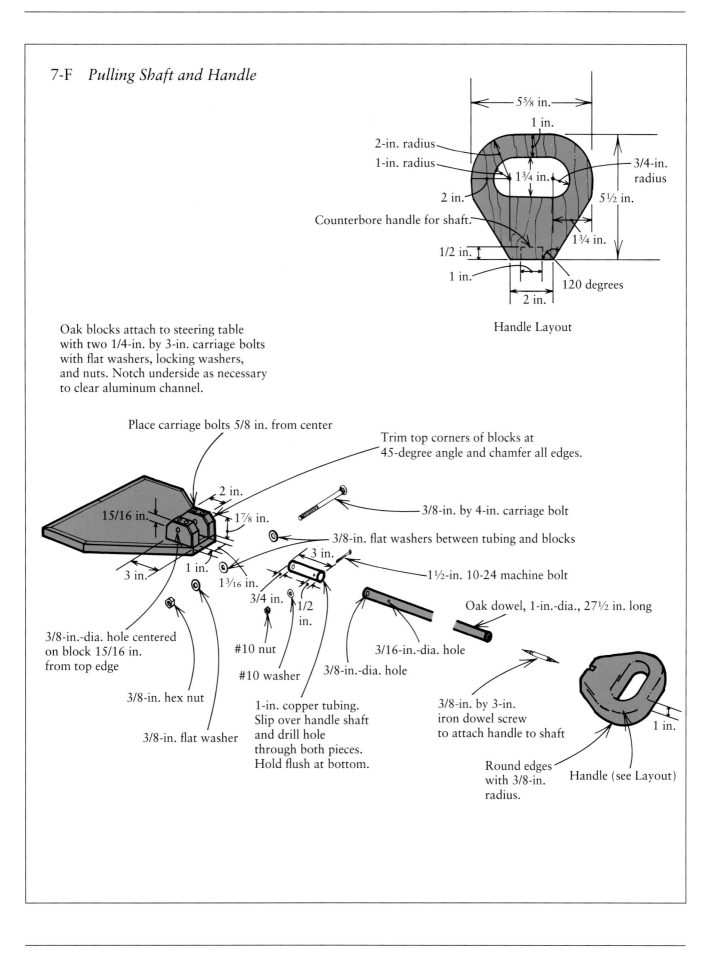

## 7-F  *Pulling Shaft and Handle*

5⁵⁄₈ in.

1 in.

2-in. radius

1-in. radius

1¾ in.

3/4-in. radius

2 in.

5½ in.

Counterbore handle for shaft.

1¾ in.

1/2 in.

1 in.

2 in.

120 degrees

Handle Layout

Oak blocks attach to steering table with two 1/4-in. by 3-in. carriage bolts with flat washers, locking washers, and nuts. Notch underside as necessary to clear aluminum channel.

Place carriage bolts 5/8 in. from center

Trim top corners of blocks at 45-degree angle and chamfer all edges.

2 in.

15/16 in.

1⁷⁄₈ in.

3/8-in. by 4-in. carriage bolt

3/8-in. flat washers between tubing and blocks

3 in.

1 in.

1³⁄₁₆ in.

3/4 in.

1/2 in.

3 in.

1½-in. 10-24 machine bolt

Oak dowel, 1-in.-dia., 27½ in. long

3/8-in.-dia. hole centered on block 15/16 in. from top edge

#10 nut

#10 washer

3/16-in.-dia. hole

3/8-in.-dia. hole

3/8-in. hex nut

3/8-in. by 3-in. iron dowel screw to attach handle to shaft

1 in.

3/8-in. flat washer

1-in. copper tubing. Slip over handle shaft and drill hole through both pieces. Hold flush at bottom.

Round edges with 3/8-in. radius.

Handle (see Layout)

**7-13** A 3-in. length of 1-in. copper tubing reinforces the bottom end of the handle shaft. The main bolt fits in a 3/8-in. hole near the end, but I drill a second 3/16-in.-dia. hole for a 10-24 machine bolt 1/2 in. from the top end of the tubing (shown here). A straightedge clamp keeps the shaft from rolling.

To complete the blocks, I have to "nibble out" a 1/16-in.-deep section from the front end of each block so it fits over the aluminum edging on the yoke. When installed, the front ends of the blocks should be flush with the front of the yoke (*drawing 7-F*) and the blocks must sit flat on the plywood. I set the table-saw blade 1/16 in. above the table and use my miter gauge with a wooden auxiliary fence to feed the stock into the blade. Now I can place the blocks on the yoke, carefully spacing them parallel to each other and 1¹³/₁₆ in. apart. Then I drill 1/4-in. holes through the bolt holes and the MDO board, and bolt the blocks to the yoke.

The handle shaft is a 27½-in. length of 1-in.-dia. oak dowel, which I cut from a 3-ft.-long piece. A bolt will connect one end of the shaft to the yoke blocks, but the shaft would probably split without a little extra reinforcement. I cut a 3-in. length of 1-in. I.D. copper tubing and slip it over one end of the shaft. Then I make a center punch mark 3/4 in. from the end and drill a 1/4-in.-dia. pilot hole through the tubing and shaft at once. I hold the piece against a straightedge clamp clamped across my drill-press table to keep the handle from rolling as I drill. Next I enlarge the 1/4-in. hole with a 3/8-in.-dia. bit.

I also need to drill a 3/16-in.-dia. hole 1/2 in. from the top end of the copper tubing for a 1½-in. 10-24 machine bolt (*photo 7-13*). When the wagon's being pulled, this second bolt will take some of the strain off the 3/8-in.-dia. bolt at the bottom end.

Now for a little assembly. Installing the shaft to the yoke takes some pretty good hand-eye coordination. The idea is to fit the shaft between the 2 blocks with a washer on each side of the shaft. To do this, I place a short 3/8-in.-dia. bolt in one block hole just far enough to hold a washer on the inside of the block. Next I insert a 3/8-in. by 4-in. carriage bolt through the other block just far enough to hold a washer on the end. Now I slip the shaft in place and tap the long bolt through with a hammer, pushing out the temporary bolt (*photo 7-14*). All I have to do now is put a washer and nut on the end.

**7-14** There's a trick for getting washers on the bolt between the shaft and the blocks. I insert a short bolt just far enough to hold a washer on the end. Then I put the long bolt through the opposite hole just far enough to hold a washer. With the shaft in place, I tap in the long bolt, pushing the short bolt out.

## Making the Handle

With a compass and square, I lay out the handle shape on a piece of 1-in.-thick oak, which I've planed from some 8/4 stock (see Project Planner and *drawing 7-F*). I'll cut out the inside with my jigsaw. I drill a couple of holes inside the handle so I can start the cut with the jig-saw. I saw out the inside first. Then, on my miter saw, I set the blade to 30 degrees and make the 2 angled cuts on the sides, holding the 2-in.-wide end of the handle against the fence. After this, I saw the outer shape of the handle on the band saw. I sand the inside and out-side edges next with the drum-sander attachment on my drill press.

At the bottom end of the handle, I have to drill a 1-in.-dia. hole for the shaft. I clamp a high wooden fence across my drill-press table to hold the stock firmly on end (*photo 7-15*). Then, with a 1-in.-dia.

7-16 A square helps me hold the bit
straight as I drill a pilot hole in the
shaft for the double-ended iron dowel
screw that holds the handle in place.

7-16 A square helps me hold the bit
straight as I drill a pilot hole in the
shaft for the double-ended iron dowel
screw that holds the handle in place.

7-17 I thread the dowel screw into
the handle shaft with a pair of pliers
and then spin the handle onto the
shaft.

forstner bit, I drill a 1/2-in.-deep hole for the handle. I round the edges
of the handle, except for the bottom, with a 3/8-in.-radius roundover
bit in my router and sand the edges smooth.

I'm gong to secure the handle to the shaft with a 3/8-in. by 3-in.
iron dowel screw. This piece of hardware has a wood-screw thread at
each end. On the drill press, I drill a 1/4-in. pilot hole in the handle. I
switch to a hand-held electric drill to bore a second hole in the end of
the handle shaft. I hold a square against the handle shaft to make sure
the bit stays straight (*photo 7-16*). Then I thread the dowel screw into
the handle shaft with a pair of slip-joint pliers (*photo 7-17*), apply
some glue, and spin on the handle.

### Side Boards

Now for the side boards of the wagon. They consist of slats and stakes
that fit into the mortises in the wagon sides (*drawings 7-A and 7-G*). I
cut the 10 stakes from some 1 × 4 oak (see Project Planner). Each
stake gets a 1½-in.-long tenon on the bottom end, which I'll cut on
the table saw.

To cut the tenon shoulders, I set the blade for a 3/16-in.-deep cut.
Then I clamp a 3/4-in.-thick gauge block to my rip fence and position
the rip fence 2¼ in. from the blade. I place a scrap piece against the
miter gauge and butt one end against the gauge block. I make a test
cut and adjust the fence as necessary to give me a 1½-in.-long tenon.
When the setting's right, I make a cut on both sides of each stake at
one end only. These cuts form the shoulders of the tenons.

Next I lower the saw blade a little for a 3/32-in.-deep cut. Without
changing the rest of the setup, I turn the stakes on edge and make a
shoulder cut on each edge. The cheek cuts come next and I make these
with my table-saw tenoning jig, raising the blade 1½ in. above the

table. All that's left is to make a rip cut at the top and bottom of each tenon. I do this on the band saw, guiding the stake against the fence. To finish the stakes, I chamfer the ends and edges with a block plane.

The slats are made from 5/16-in.-thick oak, which is nearly impossible to buy in a store. With a thickness planer, though, it's easy enough to make in the shop. First I rip, joint, and crosscut the slat stock to size from 3/4-in. oak (see Project Planner). Next, on the table saw, I saw the 3/4-in.-thick stock right down the middle to get 2 thinner pieces (*photo 7-18*). Sawing a thick board into thinner boards like this is referred to as "resawing." It's most often done on the band saw because the narrow blade wastes very little wood and there's no chance of kickback. If the wood is narrow enough, as it is with these slats, it's also possible to resaw on the table saw using a thin-kerf saw blade. After sawing the slats, I run them through my thickness planer sawn side up to take them down to a 5/16-in. thickness. Finally, I round the ends and edges with a 1/4-in.-radius roundover bit in my router table, exposing only a portion of the bit.

The slats attach to the stakes with 3/4-in. #6 screws. On the drill press, I predrill and countersink holes in the slats. I clamp a straight-edge clamp to the drill-press table to use as a stop to locate the screw holes so I don't have to measure every slat (*photo 7-19*). On the side slats, I center the holes 1⁹/₁₆ in. from the ends. On the front and rear slats, I center the holes 1¾ in. from the ends. The 2½-in.-wide slats get 2 screw holes for each stake; the 1⅜-in.-wide slats get only one. The screw holes are centered in the stakes (*drawing 7-A*).

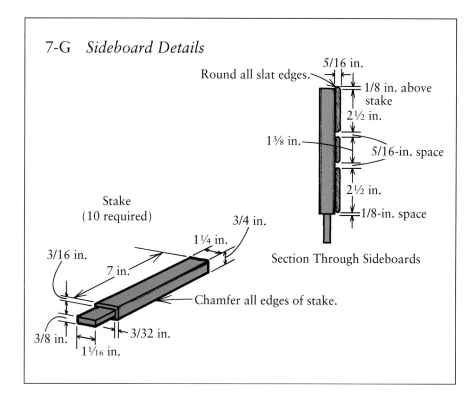

7-G  *Sideboard Details*

Round all slat edges.
5/16 in.
1/8 in. above stake
2½ in.
1⅜ in.
5/16-in. space
2½ in.
1/8-in. space

Section Through Sideboards

Stake (10 required)
3/4 in.
1¼ in.
3/16 in.
7 in.
Chamfer all edges of stake.
3/8 in.
3/32 in.
1¹/₁₆ in.

**7-18** 5/16-in.-thick oak is easy to get by splitting 3/4-in. stock down the middle. After making the cut, I run the wood through the planer, sawn side up, to take it down to 5/16 in.

**7-19** I clamp a straightedge clamp to the drill-press table to use as a stop for drilling screw holes in the wagon side slats.

The easiest way to assemble the side boards is to do it in place on the wagon. First I make 4 spacers from scrap — two 1/8 in. thick and two 5/16 in. thick. Next I place the stakes in their mortises in the wagon sides with the *worst*-looking side facing out. With a square and a pencil, I mark lines on the slats to indicate the position of the stakes. Now I angle the two 1/8-in. spacers across 2 adjacent sides of the wagon bed sides and rest a 2½-in.-wide slat on top of the spacers. Then I line up the stakes along the pencil marks and screw the slat in place. I use the 5/16-in. spacers to position the middle and top slats in the same way (*photo 7-20*). When I've screwed on the slats, I just turn the whole assembly around so that the stakes face out instead of in. After all 4 sides are complete, I can stand back for a minute and admire a job well done. But not for too long — I still have some finishing to do.

*Finishing Touches*

Fire-engine red is the proper color for a wagon. But I think I'll leave the oak side boards unpainted — they'll contrast nicely with the

bright-red bed. And to make those red parts really stand out, I'll paint the undercarriage black. That way, you won't even see it.

First, I spray the undercarriage of the wagon with an aerosol gray primer (without chloroflourocarbons of course; in fact, CFCs were banned from all aerosols back in 1988). When the primer's dry, I spray it with gloss acrylic black enamel. I also paint the top of the yoke and the copper tubing on the handle shaft black. For contrast, however, I leave the 2 oak blocks on the yoke unpainted.

For the bed, I brush on a coat of acrylic latex primer. When that's dry, I brush on 2 coats of bright-red gloss latex enamel. To show off the oak on the side boards, I brush on a couple of coats of marine spar varnish. I also apply some varnish to the handle, the shaft, and the blocks on the yoke. When the finish is dry, the wagon's ready to roll. What a beauty!

**7-20** I fasten the slats to the stakes on the wagon, angling spacers across the bed to keep the slats evenly spaced. When I've screwed on the slats, I turn the side around so the stakes face outward.

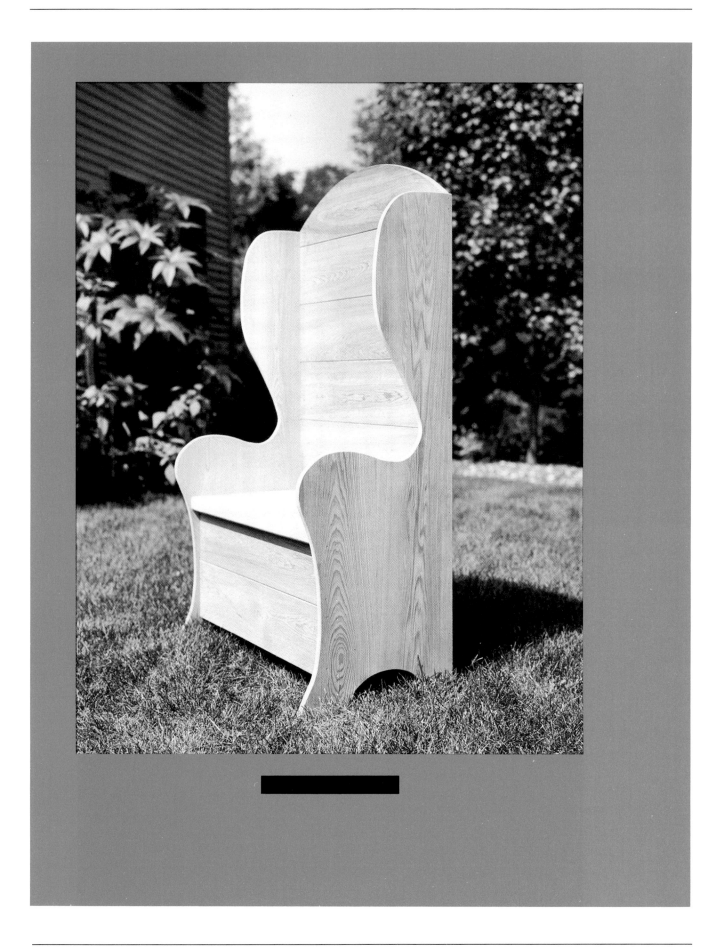

# 8

# Outdoor Lidded Bench

THIS outdoor lidded bench is an improved version of one that's been sitting on the grounds of the New Yankee Workshop for more than seventy-five years. It's really handy on the back porch as a place to park grocery bags while hunting for keys. The seat lifts off to reveal a storage compartment underneath — a good place for storing the dog's leash, the garden hose, or maybe some garden tools.

While I really liked the lines of the antique bench, I thought that I'd make a couple of improvements. The back boards on the original bench were simply butted and nailed to the side panels. This construction is fast and easy to build, but it doesn't get good marks for strength or appearance; there's a visible gap between the sides and the back. Instead of copying this construction on my version of the bench, I fit the ends of the back boards into rabbets milled along the back inside edges of the side panels (*drawing 8-D*). This joint is stronger than a butt joint and it eliminates the unsightly gap.

I also modified the joints between the back boards. The boards on the original bench were just butted together, and it's really impossible to hide a joint like that. The boards will contract when the humidity level drops, revealing gaps between the boards. I also butted the back boards on my bench, but I chose to "celebrate" the joints, instead of trying to hide them, by planing a decorative chamfer on the edges (*drawing 8-D Details*).

I thought about building the bench from pine and painting it, but I didn't want to deal with peeling paint a few years down the road. I decided to build it from cypress — a wood that's so weather-resistant it needs no finish at all. I built a couple of Adirondack chairs from unfinished cypress a few years ago and they're holding up just fine.

## PROJECT PLANNER

*Time:* 2 days
*Special hardware and tools:*
(81) 1¼-in. #8 F.H. stainless steel wood screws
Waterproof yellow glue
*Wood:*
(1) 14-ft. 1 × 10 cypress
Cut 2 pieces 52 in. long and 2 pieces 27 in. long. Edge-glue one long piece to one short piece, holding bottom ends even, to make 2 side panels.
(3) 12-ft. 1 × 8 cypress
Cut 7 pieces 35¾ in. long for back boards. Cut 2 pieces 34¾ in. long, and edge-glue to make a panel approximately 14½ in. × 34¾ in. for lid. Cut 2 pieces 34½ in. long. Rip and joint to 6⅞-in. width for 2 front boards. Cut one piece 34½ in. long for wide bottom board.
(1) 12-ft. 1 × 6 cypress
Rip and joint a 2-in. by 12-ft. piece and then cut it into the following: one piece 33 in. long for back cleat for lid; 2 pieces 13¼ in. long for side cleats for bottom; 2 pieces 13½ in. long, then cut to fit for side cleats for lid; 2 pieces 9 in. long, then cut to fit for side cleats for front; 3 pieces 12 in. long for cleats for bottom and front.
From remaining strip cut 2 pieces 48 in. long, and rip the joint to 3 in. wide for back cleats. Cut one piece 34⅜ in. long, and rip and joint to 1⅝ in. wide for front edge of lid.
(1) 6-ft. 1 × 6 cypress
Cut one piece 34½ in. long for narrow bottom board. Cut one piece 35 in. long, and then rip and joint to 1¾ in. wide for narrow back board at the bottom.

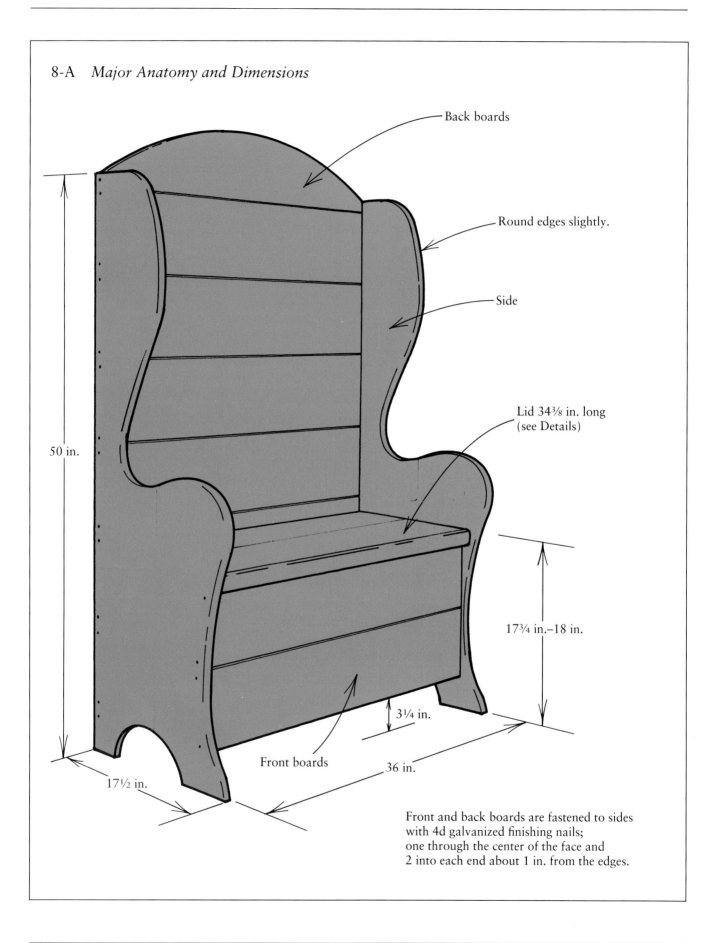

Back boards

Round edges slightly.

Side

Lid 34⅜ in. long
(see Details)

50 in.

17¾ in.–18 in.

3¼ in.

Front boards

36 in.

17½ in.

Front and back boards are fastened to sides
with 4d galvanized finishing nails;
one through the center of the face and
2 into each end about 1 in. from the edges.

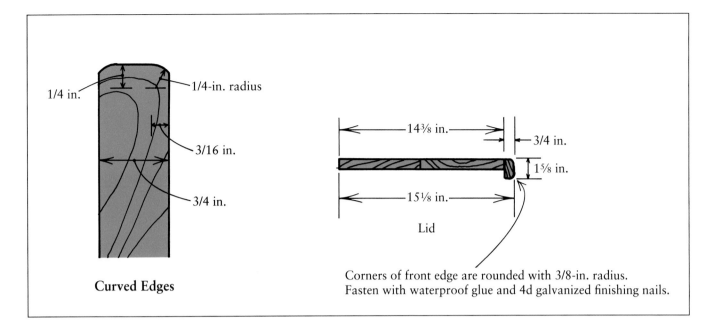

**Curved Edges**

1/4 in.

1/4-in. radius

3/16 in.

3/4 in.

14⅜ in.

3/4 in.

1⅝ in.

15⅛ in.

Lid

Corners of front edge are rounded with 3/8-in. radius.
Fasten with waterproof glue and 4d galvanized finishing nails.

My problem with cypress is that it comes from the South, so it's
difficult to find in New England, where I live. The cypress I used for
the Adirondack chairs was recycled from old brewery vats, but that
supply is long gone. After making a few phone calls, I found a source
in Florida that "mines" hundred-year-old cypress logs from rivers in
Georgia and Florida, and they agreed to ship what I wanted, already
surfaced. Cypress can also be ordered by mail from some of the lumber dealers that advertise in the classified sections of some woodworking magazines. Redwood or red cedar would be a good second choice
if you can't locate any cypress.

## Planing the Boards

As nice as my cypress was right from the mill, as always, there was a
little variation in thickness. I like to run my stock through the thickness planer to plane all the boards to a consistent thickness. This is
especially important when gluing up panels.

One thing about a planer, though: it won't remove any cup, twist,
or warp from a board. The planer's feed rollers press the board down
against the bed of the planer with enough force to flatten out the curve
during the cut. When the board comes out the other end, however, it
springs back to its original shape. The board will be thinner all right,
but the cup, twist, or warp will still be there. To avoid this problem,
you have to flatten one face of the board with a jointer, belt sander, or
hand plane first. Then place the flattened side down against the bed of
the thickness planer when you run it through. You can save yourself a
lot of trouble if you carefully select boards that are flat to begin with.

I run all the boards for the bench through the planer, taking off
about 1/32 in. of wood. Whenever I use my planer these days, I'm

**8-1** To straighten a bowed board on the table saw, I place the concave edge against the fence and trim off enough to straighten the opposite edge. Then I move the fence 1/16 in. closer to the blade, flip the board, and straighten the concave side.

thankful for the dust-collection chute I installed. Before I put on the chute, shavings and dust would spew all over the shop. The chute hooks up to my dust-collection vacuum and keeps the shop floor (not to mention my lungs) free of chips and dust.

After planing the boards, I crosscut 4 pieces of 1 × 10 to make the side panels: 2 pieces 52 in. long and 2 pieces 27 in. long (see Project Planner).

## "Jointing" on the Table Saw

Normally I square and straighten the edges of boards on the jointer. But for the side-panel boards, I resurrected a technique I used to use before I owned a jointer. In a pinch, you can get pretty respectable edges by "jointing" boards on the table saw. This technique works only with boards that are shorter than the rip fence. Here's how I do it.

First I hold one edge of the board against the rip fence to see which way it curves. Most boards bow slightly from end to end — that is, they have one concave edge and one convex edge. For the first cut, I place the concave edge against the fence. Then I run it through, taking off just enough wood to straighten the opposite (convex) edge (*photo 8-1*). Then I move the fence 1/16 in. closer to the blade, and rip the opposite edge. That's all there is to it. With a 40- to 60-tooth blade, the edges are smooth enough to glue — right off the saw.

## Gluing up the Panels

Now I'm ready to glue up the side panels. Because the bench will get wet outside, I use a new waterproof yellow glue. I clamp the boards together, lining up the bottom ends, then put the clamped-up side panels aside to dry. When the glue has cured, I take off the clamps, scrape off any excess glue with my scraper, and smooth up the panels with my belt sander.

## Side Panels

The first thing I want to do is square up the bottom edge of the side panels. My homemade panel cutter is perfect for the job. I take off about 3/4 in., holding the long back edge of the panel against the fence of my panel cutter (*photo 8-2*).

8-2 I square up the bottom ends of the side panels with my homemade panel cutter.

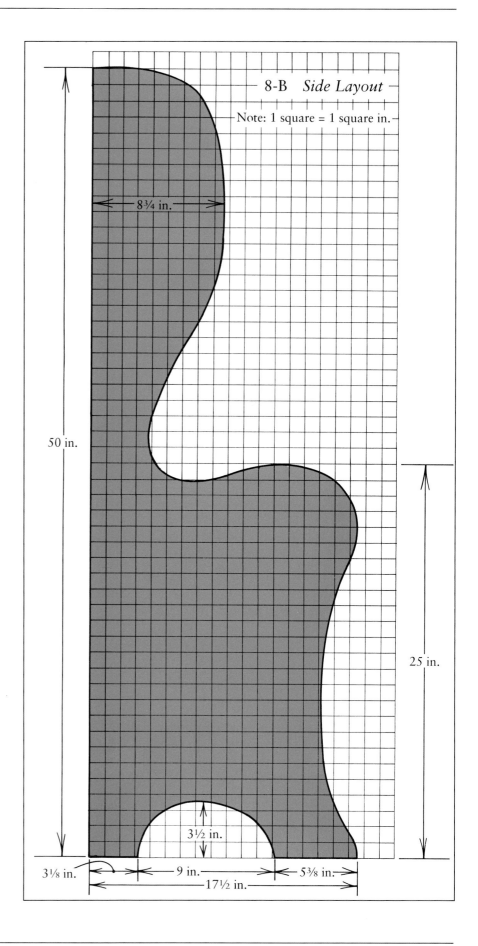

8-B  *Side Layout*

Note: 1 square = 1 square in.

8¾ in.

50 in.

25 in.

3½ in.

3⅛ in.

9 in.

5⅜ in.

17½ in.

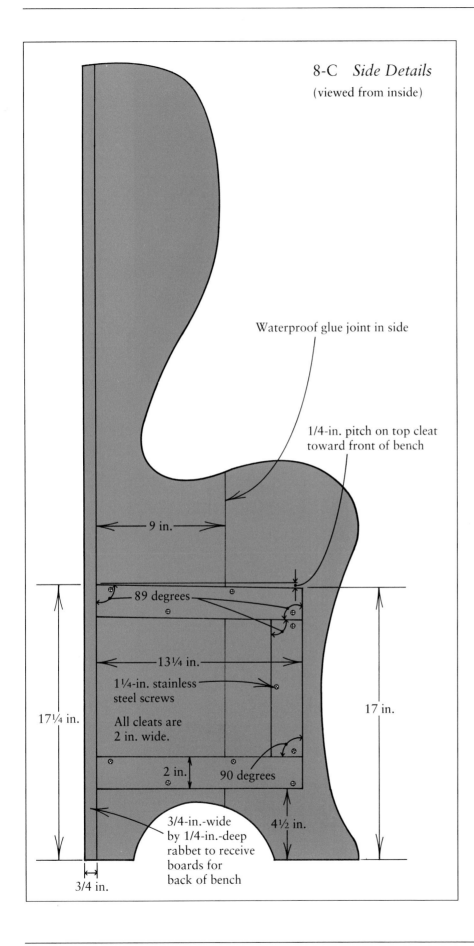

8-C  *Side Details*
(viewed from inside)

Waterproof glue joint in side

1/4-in. pitch on top cleat
toward front of bench

9 in.

89 degrees

13¼ in.

1¼-in. stainless
steel screws

17 in.

17¼ in.

All cleats are
2 in. wide.

2 in.

90 degrees

4½ in.

3/4-in.-wide
by 1/4-in.-deep
rabbet to receive
boards for
back of bench

3/4 in.

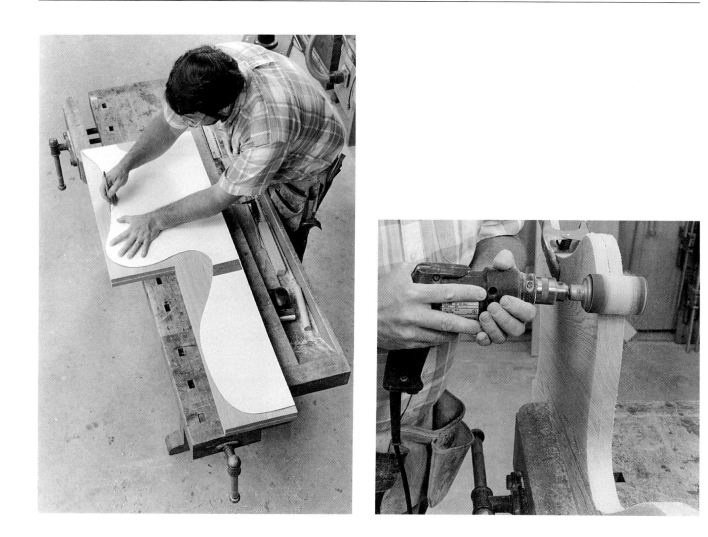

8-3   I trace the side panels from a pattern I made out of poster board. I had to tape 2 sheets of poster board together to make a pattern that's long enough.

8-4   After sawing out the sides, I clamp them together edge up and sand the edges with a drum sander in a drill.

If I were planning to build only one bench, I'd lay out the curved pattern directly on one of the side panels and saw both sides at once. But because I'll be building several of these benches, I made a pattern out of poster board (*drawing 8-B*).

I trace the pattern onto one of the side panels (*photo 8-3*) and clamp the 2 sides together on my bench with the curved edge over-hanging the bench top. Then I saw out both sides at once with my jigsaw.

After sawing out the sides, I clamp them together edge up and sand the edges with a drum sander in a hand-held drill (*photo 8-4*). I like to sand both pieces at once. This gives me a wider working surface and makes it easier to keep the sanding drum perpendicular to the side of the panel. If I were sanding only one piece at a time, the drum might rock back and forth, making the edge uneven.

The next step is to lay out the 1 × 2 cleats that screw to the sides (*drawing 8-C*). Each side has 3 cleats — one at the top that supports the lid, one to attach the bottom, and one to attach the front panel.

The top cleat slopes slightly to the front so that water will run off the lid instead of just sitting there. It's very easy to lay out (*drawing*

8-5  With a stack dado head in the table saw, I mill a 1/4-in. by 3/4-in. rabbet along the back inside edge of each side panel. The ends of the back boards will fit into these rabbets.

8-C). I measure up 17¼ in. from the back bottom corner of the side. Placing my framing square against the back edge, I draw a 13¼-in.-line square across the side. Then, at the front end of the line, I measure down 1/4 in., which is the amount of pitch I want at the front edge, and make a mark. Now I use my square to connect the back end of the line with the mark I just made. This line forms an angle of approximately 89 degrees with the back edge of the side. I lay out an identical line on the opposite side panel, keeping in mind I must lay out a mirror image.

With the cleat layout done, I ease the edges of all the curved sections with a 1/4-in. roundover bit in my router. I only want to ease the edges a little bit, so I extend only a part of the bit below the router base.

I mill a rabbet along the inside back edges of the side panels to receive the ends of the back boards (*drawings 8-C, 8-D, and 8-E*). The rabbets run the entire length of the sides. I mill these 1/4-in. by 3/4-in. rabbets on the table saw with my stack dado head set for a 3/4-in.-wide cut. To keep the cutter from hitting the rip fence, I screw an auxiliary wooden fence to the metal rip fence. This allows me to position the fence right up against the cutter without damaging the fence or the blade. I raise the dado head 1/4 in. above the table and mill the rabbet along the inside back edges of both side panels (*photo 8-5*).

## Attaching the Side Cleats

Now I'm ready for the side-panel cleats — 3 on a side. I rip and joint the 2-in.-wide cleats from 1 × 6 cypress and crosscut the pieces to length (see Project Planner and *drawing 8-C*). Then I predrill and countersink holes for the stainless steel screws that will hold the cleats to the sides. Working on one side panel at a time, I screw on the top

**8-6** I predrill and countersink for the stainless steel screws that hold the side cleats in place. I install the top cleat first (shown here), aligning the top edge with my layout line. The front cleat goes on next, the bottom cleat last.

cleat first, aligning the top edge with my sloped layout line (*photo 8-6 and drawing 8-C*). It has an angled cut at both ends.

I want the front cleat to be parallel to the back of the bench. This means I have to cut the top end at an angle where it butts against the underside of the top cleat (*drawing 8-C*). It isn't much of an angle — just about 1 degree. I make this cut on my power miter box and screw the front cleat in place. The bottom cleat goes on last. With one side complete, I repeat the procedure on the other side panel.

### Back Boards

There are 7 boards that make up the back of the bench (*drawing 8-E*). On the radial-arm saw, I cut these boards a little longer than what I need (see Project Planner). I'll trim them to final length a little later.

Now I'm ready to chamfer the edges. I could use a router with a chamfering bit, but it's faster to mill these chamfers on the jointer. I tilt the jointer fence 45 degrees and make one pass along each front edge.

With the chamfers complete, I can trim the boards to finished length. I do this on the radial-arm saw. As you can see in the photo (*photo 8-7*), I built a wooden table to the left of my radial-arm saw exactly the same height as the radial-arm saw table. This table is handy for supporting long stock. It also comes in handy in a situation like this, when I have to cut a whole run of boards exactly the same length.

Measuring 35 in. from the side of the blade, I fasten a piece of scrap to the table with screws to serve as a stop. I angle the stop block so it just contacts the workpiece at a point (*photo 8-7*). This makes it impossible for sawdust to build up between the stop and the work-

8-7 A piece of scrap tacked to the saw table serves as a stop so all the back boards are exactly the same length. I angle the stop block so it just contacts the workpiece at one point. This makes it impossible for sawdust to build up between the stop and the workpiece.

piece, preventing the board from going all the way to the stop. The result, when this happens, is a board that's too short.

With the stop in place, I square up the left end of the back board. Then I slide the board to the left so the end touches the stop and cut off the right end. With this system, all the back boards are *exactly* the same length.

With a similar setup on the radial-arm saw, I cut the 2 bottom boards and the 2 front boards to length (*drawing 8-D*).

## Installing Back Boards and Bottom Boards

Now I'm ready for a little assembly. I start by tacking the back boards to one of the sides. I clamp the sidepiece flat on my bench and nail the boards on one at a time. I measure up 3½ in. from the bottom and nail on the narrow bottom board first (*drawing 8-E*). All I do is put one 4d nail in the center of each board to hold it in place. The top board — the one with the arch — goes on later, after I've sawn out the arch.

The 2 bottom boards go on next (*drawing 8-D*). I space the boards evenly with uniform gaps between the boards to allow air to circulate in the storage compartment and make sure any water that gets in there has a way to run out. I drill and countersink for 2 screws in each end, and screw the boards to the bottom cleat with stainless steel screws.

The other side of the bench goes on top. I place it over the ends of the boards and tack each back board to the second sidepiece as I did to the first. Then I screw the opposite ends of the bottom boards to the bottom cleat, making sure to keep the bottom boards square to the sides.

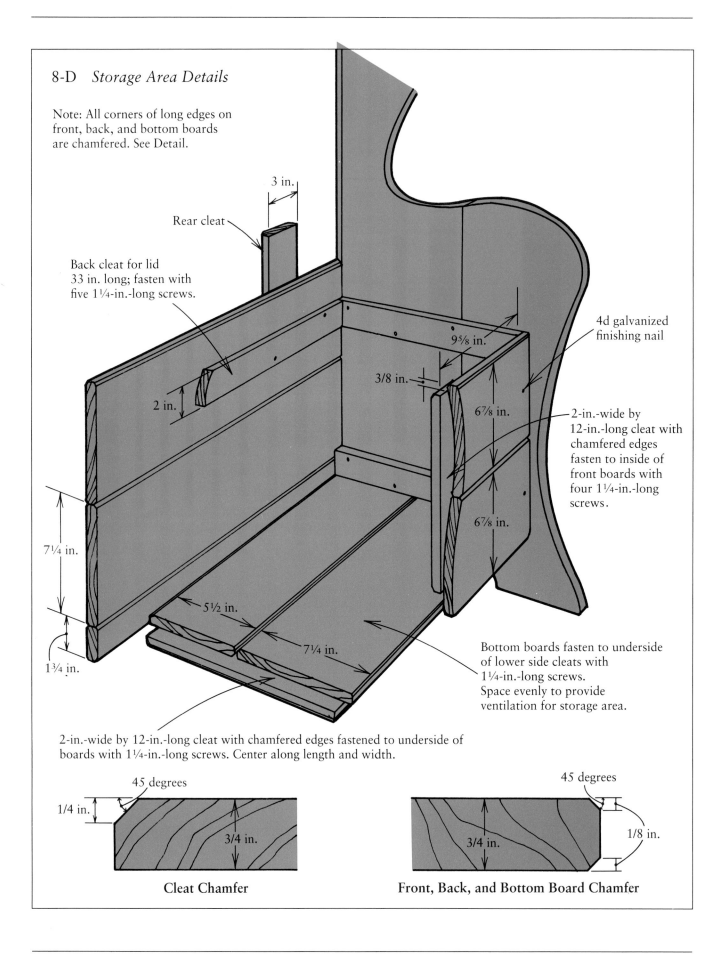

## 8-D  *Storage Area Details*

Note: All corners of long edges on front, back, and bottom boards are chamfered. See Detail.

3 in.

Rear cleat

Back cleat for lid 33 in. long; fasten with five 1¼-in.-long screws.

2 in.

9⅝ in.

3/8 in.

4d galvanized finishing nail

6⅞ in.

2-in.-wide by 12-in.-long cleat with chamfered edges fasten to inside of front boards with four 1¼-in.-long screws.

6⅞ in.

7¼ in.

1¾ in.

5½ in.

7¼ in.

Bottom boards fasten to underside of lower side cleats with 1¼-in.-long screws. Space evenly to provide ventilation for storage area.

2-in.-wide by 12-in.-long cleat with chamfered edges fastened to underside of boards with 1¼-in.-long screws. Center along length and width.

45 degrees

1/4 in.

3/4 in.

**Cleat Chamfer**

45 degrees

3/4 in.

1/8 in.

**Front, Back, and Bottom Board Chamfer**

## 8-E  *Back of Bench*

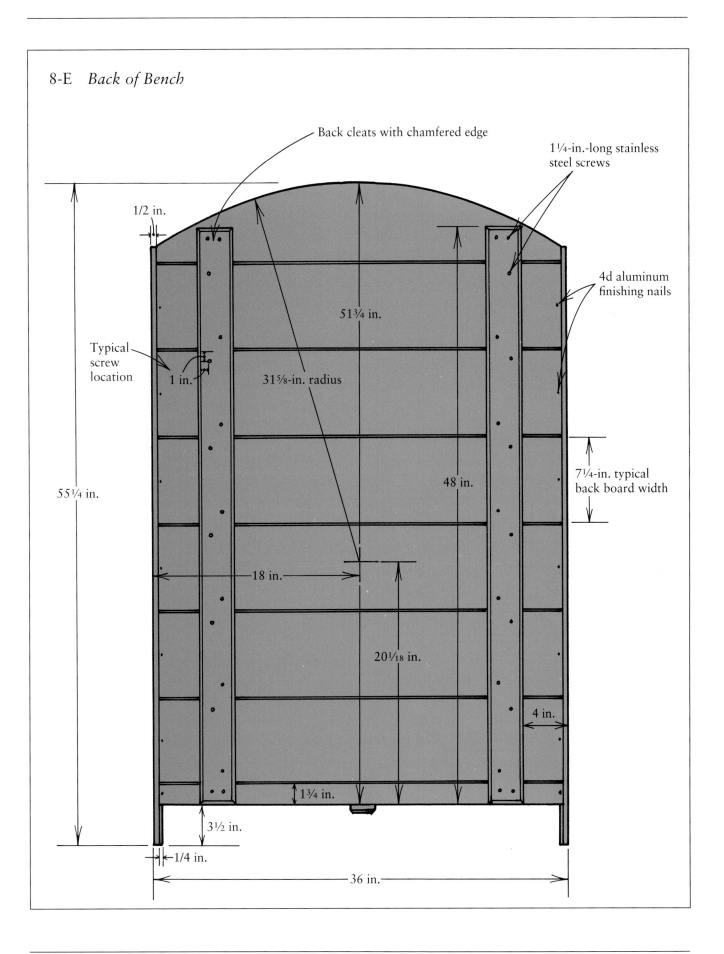

Back cleats with chamfered edge

1¼-in.-long stainless
steel screws

4d aluminum
finishing nails

1/2 in.

51¾ in.

31⅝-in. radius

48 in.

7¼-in. typical
back board width

Typical
screw
location

1 in.

55¼ in.

18 in.

20¹⁄₁₈ in.

4 in.

1¾ in.

3½ in.

1/4 in.

36 in.

8-8 To draw the arc on the top back board, I use a long stick as a compass. I hold one end of the stick on the top of the arc and drive a nail through the stick into a center point I marked on the back of the bench. I place a pencil against the end of the stick and pivot the stick on the nail to draw the arc.

8-9 The two 3-in. by 48-in. back cleats get screwed to the back boards. I drill and countersink holes in the cleats — 2 for each back board — staggering the holes as shown.

## Laying Out the Arch

Now I'm ready to lay out the arch on the top of the back board. To draw this large-radius arc I use a long stick, my framing square, and a little basic geometry.

First I mark a centerline down the middle of the back, from top to bottom. Next, I place the top board in position in the side rabbets. I want to lay out an arc starting from points 1/8 in. above the top ends of the sidepieces, so I make pencil marks to locate these 2 points. Then I establish the top of the arc by measuring up 51¾ in. from the bottom back board along the centerline of the bench (*drawing 8-E*).

With my framing square, I draw a line between the top of the arc and one of the starting points at the end of the board. Next, I measure the length of this line and make a mark at its center point. Holding my framing square on this center point, I draw a second pencil line perpendicular to the first one. I extend this second line until it intersects with the centerline along the back of the bench. This point, where the second pencil line intersects the centerline, is the center point for my arc.

To draw the arc, I use a long stick as a compass (*photo 8-8*). I hold one end of the stick on the top of the arc and drive a nail through the stick into the center point I marked on the back of the bench. I place a pencil against the end of the stick and pivot the stick on the nail to draw the arc.

Now I remove the stick and the top board and saw out the arch with my jigsaw. I clean up the curve with the drum-sander attachment on my drill press and round the edges of the curve the same as I did on the sides with a 1/4-in. roundover bit in my router. With the top board finished, I tack it in place with a nail through each end.

## Cleats and Front Boards

Now I can mill and install all the remaining cleats: 2 for the back, 2 for the front, one for the bottom, and one to support the back edge of the lid. I rip, joint, and crosscut these parts to size (see Project Planner). Except for the cleat that supports the lid, I chamfer all 4 edges on one side of each cleat with a chamfering bit in my router. As always, I rout the end grain first to minimize tearout at the corners and feed the router from left to right against the rotation of the bit.

With the chamfers all milled, I install the two 3-in. by 48-in. cleats that support the back boards. I drill and countersink screw holes in the cleats — 2 for each back board — staggering the holes as shown (*drawing 8-E and photo 8-9*). Then I screw the cleats to the back boards with stainless steel screws.

Next I screw the two 2-in. by 12-in. cleats to the inside faces of the front boards (*drawing 8-D and photo 8-10*). With the cleats in place, I nail the front assembly across the front of the bench with a couple of 4d galvanized finishing nails (*photo 8-11*).

While the bench is still clamped on its side, I screw on the bottom cleat that supports the bottom boards. I center it in the middle of the bench and install 2 screws in each board.

**8-10** Two 2-in. by 12-in. cleats get screwed to the insides of the front boards.

**8-11** With the cleats in place, I nail the front assembly to the front of the bench.

**8-12** To dress up the front edge of the lid and give it a thicker look, I glue and nail on a 1⅝-in.-wide strip of cypress with the front edges rounded over.

Now I take the assembly off the workbench and place it on its side on the floor. To reinforce the back boards, I shoot a couple of 4d galvanized finishing nails into each board, nailing through the sidepieces into the ends of the back boards. I space the nails about 1¼ in. in from the edges of the boards.

The last cleat to install is the 2-in. by 33-in.-long cleat that supports the back edge of the lid. With the bench right-side up on the floor, I drill and install 5 stainless steel screws to secure the cleat to the back. I make sure that the top of the cleat is flush with the tops of the side cleats (*drawing 8-D*).

## Making the Lid

All that's left is the lid. To make it, I rip and joint 2 pieces of 1 × 8 cypress and edge-glue them with waterproof glue to make a panel approximately 14½ in. × 34¾ in. (see Project Planner). When the glue has dried, I square up one end on the table saw with my homemade panel cutter. Then I rip and joint the panel to a width of 14⅜ in. (see *drawing 8-A Lid Detail*).

To determine the finished length of the lid, I measure from one side of the bench to the other. I subtract 1/8 in. from this measurement to allow side clearance and cut the lid to length — 34⅜ in. for my bench.

To dress up the front edge of the lid and give it a thicker look, I mill a 1⅝-in.-wide strip of cypress (*photo 8-12 and drawing 8-A Lid Detail*). I round over the 2 front edges of the strip with a 3/8-in.-radius roundover bit in my router. Then I glue it to the strip and the edge of the lid and tack the strip in place with some 4d galvanized finishing nails.

Next morning, when the glue is dry, I smooth up the lid with my belt sander and put the lid in position on the bench. I don't need a finish — that cypress will stand up to even the worst New England weather.

At times like this, it's always nice to sit back and admire your work. In this particular case, I believe I'll sit *on* my work and think about where to put it.

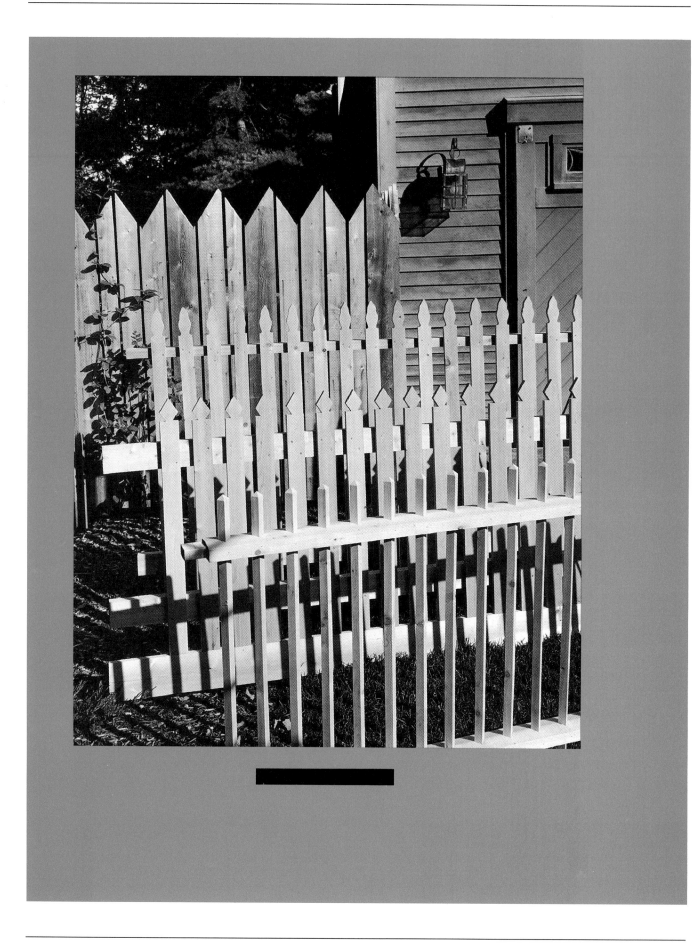

# 9

# *Four Colonial Fences*

W HEN I decided to show how to build a variety of fences on *The New Yankee Workshop*, there was no question where I would turn to seek inspiration: colonial Williamsburg — the re-created eighteenth-century village in Williamsburg, Virginia. There I found dozens of fence styles to choose from. Like most colonial towns, Williamsburg had a law that required every homeowner to put up a fence. With good reason, too, because fences helped to keep the peace in a way. They kept the livestock out of the garden and marked off the property boundaries for all to see. Fences also provided a reassuring touch of order, in sharp contrast to the untamed wilderness just outside town.

In this chapter I'll explain how to build four different fence sections from colonial Williamsburg. Two of these — the flame-top fence and the diamond-top fence — are traditional flat picket fences. They're easy to build and they'll look great around any traditional home. The mortised fence, another picket design, is a little more challenging to build, but it will really add a lot to your home, yard, or garden. The garden fence is a much taller fence built of random-width rough boards with an unusual saw-tooth pattern at the top. It's a copy of the fence that encloses the kitchen garden of the Governor's Palace at colonial Williamsburg. It too is easy to build and is just the thing for some extra privacy or security around a pool.

The procedures in this chapter are for building one 8-ft. section of each type of fence. These sections are designed for level ground only. Sloping fences must be custom-built for a specific site. For information about installing fences and dealing with sloped sites, I suggest that you turn to one of the many good books available on fencing.

## PROJECT PLANNER

NOTE: Quantities given are for building one 8-ft.-long section of fence. Multiply as necessary for additional sections. Each additional fence section attached to the first section requires only one more post.

### FLAME-TOP FENCE
*Time:* 1/2 day per section
*Special hardware and tools:*
6d galvanized common nails
*Wood:*
(2) 8-ft. full rough-cut 2 × 4 white cedar

Plane, rip, and joint to $1^5/8$ in. × $3^5/8$ in. and cut to $95^1/2$ in. long for stringers/rails.
(2) $6^1/2$-ft. full rough-cut 6 × 6 white cedar

Surface plane all sides until post is 5 in. square. Cut top and dado according to plan. (Note: For a corner post, mill dadoes on adjacent sides and leave top flat.)
(9) 10-ft. 1 × 3 white cedar

Cut 18 pieces 52 in. long. Shape tops according to pattern for pales/pickets.

### DIAMOND-TOP FENCE
*Time:* 1/2 day per section
*Special hardware and tools:*
6d galvanized common nails
*Wood:*
(2) 8-ft. full rough-cut 2 × 4 white cedar

Plane, rip, and joint to $1^5/8$ in. × $3^5/8$ in. and cut to 95 in. long for stringers/rails.
(2) 5-ft. full rough-cut 6 × 6 white cedar

Surface plane all sides until post is 5 in. square. Cut dadoes and top according to plan. (Note: For a corner post, mill dadoes on adjacent sides.)
(5) 14-ft. 1 × 4 white cedar

Rip and joint all lengths to $2^3/4$ in.

wide. Then cut into twenty 36½-in. lengths. Cut tops according to plan for pales/pickets.

(1) 8-ft. 1 × 6 cedar

Cut to 95 in. long for skirtboard.

## MORTISED FENCE

*Time:* 3/4 day per section
*Special hardware and tools:* None
*Wood:*

(2) 8-ft. full rough-cut 2 × 4 white cedar

Plane, rip, and joint to 1¹³/₁₆ in. × 3⅜ in., and cut to 95¾ in. long for stringers/rails.

(2) 6-ft. full rough-cut 6 × 6 white cedar

Surface-plane all sides until post is 5 in. square. Cut top and mortise according to plan. (Note: For a corner post, mill mortises on adjacent sides.)

(2) 10-ft. 5/4-in. by 6-in. rough-cut white cedar

Surface-plane to 1-in. thickness. Then rip and joint each board into four 1-in. strips. Crosscut strips into 38-in. lengths for pales/pickets.

## GARDEN FENCE

*Time:* 1/2 day per section
*Special hardware and tools:*
6d galvanized common nails
chalkline
*Wood:*

(3) 8-ft. full rough-cut 2 × 4 white cedar

If necessary, rip to 4-in. width for stringers/rails. Keep ripped edges down when assembling.

random widths of full rough-cut 1 × 4s, 1 × 6s, and 1 × 8s

Select enough boards to cover 96 in. with a 5/8-in. space between boards. Square one end of each board and assemble in random order for pales.

(2) 8-ft. full rough-cut 6 × 6 white cedar

Cut top and dadoes according to plan. (Note: For a corner post, mill dadoes on adjacent sides.)

## Wood for Fences

Surrounded as they were by an "endless" virgin forest, colonists in the 1700s had an intimate knowledge of wood. They knew exactly which wood was best suited for a particular purpose. In Virginia, fences were often made of old-growth southern yellow pine, which, because of its tight growth rings, was fairly resistant to decay.

Modern yellow pine is not very resistant to decay, which is why most southern yellow pine sold today is pressure-treated. Pressure-treated wood holds up extremely well outdoors and in the ground, but thin fence boards cut from pressure-treated wood tend to twist unless you buy the premium grade or add extra rails or stringers for support. After talking to some of the most respected fence manufacturers in the country, I decided that the best wood to use was eastern white cedar (*Thuja occidentalis*). It's highly resistant to decay, light in weight, and real nice to work with. Being in New England, I was lucky enough to get my cedar from a sawmill in Maine that sold me full dimension, rough-cut lumber.

## FLAME-TOP FENCE

This picket patterns (see fence third from front on page 162) dates from the early 1700s and was found in Robinson, South Carolina. The tops of the pickets, or pales, are cut in the shape of a flame. Back in the old days, the flames were all cut by hand with a bow saw, a type of narrow-bladed saw with a wooden frame that held the blade under tension. The craftsmen at colonial Williamsburg still use bow saws today, but I'm thankful I have a few power-tool alternatives.

For each 8-ft. section of fence, I cut 18 pieces of 1 × 3 white cedar 52 in. long to make the pales. Then I rip and joint two 8-ft. rough cedar 2 × 4s to 1⅝ in. × 3⅝ in. and cut them exactly 95½ in. long on the radial-arm saw.

### Routing the Flames

I could saw out the flames with a band saw or hand-held jigsaw, but that would require me to mark out the flame on each and every pale. I suppose I could save a little time by cutting 2 pales at once, but even that would be pretty slow going. In order to speed up production, I'll use a pattern-routing technique that's faster than sawing. All I need is my router, a plywood template, and a flush trim bit with a 1½-in.-long cutter. This type of bit is commonly used for trimming the edges of plastic laminate.

First, I make a template the exact shape of the flame. I cut a piece of 3/8-in. plywood 8 in. × 10 in. and draw a centerline down the middle. Then I make a pattern by folding a piece of paper in half and cutting out half of the flame pattern with a pair of scissors (*drawing 9-B*). When I unfold the paper, I have a symmetrical flame 2½ in. wide — the width of my pales. I trace this pattern onto the plywood

## 9-A  Flame-Top Fence

Maximum recommended fence section 95 in. long including half laps.
For other lengths adjust centers for pickets/pales if necessary.
Lap joints at corners must be modified.

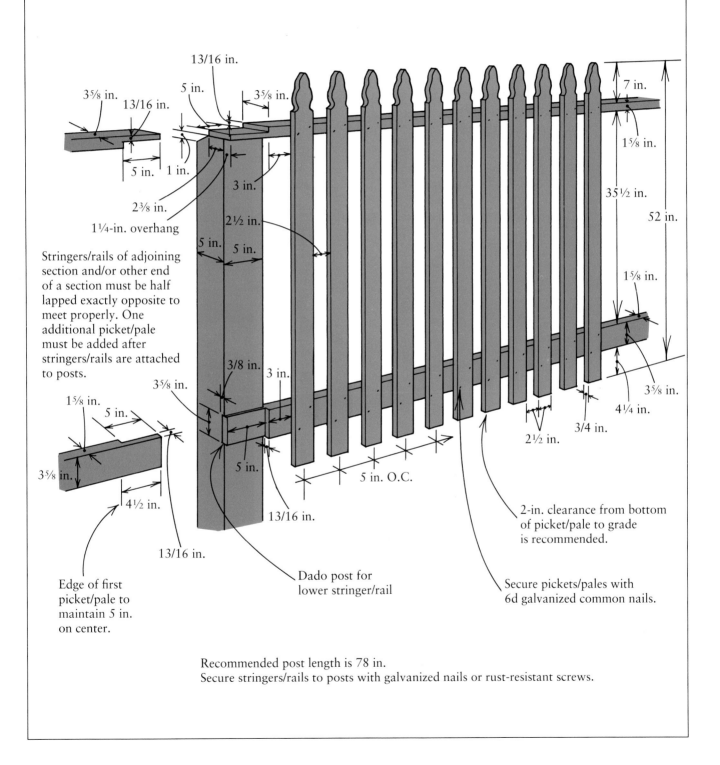

13/16 in.

5 in.

3⁵⁄₈ in.

3⁵⁄₈ in.

13/16 in.

3⁵⁄₈ in.

5 in.

1 in.

2³⁄₈ in.

1¼-in. overhang

3 in.

2½ in.

5 in.

5 in.

7 in.

1⁵⁄₈ in.

35½ in.

52 in.

1⁵⁄₈ in.

Stringers/rails of adjoining section and/or other end of a section must be half lapped exactly opposite to meet properly. One additional picket/pale must be added after stringers/rails are attached to posts.

3/8 in.

3 in.

3⁵⁄₈ in.

1⁵⁄₈ in.

5 in.

3⁵⁄₈ in.

4½ in.

13/16 in.

5 in.

13/16 in.

5 in. O.C.

3⁵⁄₈ in.

4¼ in.

3/4 in.

2½ in.

2-in. clearance from bottom of picket/pale to grade is recommended.

Edge of first picket/pale to maintain 5 in. on center.

Dado post for lower stringer/rail

Secure pickets/pales with 6d galvanized common nails.

Recommended post length is 78 in.
Secure stringers/rails to posts with galvanized nails or rust-resistant screws.

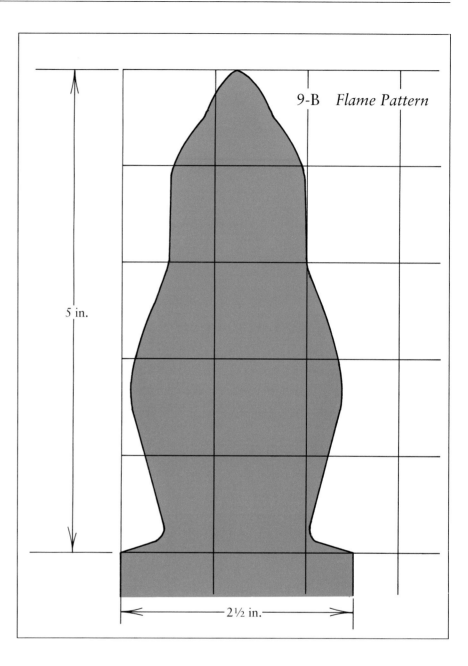

9-B *Flame Pattern*

5 in.

2½ in.

and saw out the template with my band saw. Next, I fasten a scrap pine block to the template with glue and brads 1¼ in. from the centerline on either side. These scrap blocks position the workpiece side to side.

To rout the flames, I clamp the template to my workbench with the flame end overhanging the bench. I place one of the pales on top of the template and flush the end up with the end of the template. I clamp the other end of the pale to the bench to keep it from shifting around. Then I place the router on top of the pale and adjust the depth of cut so that the bearing will ride against the template. When I've got things set up properly, I rout the flame, starting at the right-hand base of the flame and routing counterclockwise around the flame (*photo 9-1*). When I'm finished, I remove the pale from the jig and knock off the sharp corners with a piece of sandpaper. That's all there is to it.

## Stringer Half Laps

The stringers or rails of the flame-top fence get half laps at each end so stringers on adjacent sections of fence will overlap (*drawing 9-A*). The half laps overlap at the posts and must be as long as the fence posts are wide — in this case, 5 in. I cut these joints on the radial-arm saw with my stack dado head set for a 3/4-in.-wide cut. I mark off 5 in. from the ends of the stringers and set the dado head for a 13/16-in.-deep cut. I make repeated crosscuts to "nibble out" a half lap at one end of each stringer. At the other end of each stringer, I cut a half lap on the opposite side from the first. These half laps, too, are 13/16 in. deep (*drawing 9-A*).

## Installing the Pales

Nothing could be easier than putting this fence section together. Before I can nail on the pales, I have to mark the locations of the pales on the stringers. On the left-hand end of each stringer, I make a mark 3 in. from the half lap to position the left-hand edge of the first pale (*drawing 9-A*). Then I make a mark every 5 in. to space the pales 5 in. on center (O.C.). The right-hand edge of the last pale on the right should end up 4½ in. from the right-hand end of the stile (*drawing 9-A*).

With the layout complete, I place the top stringer on edge on the floor and place the bottom stringer on top of a third 2 × 4. I space the 2 stringers 35½ in. apart and nail a pale at each end with 6d galvanized common nails — 4 nails to a pale. The top ends of the pales project 7 in. above the top stringer. The bottom ends extend 4¼ in. below the bottom stringer. With the 3 pales in place, I check the section for square by measuring across the diagonals. If necessary, I rack the fence slightly until the diagonals are equal. Then I nail on all the other pales.

## Posts

This fence is rather high, so I'll make the posts from 78-in. lengths of rough-sawn white cedar 6 × 6 (see Project Planner). I surface-plane all 4 sides until the posts are 5 in. square. Then I mill a 3/8-in. by 3⅝-in. dado 35½ in. from the top of the post for the bottom stringers (*drawing 9-A*). Corner posts need dadoes on adjacent sides.

At the top of the post, I cut a bevel on the opposite side from the dado as shown in the drawing. I lay out the bevel and make the cut on my radial-arm saw. I don't bevel the corner posts — the top just stays flat.

9-1  I use a pattern-routing technique to shape the tops of the pales on the flame-top fence. I make a plywood template the shape of the flame and clamp it to my bench. I place a pale on top of the template. With a flush-trim bit, I rout counterclockwise around the flame. The bit's pilot bearing rides against the template to rout a matching shape on the pale above.

# DIAMOND-TOP FENCE

This fence (see fence second from front on page 162) has a nice diamond shape at the top of the pickets or pales (*drawing 9-C*). The stringers, or rails, are even simpler than those on the flame-top fence since there are no half laps to contend with. Adjacent fence sections just butt against each other. This fence also has a skirtboard beneath the pales to keep cats and other small critters from scurrying under the fence.

To get started, I cut the stringers, pales, and skirtboard from white cedar (see Project Planner). For each 8-ft. section of fence I need to cut two 95-in. stringers and twenty 3/4-in. by 2¾-in. by 36½-in. pales. I also need one 1 × 6 skirtboard 95 in. long.

## Cutting the Pales

On the original fence at Williamsburg, I'm certain that the diamond tops were all cut by hand, one at a time. I want to speed things up a bit so I'm going to gang several pales together (9 in this case) and cut them with my radial-arm saw.

First, I clamp 9 pales together on edge with a single clamp at the bottom ends. I measure down 1¹⁵⁄₁₆ in. from the top and square a line across the edges of the pales. This line marks the corners of the diamonds (*drawing 9-C*). Next, I measure down 3³⁄₁₆ in. from the top and square a second line across to mark the bottoms of the diamonds (*drawing 9-C*). I turn the pales over and make identical marks on the opposite edges.

The first cut I'll make forms the bottom of the diamond. I tilt the radial-arm saw blade 55 degrees to the right and adjust the blade so it's 2 in. above the table. Then I make a cut along the first line I marked — the one that's 1¹⁵⁄₁₆ in. from the top. I turn the pales over and make an identical cut on the opposite sides (*photo 9-2*).

With the blade still at 55 degrees, I lower the saw a little bit and saw the top of the diamond, first on one side, then on the other (*photo 9-3*). The 2 cuts should meet right at the centerline (*drawing 9-C*). Now I can raise the saw, tilt the blade back to 90 degrees, and make the shoulder cuts at the bottoms of the diamond (*photo 9-4*). I don't cut all the way into the corners. Instead I use a backsaw to clean up the corners for a nice sharp point (*photo 9-5 and drawing 9-C*). Now I can unclamp the 9 pales and cut the others in the same way, 9 at a time. Each 8-ft. section of fence requires 20 pales.

## Assembling the Fence

As I did with the flame-top fence above, I mark out the locations of the pales on the stringers. For this fence, the right-hand pale is positioned 3⅜ in. from the end of the stringers, and the rest of the pales are spaced on 4¾-in. centers (*drawing 9-C*). I place the 2 stringers on the bench and line them up parallel to each other and 18⅜ in. apart.

**9-2** To speed production, I cut 9 diamond-top fence pales at once. The first cut forms the bottom of the diamond. With the radial-arm saw blade tilted 55 degrees and 2 in. above the table, I make a cut along a line marked 1¹⁵/₁₆ in. from the top of the pale. Without changing the setting, I turn the pales over and make an identical cut on the opposite sides.

**9-3** With the blade still at 55 degrees, I lower the saw a little bit and saw the top of the diamond, first on one side, then on the other. The 2 cuts should meet at the centerline.

**9-4** To cut the shoulders of the diamonds, I raise the blade and make a 90-degree cut for each shoulder.

**9-5** I clean up the shoulder corners with a backsaw for a nice sharp point.

## 9-C *Diamond-Top Fence*

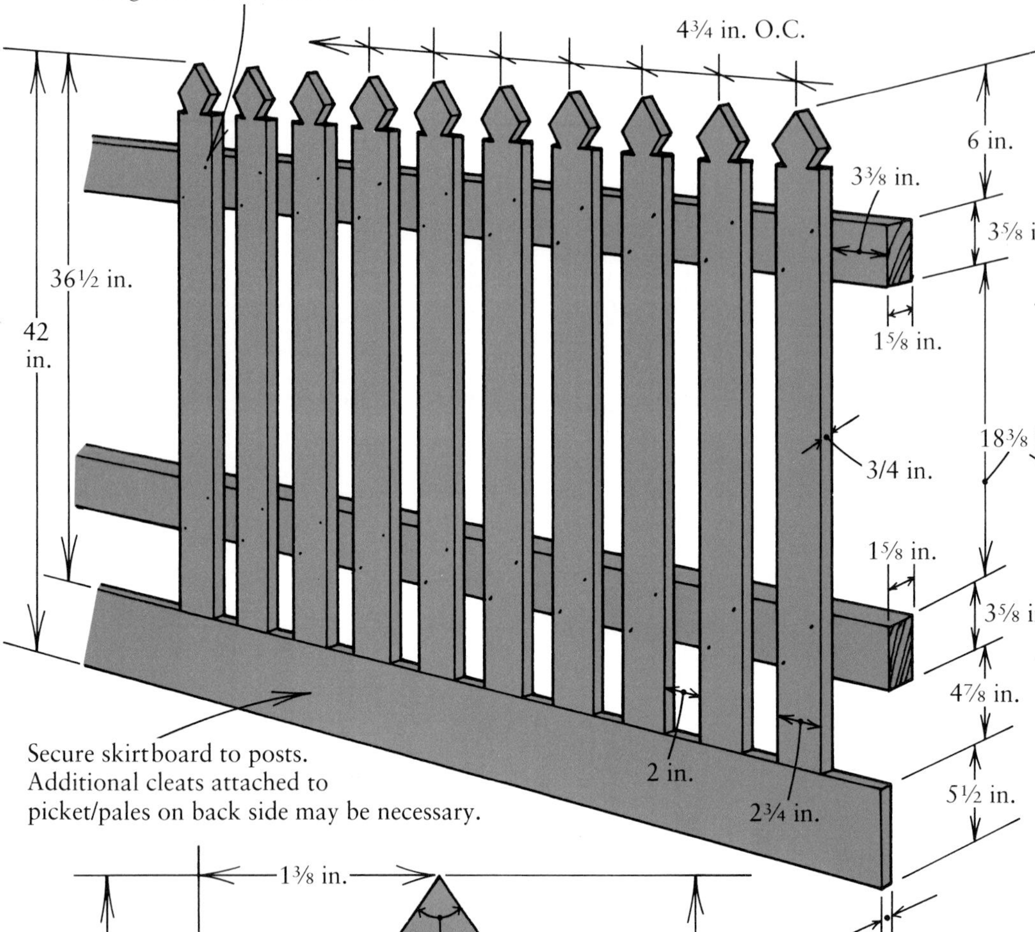

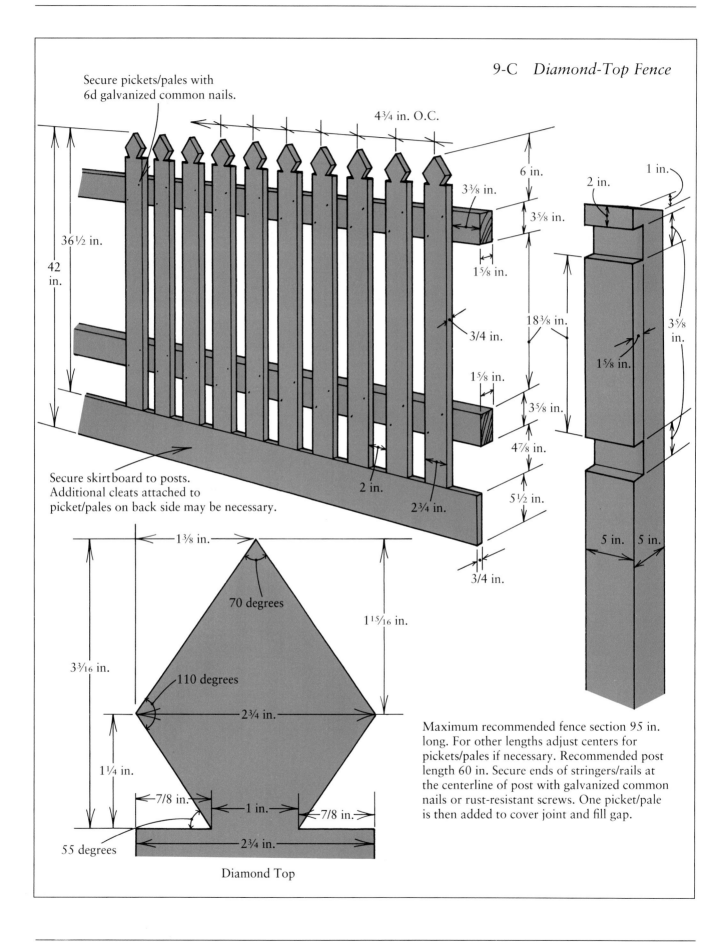

Secure pickets/pales with
6d galvanized common nails.
4¾ in. O.C.
36½ in.
42
in.
6 in.
3⅜ in.
3⅝ in.
1⅝ in.
18⅜ in.
3/4 in.
1⅝ in.
3⅝ in.
4⅞ in.
5½ in.
2 in.
2¾ in.
3/4 in.
Secure skirtboard to posts.
Additional cleats attached to
picket/pales on back side may be necessary.


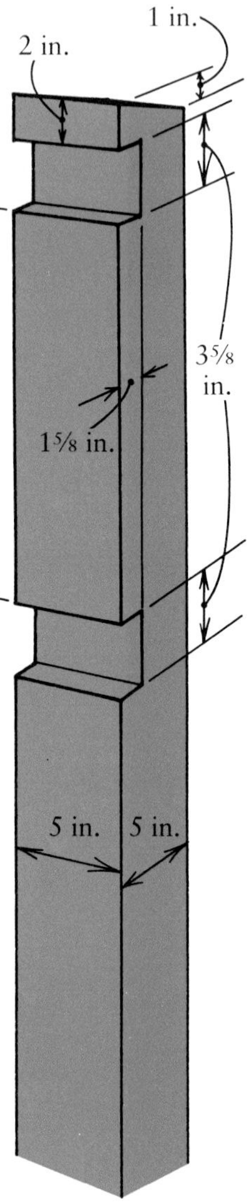

1 in.
2 in.
3⅝
in.
1⅝ in.
5 in.
5 in.


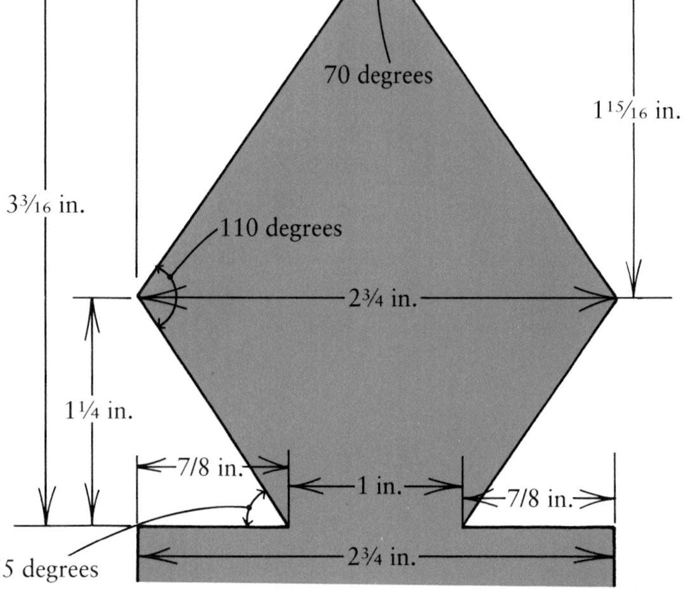

1⅜ in.
70 degrees
1¹⁵⁄₁₆ in.
3³⁄₁₆ in.
110 degrees
2¾ in.
1¼ in.
7/8 in.
1 in.
7/8 in.
2¾ in.
55 degrees


Diamond Top

Maximum recommended fence section 95 in. long. For other lengths adjust centers for pickets/pales if necessary. Recommended post length 60 in. Secure ends of stringers/rails at the centerline of post with galvanized common nails or rust-resistant screws. One picket/pale is then added to cover joint and fill gap.

9-6 To hold the skirtboard in place temporarily, I fasten temporary scrapwood cleats to the bottoms of 2 pales with screws (the corner of one cleat is partially visible in the foreground). I nail these pales to the stringers and fasten the skirtboard to the cleats temporarily as a guide for installing the pales.

Because the diamond-top fence has a skirtboard, there's an extra step to perform before I can nail on the pales. I screw a temporary scrapwood cleat to the bottom ends of 3 of the pales (for an 8-ft. section). Next, using 6d galvanized common nails, I nail these pales to the stringers — one at each end and one near the middle. I measure to make sure that the tops of the pales are 6 in. above the top stringer and the bottoms are 4⅞ in. below the bottom stringer (*drawing 9-C*).

The skirtboard goes on next, but only temporarily until all the pales are in place. It gets nailed on permanently across the fence posts when the fence is installed. For now, I want the skirtboard in place just as a guide for installing the pales. I screw through the cleat into the skirtboard, making sure the edge of the skirtboard butts against the bottoms of the pales (*photo 9-6*). When the skirtboard's in place, I nail on the rest of the pales, placing the ends against the skirtboard. When the pales are installed, I unscrew the skirtboard. Pretty simple.

## Posts

I recommend 60-in. posts for a low fence like this. I cut them from rough-sawn 6 × 6 white cedar and then surface-plane all 4 sides until the posts are 5 in. square. Next, on the radial-arm saw, I bevel the top of each post so the rain will run off (*drawing 9-C*). I swing my radial-arm saw about 12 degrees to the right to make the cut.

Next I have to mill dadoes for the stringers (*drawing 9-C*). Each post gets 2 dadoes 3⅝ in. wide and 1⅝ in. deep (corner posts, of course, need dadoes on adjacent sides). The top dado starts 2 in. down from the top edge (*drawing 9-C*). The bottom dado is 18⅜ in. below the top one. I cut the dadoes on the radial-arm saw with my stack dado head set for a 3/4-in.-wide cut. I make repeated crosscuts to cut the width of the dadoes. Because the dadoes are deep, I cut them in two 13/16-in. deep passes, lowering the saw for the second pass.

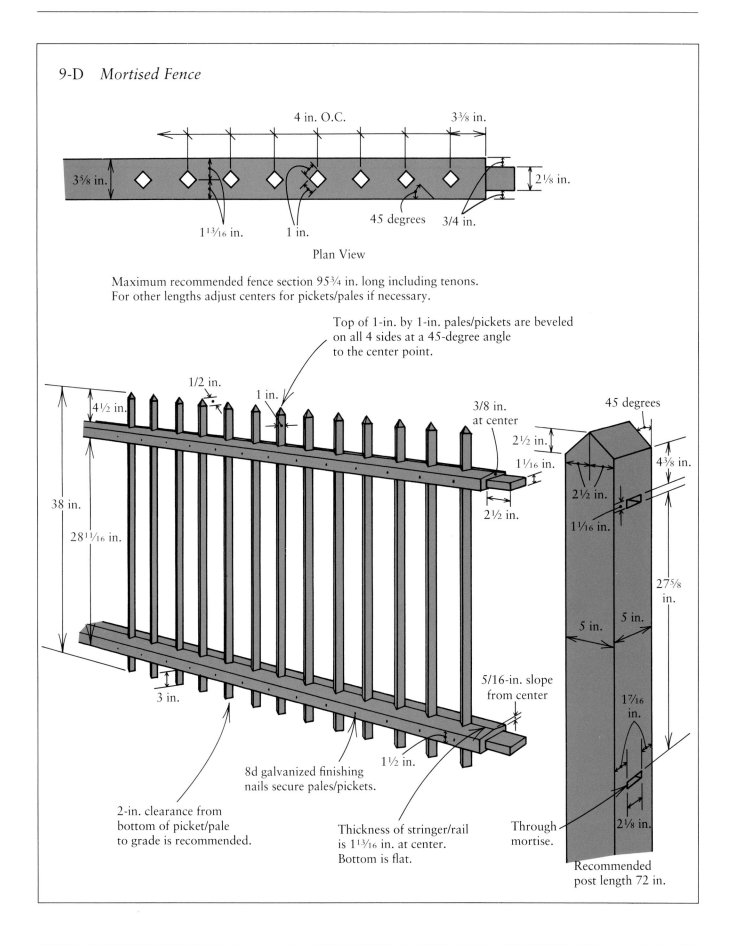

4 in. O.C.

3⅜ in.

3⅝ in.

2⅛ in.

1¹³⁄₁₆ in.

1 in.

45 degrees

3/4 in.

Plan View

Maximum recommended fence section 95¾ in. long including tenons.
For other lengths adjust centers for pickets/pales if necessary.

Top of 1-in. by 1-in. pales/pickets are beveled
on all 4 sides at a 45-degree angle
to the center point.

1/2 in.

1 in.

4½ in.

3/8 in.
at center

45 degrees

2½ in.

1¹⁄₁₆ in.

4⅜ in.

38 in.

28¹¹⁄₁₆ in.

2½ in.

2½ in.

1¹⁄₁₆ in.

27⅝ in.

5 in.

5 in.

3 in.

5/16-in. slope
from center

1½ in.

1⁷⁄₁₆ in.

8d galvanized finishing
nails secure pales/pickets.

2-in. clearance from
bottom of picket/pale
to grade is recommended.

Thickness of stringer/rail
is 1¹³⁄₁₆ in. at center.
Bottom is flat.

Through
mortise.

2⅛ in.

Recommended
post length 72 in.

## MORTISED FENCE

Here's a good example of a highly crafted colonial fence (see fence in forefront on page 162). Square pickets, set at a 45-degree angle, pass through mortises cut in the stringers. The tops of the stringers are sloped so that water will shed. It's a very attractive fence. I can't imagine what it would be like to cut dozens of mortises with hand tools, but that's how the original fence was built. The job will be a little easier with the power tools in my shop.

The stringers or rails start out as full rough-cut 8-ft. white cedar 2 × 4s (see Project Planner). I plane both sides in my thickness planer to a 1¹³⁄₁₆-in. thickness. Then I joint one edge straight and rip the stringers 3⅝ in. "strong." A pass through the jointer cleans up the sawn edge. After that, I crosscut each stringer to a length of 95¾ in. on my power miter box.

### Mortising the Stringers

Next I want to lay out the locations of the mortises (*drawing 9-D*). Starting at the right-hand end of the stringer, I square a line 2½ in. from the end to mark the length of the tenon that will connect to the post. I draw a second line 3⅜ in. from the first to mark the center of the first mortise. I space the other mortises 4 in. on center from the first and draw lines across. At the opposite end of the stringer, I lay out another 2½-in.-long tenon. I mark the other stringer in the same way. I also need to draw a centerline the full length of the stringer to locate the centers and corners of the mortises (*drawing 9-D*).

With a combination square I lay out a mortise at 45 degrees to the edges of the stringer (*drawing 9-D*). The sides of the mortises are 1 in. long.

To cut the mortises, I'll use my new hollow-chisel mortising machine. It's a single-function machine that works just like the hollow-chisel mortising attachment on my drill press. The nice thing about it is that it frees up my drill press for drilling holes.

The first thing I want to do is drill a 1-in.-dia. hole all the way through the stringer at each mortise location. I set up my drill press with a 1-in.-dia. forstner bit and put a piece of scrap plywood on the table so the bit won't break out the wood as it goes through the stringer. I clamp a straightedge clamp across the table so that the centerline of the stringer falls right under the bit. I adjust an outboard roller stand to support the end of the stringer. Then I drill a hole through each mortise location on both stringers.

Now I'm ready to square off the corners of the mortises. I install a 1/2-in. mortising bit with the chisel turned at 45 degrees to the mortising machine's fence — that is, with one corner facing the operator (*photo 9-7*). Then I put a piece of masking tape on the mortising machine's fence, which aligns with the back corner of the mortising chisel. I'll align this tape with the center mark for the mortise. Then I

9-7  I square off the mortise corners with a 1/2-in. hollow-chisel mortising bit in my mortising machine. I install the chisel at a 45-degree angle to the fence. I align the center mark for the mortise with a centerline drawn on the fence, which aligns with the back corner of the mortising chisel. Then I adjust the fence from front to back so the bit cuts the back corner of the mortise. Then I cut the back corner of every mortise.

9-8  With 2 corners of each mortise complete, I reset the fence so the corner of the bit falls on the centerline of the stringer. Then I cut the other 2 corners of each mortise.

adjust the fence to position the corner of the bit over the back corner of the mortise. I cut one corner and continue along the whole length of the stringer, cutting just this back corner of every mortise (*photo 9-7*).

Next I just flip the stringer end-for-end and cut the opposing corner with the same setup. Then I repeat these 2 cuts on the other stringer. If I'm making several sections of fence at once I'll make these 2 corner cuts on all the stringers before changing the setup for the next step in the procedure.

With 2 of the 4 corners complete I reset the fence so the corner of the bit falls on the centerline of the stringer. Then I cut the other 2 corners of each mortise, lining up the side of the bit with the first 2 cuts (*photo 9-8*).

### Stringer Tenons

There are a lot of different ways to join the fence sections to the post. One of the strongest and nicest is a mortise-and-tenon joint, and that's what I'll use for the mortised fence. Now's the time to cut the tenons.

To cut the cheeks of the tenons I set up my radial-arm saw with a stack dado head and adjust the blade height to make a 3/8-in.-deep cut on the top of the stringer. I make repeated crosscuts to complete one cheek. Then I flip the stringer over and cut the opposite cheek (*photo 9-9*). The resulting tenon should be $1\frac{1}{16}$ in. thick (*drawing 9-D*). I repeat this procedure to cut the cheeks on the opposite end as well as on the other stringer.

The next step is to cut the tenon sides. I turn the stringer on edge and raise the blade to make a 3/4-in.-deep cut (*photo 9-10 and drawing 9-D*). I cut one edge, then flip the stringer over to cut the other edge. The finished tenon should be $2\frac{1}{8}$ in. wide. I repeat the process on the other end as well as on any other stringers I'm making.

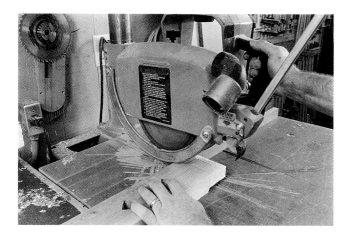

## Beveling the Stringers

One of the things I like best about this fence is that the tops of the stringers are beveled to let the water run off. To cut these bevels, I set up my table saw with the fence on the left side of the blade and the blade tilted 10 degrees. I adjust the fence so it's 1$\frac{17}{32}$ in. from the blade, measured at the table surface. I make a rip cut on one edge, then flip the stringer end-for-end and make a second cut (*photo 9-11*). I clean up the saw marks on the jointer with the blade set for a 1/32-in. cut and the fence tilted 10 degrees. The 2 bevels should meet at the centerline.

**9-9**   I use a mortise-and-tenon joint to join the mortised fence's stringers to the posts. I cut the tenon cheeks on my radial-arm saw with a stack dado head set to make a 3/8-in.-deep cut on the top of the stringer. I make repeated crosscuts to complete one cheek. Then I flip the stringer over and cut the opposite cheek to make a 1$\frac{1}{16}$-in.-thick tenon.

**9-10**   To cut the sides of the tenon I turn the stringer on edge and raise the blade to make a 3/4-in.-deep cut. I cut one edge, then flip the stringer over to cut the other edge. The finished tenon is 2$\frac{1}{8}$ in. wide.

**9-11**   On the table saw, I bevel the tops of the stringers so the rain will run off. I set up the fence on the left side of the blade and tilt the blade 10 degrees.

## Making the Pales

I cut the pales from 5/4 × 6 rough-cut white cedar (see Project Planner). First I plane the boards down to a 1-in. thickness and crosscut the boards into 38-in. lengths. I set a stop on my miter-box fence so the pales are all the same length. Then I rip and joint the boards into 1-in. strips.

The tops of the pales are pointed, and I do this on my power miter box. I square a line across one pale 1/2 in. down from the top. Then I swing the miter-box blade 45 degrees to the right and adjust the fence stop so the cut falls on the line. I set the stop and make four 45-degree cuts, turning the pale 90 degrees for each cut. The cuts all meet at the center for a nice 4-sided point.

## Assembling the Fence

Now I'm ready to put the section together. I put a long straight 2 × 4 on the top of my bench. On top of the 2 × 4 I stand a few 3-in.-long spacers, cut from scrap 2 × 4. The bottom stringer goes on top of the spacers, and I clamp the whole assembly to the bench (*photo 9-12*). The spacers allow just 3 in. of pale to drop below the stringer. Now I slip the pales into their mortises until the bottom end stops on the 2 × 4 (*photo 9-12*).

To position the top stringer, I cut scrap spacers 26⅞ in. long and clamp them, with spring clamps, to a few of the pales (*photo 9-13*). Now I fit all the pales into the holes in the top stringer. It's times like these when I could use the help of my 12 closest friends, but I just take my time and slip them in from one end to the other. Then I tap the stringer down with my shot-filled mallet until it's seated on top of the spacers (*photo 9-13*). I measure across the diagonals to see if the fence is square. When it is, I pin it all together with one 8d galvanized finishing nail in each pale.

## Making the Posts

Like the other fences, the posts for the mortised fence are milled from rough-cut white cedar 6 × 6 planed on all 4 sides to a 5-in. square. For this fence I recommend a 72-in. long post. I cut 2 through-mortises with my hollow-chisel mortiser for the tenons on the stringers (*drawing 9-D*). Then I bevel the tops of the posts by making two 45-degree cuts on my radial-arm saw.

Corner posts will need mortises on 2 adjacent sides. These corner mortises won't go clear through the post but will intersect inside. The tenons of adjacent corner sections of fence will need to be cut off at a 45-degree angle before being inserted into the post.

**9-12** To assemble the mortised fence, I place a long 2 × 4 on the bench. On the 2 × 4 I stand some 3-in.-long spacers cut from scrap 2 × 4. The bottom stringer goes on top of the spacers, and I clamp the assembly to the bench. Now I slip the pales into their mortises until the bottom end stops on the 2 × 4. The spacers allow 3 in. of pale to drop below the stringer.

**9-13** To position the top stringer, I cut scrap spacers 26⅞ in. long and clamp them to a few of the pales with spring clamps. Now I fit the pales into the top stringer mortises and tap the stringer down until it's seated on the spacers.

# GARDEN FENCE

The garden fence (see fence in back on page 162) is the simplest of all these fences to build. It consists of random-width rough cedar boards nailed to 3 rough 2 × 4 stringers (see Project Planner). The only decorations are the cutouts at the top, which are done after the boards have been nailed to the stringers.

I crosscut all the boards to 72 in. and sort them according to width. Then I square up one end of each stringer and cut them all 96 in. long. (This is the maximum recommended length. The stringers can be shorter.) I place 2 stringers on the shop floor 50 in. apart and parallel to each other. In between these I center the third stringer 19 in. from the other 2 (*drawing 9-E*).

Now I'm ready to nail on the boards. The procedure I use is for building fence sections from the right and working toward the left. If you start building the left-hand section of the fence first, you'll need to reverse the procedure explained below.

For the very first section of fence, I tack on the right-hand board flush with the ends of the stringers (using 6d galvanized common nails). The right-hand board can be any width at all. Each adjacent section of fence will start out a little differently, as I'll explain later.

At the other end, I temporarily nail on a board so that it overhangs the left-hand ends of the stringers by a couple of inches. I have to remove this board later when I install the fence, so I just tack it in place for now. The bottom ends of these boards should be 4 in. below the bottom stringer, and the top ends should be 19 in. above the top stringer (*drawing 9-E*). With the 2 boards in place, I measure the diagonals to check for square.

So that the fence boards will be straight across the bottom, I tack a nail in each fence board and stretch a string across the bottoms of these 2 outer boards as a guide. Now I just nail on the other boards, choosing widths at random and aligning the bottom ends on the string. I use a few scrapwood spacers to space the boards 5/8 in. apart and usually have to rip the last board to width to get the proper spacing.

With the boards all in place, I'm ready to lay out for the cuts at the top. The peaks are all 18 in. above the top rail. The valleys are all 8½ in. below the peaks. Both peaks and valleys are spaced 12 in. on center with the valleys offset 6 in. from the peaks (*drawing 9-E*). With my chalkbox I snap 2 lines: one for the peaks, one for the valleys.

For the very first fence section, I start the first valley at the extreme right-hand end of the fence and space the other valleys 12 in. on center from there. I offset the peaks 6 in. from the valleys and connect the peaks and valleys with a pencil and a framing square (*photo 9-14*). So the peaks and valleys will match up from one fence section to the next, I always use the peak, valley, or the portion of the slope (whichever is there) from the left-hand board on the previous section as a

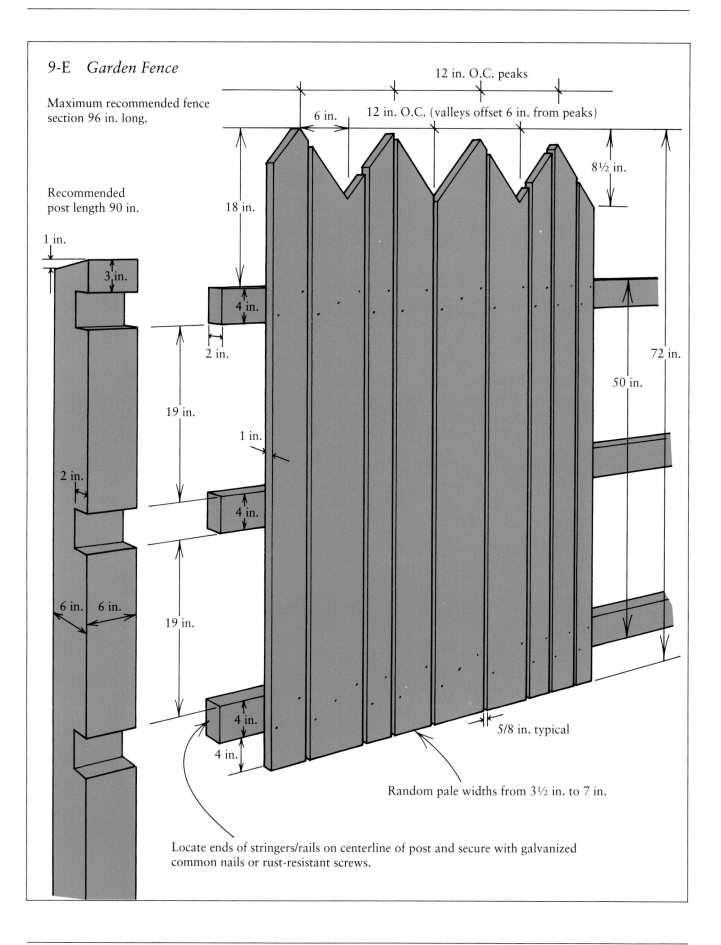

9-E  *Garden Fence*

Maximum recommended fence
section 96 in. long.

Recommended
post length 90 in.

12 in. O.C. peaks

12 in. O.C. (valleys offset 6 in. from peaks)

6 in.

8½ in.

1 in.

3 in.

18 in.

4 in.

2 in.

19 in.

72 in.

50 in.

1 in.

2 in.

4 in.

6 in.    6 in.

19 in.

4 in.

4 in.

5/8 in. typical

Random pale widths from 3½ in. to 7 in.

Locate ends of stringers/rails on centerline of post and secure with galvanized
common nails or rust-resistant screws.

guide to space the peaks and valleys on the section I'm building. This way, when the fence sections are all fastened together, the 12-in. spacing remains consistent across all sections.

Now, with my circular saw, I cut out the peaks and valleys, finishing up the corners with my jigsaw. I'll remove the left-hand board to nail the fence stringers to the posts (*drawing 9-E*) and nail it permanently in place after the fence is installed.

Adjacent sections of fence start out a little differently. To mark the location of the right-hand edge of the board on the right, I measure how far the left-hand board on the previous section overhangs the ends of the stringers. I add 5/8 in. (the width of the space between boards) to this measurement to locate the edge of the right-hand board. Other than this, each section is built the same way.

## Garden-Fence Posts

A high fence like this one needs 90-in. posts. I cut them from rough 6 × 6 white cedar posts. I cut a dado for each stringer with the dado head on my radial-arm saw (*drawing 9-E*). As with all fences, the corner posts need dadoes on adjacent sides. At the top, I cut a 12-degree bevel so water can run off.

Now, a section of this garden fence would look good outside the New Yankee Workshop.

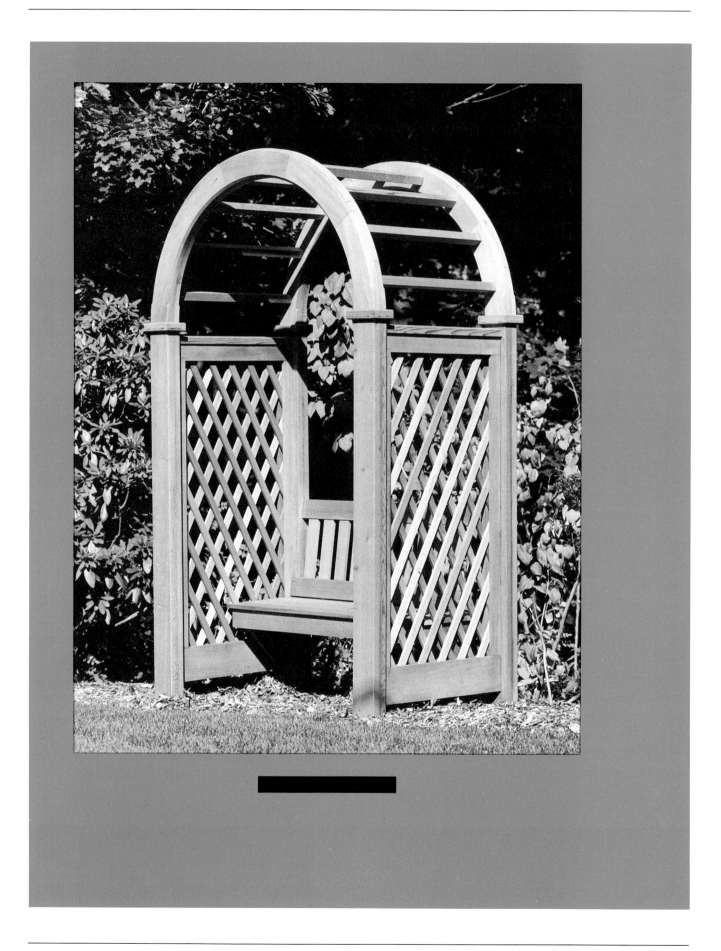

# 10

# Redwood Arbor

PROJECT PLANNER

*Time:* 6 days
*Special hardware and tools:* None
*Wood:*
(4) 6-ft. 4 × 6 redwood
Rip and plane to 3 in. × 5 in. and cut to 66 in. long for posts.
(2) 12-ft. 2 × 8 redwood
From each board, cut one piece 21 in. long with an 18-degree angled cut on one end (measure to the long point) for segments at arch ends. Then cut 7 pieces 19¼ in. long with 18-degree angled cuts on both ends for arch segments.
(1) 8-ft. 2 × 8 redwood
Cut 2 pieces 21 in. long and 4 pieces 13 in. long with an 18-degree angle on one end (measure to the long point) for segments at arch ends.
(3) 14-ft. 2 × 4 redwood
Cut one board into 5 pieces 32½ in. long. Then rip and joint 9 pieces 1½ in. × 1½ in for rungs.
From one board, cut 2 pieces 50½ in. long for seat-frame front rails. From remainder, cut 2 pieces 30 in. long for side-frame cap rails.
From third board, cut one piece 52 in. long for backrest top rail; one piece 50½ in. long for backrest bottom rail; one piece 48 in. long for seat-frame back rail; and one piece 16½ in. long for seat-frame end piece.
(1) 8-ft. 2 × 4 redwood
Cut one piece 16½ in. long for seat-frame end piece; 2 pieces 11¼ in. long for seat-frame crosspieces; and 2 pieces 22 in. long for seat-frame angle braces.
(1) 12-ft. 1 × 8 redwood
Cut 4 pieces 30 in. long. Then rip and joint to 6 in. wide for side-frame bottom rails. Rip and joint scrap into 4 pieces 1½ in. wide for molding between arches and posts.
(3) 10-ft. 1 × 8 redwood
Rip and joint each piece into 5 pieces 1¼ in. wide. Rip these to 9/16-in. thickness and surface-plane to 1/2-in. thickness for lattice.

TWENTY-FIVE miles off the south of Cape Cod lies the beautiful isle of Nantucket. Rich in seafaring history, this tiny island was an important whaling center in the heyday of sail. Tourists come in by the boatload today but the charm of the place is unspoiled. The village of Siasconset on the southeastern shore boasts some of the oldest seaside cottages on the entire east coast.

While strolling around the village, I was intrigued by the number of arbors I found — it seemed as though every other house had one. Most were built into a fence or a hedge and designed as a pass-through. One that I noticed had a bench where you could sit and relax. I was so intrigued by the arbors of Siasconset that I decided to build one for my own garden. I boarded the ferry boat back to the mainland full of ideas.

Back at my drawing board, I worked out the design. It's about 4 ft. wide with a 2-ft.-radius arch at the top. There are rungs across the top and lattice on the sides so that we can train a vine to climb up over it. I also added a bench so we could relax and enjoy our garden on a balmy summer evening.

## Making the Arches

The most difficult and time-consuming part of this project is building the arches. There were a couple of different ways it could be done. I could have ripped thin strips of wood, and bent them around a form all glued up together. This technique is known as laminate bending, and it makes a good, strong job. But the arches of the arbor are so wide that I'd have had to rip about twenty 1/4-in. strips to glue up the 5-in. width. Instead of strips, I decided to save time and material by gluing up segments of the arch instead of strips -— 2 × 8 redwood,

(1) 6-ft. 1 × 6 redwood

Rip and joint 2 pieces 2½ in. wide. Then cut 11 pieces 11 in. long for backrest slats.

(1) 14-ft. 1 × 4 redwood

Cut 3 pieces 50½ in. long for seat slats.

(4) 12-ft. 1 × 4 redwood

From each board, cut one piece 60 in. long. From this, rip one piece 1 in. wide for post cleats (4 required) and one piece 2¼ in. wide for side-frame stiles (8 required). Joint and trim the 2¼-in. pieces 51 in. long.

From each remaining board, cut one piece 51 in. long. Then rip and joint to 2¼ in. wide for remaining side-frame stiles and cut one piece 30 in. long, and rip and joint to 3-in. width for side-frame top rails (4 required).

(1) 8½-ft. 1 × 4 redwood

Cut 2 pieces 50½ in. long for seat slats.

glued up in 2 layers (*drawing 10-B*). The joints overlap, as shown in the drawing, so the arch becomes a very strong unit.

I start with some 2 × 8 redwood, which I'll cut on my radial saw. I turn the saw to 18 degrees, the angle I want for all my segments (*drawing 10-B*). The first pieces to cut have 72-degree angles at each end and measure 19¼ in., long point to long point (*drawing 10-B*). I cut one end, then use my bevel gauge set to 18 degrees to mark the cut on the opposite end. I need to cut 14 of these segments. I also cut 8 pieces with an angled cut on only one end — 4 pieces 21 in. long and 4 pieces 13 in. long (see Project Planner). These will be the segments at the ends of the arch (*drawing 10-B*).

Next, with a pencil and a square, I draw a centerline across the width and top edge of 3 of the segments with 2 angled ends. I'll need these lines to align these first 3 segments of the arch during glue-up.

Gluing up the arches requires lots of clamps and nearly a pint of one-part waterproof glue. With my clamps and glue at hand, I'm ready to go. I choose one of the pieces with angles on both ends for the "keystone" segment — the top center segment of the arch. I cover the face that has the pencil line with a nice even coat of glue. Then I spread glue on 2 other segments that have angled cuts on both ends.

What I want to do is glue one segment to the keystone, aligning the end of this overlaying segment with the centerline on the keystone (*photo 10-1 and drawing 10-B*). Then I align the end of the keystone with the centerline on the edge of the overlying segment. When everything lines up, I nail the segments together with two 8d finishing nails. I locate the nails near the edges so they won't be in the way later when I cut out the arch (*photo 10-2*).

I glue on the second overlying segment in exactly the same way, butting one end against the first segment and lining up the end of the

10-1 I begin gluing up the arch by attaching one segment to the "keystone," aligning the end with a centerline drawn on the keystone. Then I align the centerline on the overlying segment with the end of the keystone. I nail the segments together, placing the nails near the edges so they won't be in the way when I cut out the arch.

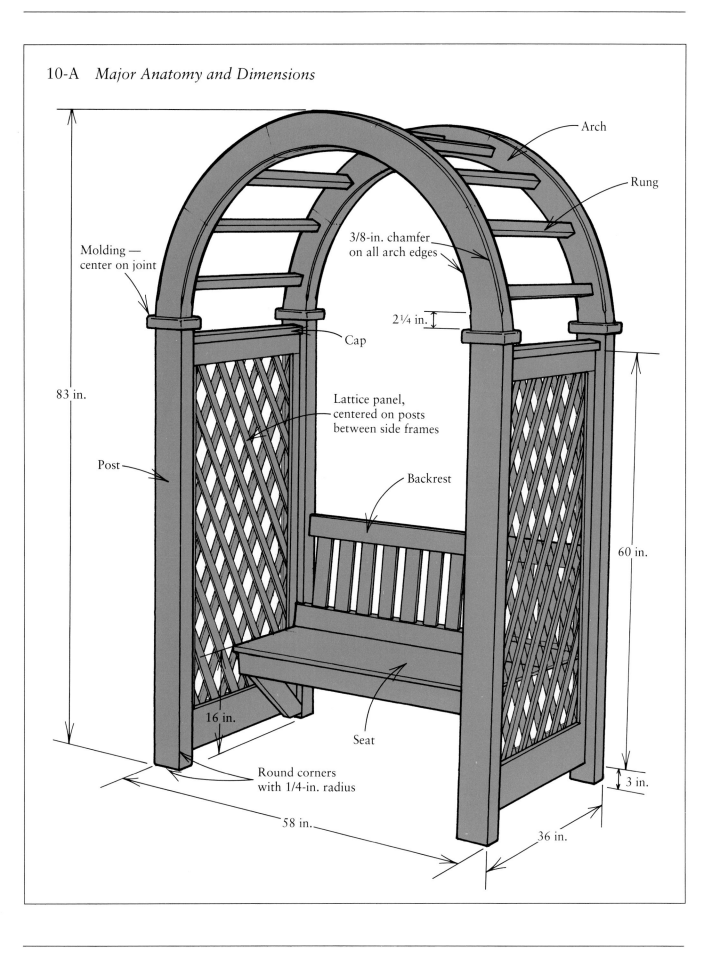

Arch

Rung

Molding —
center on joint

3/8-in. chamfer
on all arch edges

2¼ in.

Cap

83 in.

Lattice panel,
centered on posts
between side frames

Backrest

Post

60 in.

16 in.

Seat

Round corners
with 1/4-in. radius

3 in.

58 in.

36 in.

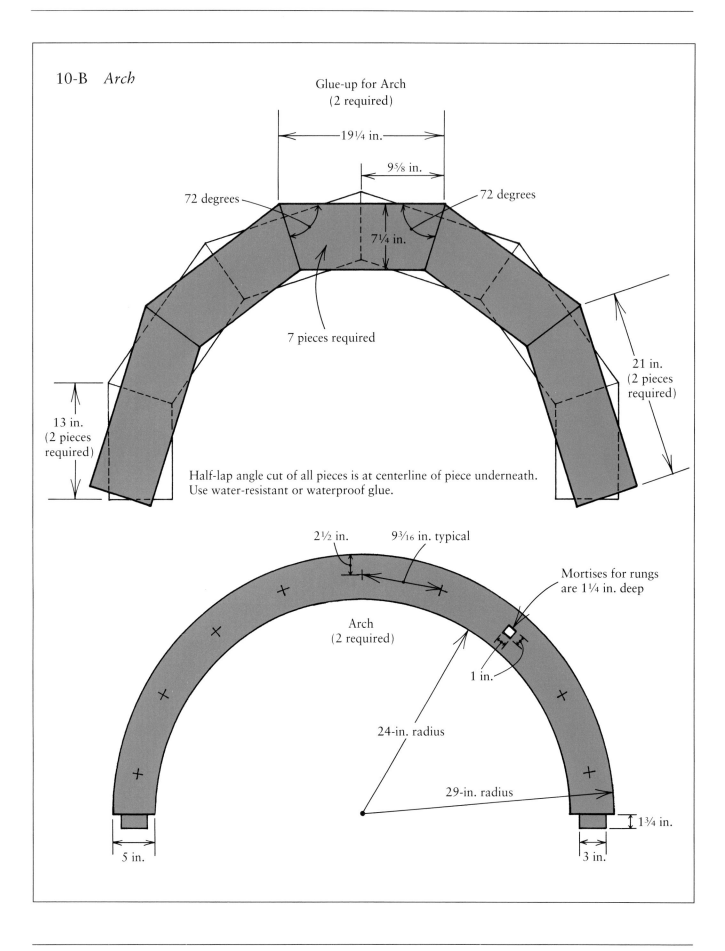

10-B  *Arch*

Glue-up for Arch
(2 required)

19¼ in.

9⅝ in.

72 degrees

72 degrees

7¼ in.

7 pieces required

21 in.
(2 pieces required)

13 in.
(2 pieces required)

Half-lap angle cut of all pieces is at centerline of piece underneath.
Use water-resistant or waterproof glue.

2½ in.

9³⁄₁₆ in. typical

Mortises for rungs
are 1¼ in. deep

Arch
(2 required)

1 in.

24-in. radius

29-in. radius

1¾ in.

5 in.

3 in.

keystone with the centerline on the second segment's edge. I nail this one in place, just like the first.

Now I can clamp the segments together and continue along, gluing and clamping as I go, holding the ends of the segments even. One layer of the arch is made up of 3 segments with 2 angled ends; the other layer has 4 (*drawing 10-B*). At the ends of the arch, I glue on the segments that have angled cuts on just one end as shown in the drawing. It sure takes a lot of clamps (*photo 10-2*)! When one arch is finished, I glue up the other in just the same way and let the glue dry overnight.

I could have sawed out the arches with my band saw or jigsaw but I decided to cut them out with a router instead. To guide the router, I need to make a plywood template in the shape of the arch. I set up my plunge router with a 13/16-in. o.d. guide collar and a 1/2-in.-dia. straight bit. The guide collar will ride against the template to make the cut.

The finished arch will be 5 in. wide, but the template must be slightly narrower in width to account for the 5/32-in. offset between the radius of the guide collar and the radius of the bit. Using this 5/32-in. offset, I calculate the inside radius of the template to be 24$\frac{5}{32}$ in. and the outside radius to be 28$\frac{27}{32}$ in.

**10-2** The arches are glued up from 2 layers of segments with the joints overlapping for strength. I've used up every clamp in the shop!

**10-3** I cut out the arches by guiding my plunge router around a plywood template. The router is set up with a guide collar and straight bit. I remove 1/4 in. with each pass. When I can't cut any deeper, I flip the arch over, attach the template to the opposite side, and rout from that side.

I lay out the template on a sheet of 1/4-in. plywood, extending the ends of the template 1¹⁹/₃₂ in. beyond 180 degrees to account for the 1¾-in.-long tenons on the ends of the arch (*drawing 10-B*). I'll just rout around the ends of the template to trim the tenons to length. After drawing the inside and outside arcs of the template, I draw a third arc at a 26½-in. radius to mark the centers of the rung mortises I'll need to cut in the arches (*drawing 10-B*). Along this arc, I mark off 9 center points 9³/₁₆ in. apart, starting at the top of the arch as shown in the drawing. I saw out the template on my band saw and smooth up the curves with my sander. Then I drill through the rung-mortise center marks with a 1-in.-dia. forstner bit.

I place the template over one of the glued-up arch blanks, centering it over the keystone piece and aligning it with a vertical line I've drawn on the arch. Then I fasten it with a couple of screws. Once the template's in place, I mark the arch where the ends of the template fall and use a try square to extend these lines down the sides of the arch blank. This makes it easier, later, for me to position the template on the opposite side of the blank.

Now I'm ready to cut out the arches. I set my router for a 1/4-in.-deep cut and go round and round the template, moving from left to right, increasing the depth by 1/4 in. at each pass (*photo 10-3*). I cut as far as I can and then I remove the template, flip the arch over, and do the same thing on the other side until the 2 cuts meet.

When I install the template on the opposite side of the arch, I position the template ends on the pencil lines I made before. It's important to flip the template over — the opposite side should face up. Flipping the template ensures that the cuts will line up, even if the template isn't *perfectly* symmetrical. Before I remove the template, I run a pencil around the rung-mortise holes to mark their location on the arch. Now I can remove the template.

After cutting out both arches, I'm ready to cut the mortises for the rungs. The first step is to drill 1-in.-dia. holes 1 in. deep on the spots that I marked through the template. I do this on the drill press with a 1-in.-dia. forstner bit (*photo 10-4*).

I'll use my router to square up the holes for the mortises, using the same methods I used for the arches. First, I make a plywood template to guide my router. I cut a 1⁵⁄₁₆-in.-square hole in some plywood and center this opening over one of the holes in the arch. Clamping the template in position, I attach a couple of scrap blocks to the underside of the template, placing them against the outer edge of the arch. The blocks allow me to quickly align the template opening over the holes.

To use the template, I position it over a hole with the blocks against the outer curve of the arch and clamp it in place. Then I rout around the hole clockwise, plunging the bit 1¼ in., the full depth of the mortise (*photo 10-5*).

Next, I need to cut tenons at the ends of the arch. These tenons will fit into mortises in the posts. I lay out the tenons as shown in the drawing (*drawing 10-C*) and cut them out with my small circular saw

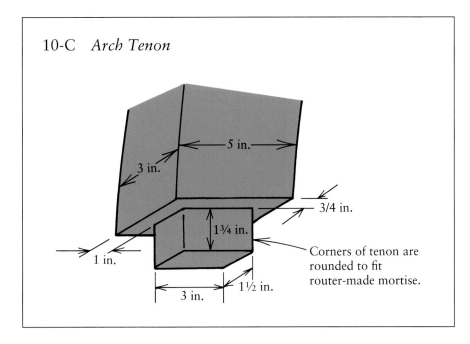

10-C   *Arch Tenon*

5 in.

3 in.

3/4 in.

1¾ in.

1 in.

Corners of tenon are rounded to fit router-made mortise.

3 in.

1½ in.

**10-4** The first step for milling the mortises for the rungs is to drill 1-in.-dia. holes with a forstner bit.

**10-5** I square up the mortises with my plunge router and the same guide collar setup I used for the arches. I position a template with a square hole over the 1-in.-dia. holes and rout out 1¼ in. of wood.

and a backsaw. First I make the shoulder cuts across the width of the arch, setting the circular saw for a 3/4-in.-deep cut. Next I make the shoulder cuts across the thickness of the arch with a backsaw. Finally, to make the cheek cuts, I return to my circular saw, setting the blade for a 1¾-in.-deep cut (*photo 10-6*). I round the corners of the tenon a little with my wood rasp. Then I smooth up the curves of the arches with my sander and ease all the corners with a 1/4-in. roundover bit in my router.

The final milling step on the arch is purely decorative. Using a chamfering bit in my router, I chamfer the edges of the arch, stopping the cut about 3½ in. from the ends. That takes care of the arches.

*Corner Posts*

To make the posts, I rip and joint some 4 × 6 redwood to 3-in. by 5-in. dimensions. Then I cut posts that measure 66 in. long.

In the ends of posts, I need to cut 1½-in. by 3-in. mortises to receive the tenons on the arches (*drawing 10-D*). First I make another jig like the one I used to rout the arch mortises (*photo 10-7*). I use the same guide collar and bit setup I used before, so I need to cut a 1¹³/₁₆-in. by 3⁵/₁₆-in. square opening in the jig. I attach some scrap blocks to the back of the jig to center the jig over the end of the post and I drill a hole for a screw so I can fasten the jig to the post.

## 10-D  *Top of Post Mortise*

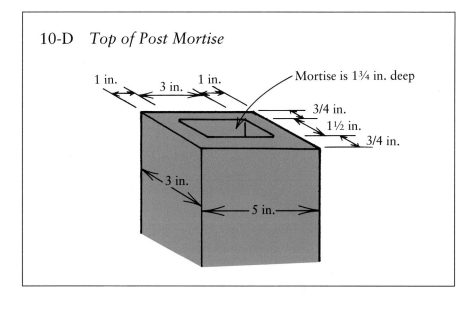

1 in.  3 in.  1 in.

Mortise is 1¾ in. deep

3/4 in.
1½ in.
3/4 in.

3 in.

5 in.

**10-6** I make the cheek cuts of the post tenons with my small circular saw, setting the blade for a 1¾-in.-depth of cut.

To rout the mortises, I clamp the post in my bench vise. I fasten the jig to the post with a screw (*photo 10-7*) and rout around the opening with my plunge router, lowering the depth of cut 1/4 in. with each pass. My shop vacuum comes in handy to remove the chips from the hole. The finished mortises should be 1¹³⁄₁₆ in. deep.

The 2 back posts also need 1-in. by 2½-in. mortises for the tenons on the top rail of the backrest (*drawings 10-A and 10-E*). These mor-

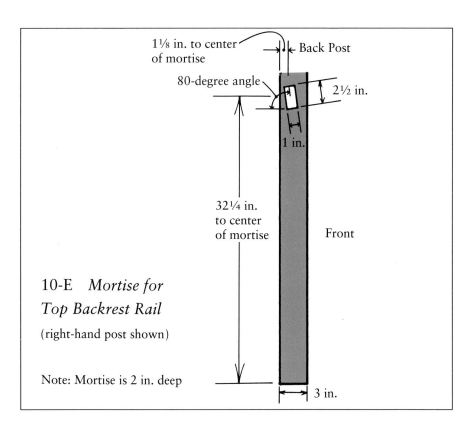

1⅛ in. to center of mortise

Back Post

80-degree angle

2½ in.

1 in.

32¼ in. to center of mortise

Front

## 10-E  *Mortise for Top Backrest Rail*

(right-hand post shown)

Note: Mortise is 2 in. deep

3 in.

**10-7** I mill the mortises in the tops of the posts with my plunge router and guide collar setup. I make another jig that attaches to the post with a screw. The opening in the jig is larger than the mortise to account for the 5/32-in. offset between the outside radius of the guide collar and the radius of the bit.

**10-8** Milling the angled mortises for the backrest top rail is a 2-step process. I remove most of the wood with a 1-in.-dia. forstner bit and then I square up the sides and corners with a chisel.

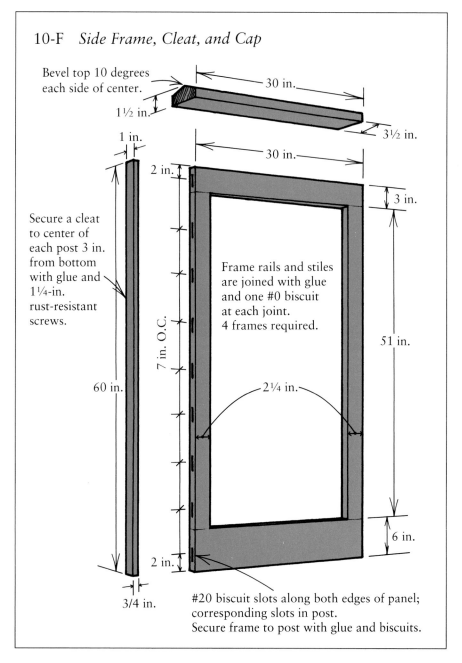

10-F *Side Frame, Cleat, and Cap*

Bevel top 10 degrees each side of center.

1½ in.

30 in.

3½ in.

1 in.

Secure a cleat to center of each post 3 in. from bottom with glue and 1¼-in. rust-resistant screws.

60 in.

3/4 in.

2 in.

2 in.

30 in.

3 in.

7 in. O.C.

Frame rails and stiles are joined with glue and one #0 biscuit at each joint. 4 frames required.

51 in.

2¼ in.

6 in.

#20 biscuit slots along both edges of panel; corresponding slots in post. Secure frame to post with glue and biscuits.

tises are cut at an 80-degree angle to accommodate the slant of the backrest. I lay out these mortises as shown in the drawing (*drawing 10-E*), measuring from a center point 32¼ in. from the bottom of the post and 1⅛ in. from the back. The mortises on opposite posts must be mirror images of each other.

I remove most of the wood from these mortises with a 1-in.-dia. forstner bit on the drill press, setting the bit for a 2-in.-deep cut. I clean up the mortises and square up the corners with a sharp chisel (*photo 10-8*). For a finishing touch, I ease all the edges on the posts with a 1/4-in.-radius roundover bit.

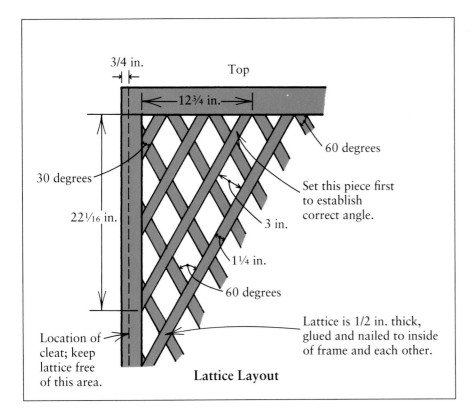

3/4 in.

Top

12¾ in.

60 degrees

30 degrees

Set this piece first
to establish
correct angle.

22¹⁄₁₆ in.

3 in.

1¼ in.

60 degrees

Lattice is 1/2 in. thick,
glued and nailed to inside
of frame and each other.

Location of
cleat; keep
lattice free
of this area.

**Lattice Layout**

## Side Frames and Lattice Panels

Now for the lattice panels (*drawings 10-A and 10-F*). These consist of
an inner side frame and an outer side frame. The lattice goes in the
middle — sort of like the ham in a sandwich.

After milling all the stock for the frames and lattice (see Project
Planner), the first thing I want to do is make one of the frames. Nothing fancy here — just butt joints reinforced with biscuits. It's amazing
how strong a simple biscuit joint is.

I mill slots for #0 biscuits in the ends of the stiles, and corresponding slots in the rails. Then I put some waterproof glue in the slots and
on the biscuits and clamp the frame together. I check for square by
measuring across the diagonals — if they're equal, I know the frame is
square.

While the frame is drying in the clamps I can start to apply the lattice. I lay out a 60-degree triangle (30-60-90 degrees) on one corner of
the frame, to mark the location of the first strip of lattice I'll install
(*drawing 10-F*). Before I get started I want to clamp a 3/4-in.-wide
cleat to the outer edge of each stile. I'll butt the ends of the lattice
against these cleats.

Each piece of lattice gets a 60-degree cut at one end and a 30-
degree cut at the other. To make these cuts efficiently, I set my miter
box to cut a 30-degree angle and my radial-arm saw to cut a 60-
degree angle.

**10-9** To install the lattice on the side frame, I mark off a 60-degree triangle on the top and side. I position the first strip on these marks and glue and nail it in place. I use the 3-in.-wide spacer (on the bench) to space the other strips. Note the 3/4-in. cleats clamped along each of the stiles. The bottom ends of the lattice strips butt against these cleats.

**10-10** A second layer of lattice strips goes on top of the first. Here I'm using the spacer to space the strips. The second side frame will go on top of the lattice.

For the first strip of lattice, I cut one end to 60 degrees. I butt this end against the cleat, line up the lattice with my triangle marks, and run a pencil along the top rail's upper edge to mark the length of the lattice. Now I cut the lattice to length and fasten it to the frame with waterproof glue and some 1-in. brads (*photo 10-9*). I install the other lattice strips, using a 3-in.-wide spacer to space the strips apart.

Now, I start from the triangle mark on the top rail again, overlaying the first layer of lattice strips with a second layer going in the opposite direction (*photo 10-10*). For this layer, I switch to 3/4-in. nails so the nails don't go all the way through the lattice strips underneath. I nail the strips wherever they cross.

Next I have to make another frame for the other side of the sandwich. When this frame's assembled, I'm ready to put the sandwich together. I apply some glue on the ends of the lattice strips where the frame will go. Now I just flip the frame over and place it on top of the lattice panel. I check with a square to make sure the 2 outer frames are aligned. Then I nail through the frame and the lattice strips into the other frame with 8d finishing nails, angling the nails so they don't come through the other side. One more lattice panel to go.

## Attaching the Lattice Panels

Now I'm ready to attach the lattice panels to the posts. The first thing I want to do is cut a series of biscuit slots in the edges of the side frames — about every 7 inches (*drawing 10-F*). I make pencil marks along the sides of the frame and line up the index mark of my biscuit joiner with these lines.

Next I need to attach a 3/4-in. by 1-in. by 60-in. cleat to the center of each post with glue and screws (*drawing 10-F*). This cleat will fit between the 2 side frames of the lattice panel. But first I need to transfer the biscuit-joiner pencil marks from the frame to the cleat. This only takes a second — I slip the cleat in between the 2 side frames and make marks with a pencil. Then I remove the cleat and fasten it to the post with waterproof glue and 1¼-in. rust-resistant screws, locating the bottom end of the cleat 3 in. from the bottom of the post (*photo 10-11*). The pencil lines should be facing up.

I remove the right-angle accessory fence from the biscuit joiner and place the biscuit joiner against the cleat to cut the corresponding slots in the posts (*photo 10-12*). There are a lot of slots, but the biscuits are the only things that hold the panels to the posts. Into each slot goes

**10-11** I attach a 3/4-in. by 1-in. by 60-in. cleat to the center of each post with waterproof glue and 1¼-in. rust-resistant screws. I locate the bottom end of the cleat 3 in. from the bottom of the post.

**10-12** I align the index mark of my biscuit joiner with the pencil marks on the cleats to cut slots that will correspond to the slots I cut in the edges of the lattice-panel side frames.

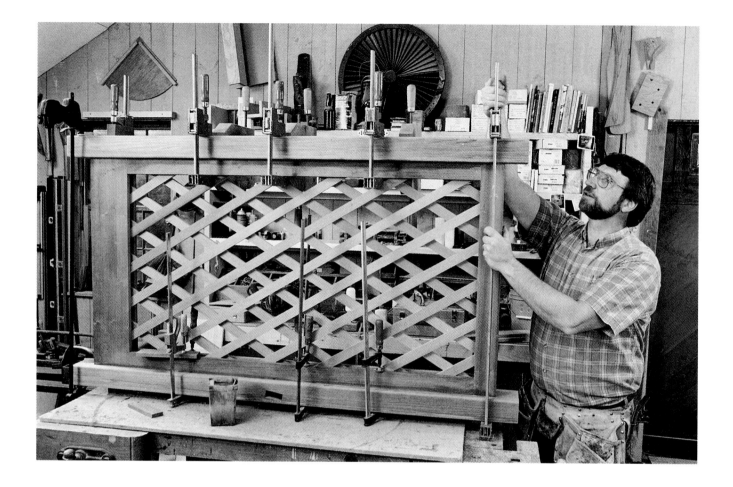

**10-13** With biscuits and glue in the slots, I slip the lattice panel over one post and then put the other on top. Clamps pull the biscuit joints tight.

some glue and a #20 biscuit. Then I lower the lattice-panel assembly onto the biscuits. The second post goes on top, and I clamp the assembly together (*photo 10-13*). The other lattice-panel assembly goes together in just the same way.

On the top of each lattice-panel frame is a 2 × 4 cap. It has a beveled top for looks but also so the rain water will run away (*drawing 10-F*). I cut the 2 × 4 redwood to a length of 30 in. and run it through the table saw with the rip fence positioned to the left of the blade and the blade tilted to a 10-degree angle. I make one cut from each side — the cuts should just about meet in the middle. After jointing, they'll meet right in the center. I clean up the cuts on the jointer and attach the caps with some 8d finishing nails, centering the cap on the frame.

### Building the Seat

Now for the seat. After milling all the pieces to dimension and length (see Project Planner) I'm ready to start on the joinery. The backrest comes first.

I need to cut a 1-in. by 2½-in. tenon, 2 in. long, on the top rail of the backrest to fit the angled mortises I cut in the posts a little earlier (*drawing 10-G*). I cut these tenons on the table saw, using a gauge block clamped to the rip fence to determine the length of the tenon. I make the shoulder cuts first, setting the blade for a 1/4-in.-deep cut. Next, I raise the blade to 1/2 in. and cut the top and bottom shoulders.

Moving to the band saw, I cut the top and bottom of the tenon, guiding the wood along a fence. The cheek cuts come next and I use the band saw for this operation as well.

The bottom rail of the backrest requires a wedge-shaped cutout at each end (*drawing 10-G*). I lay out these notches as shown in the drawing and make the cuts with my backsaw (*photo 10-14*). These notches fit around the post and give the backrest a 10-degree slant.

Glue and biscuits are all I need to assemble the back slats between the two backrest rails. I cut a biscuit slot in the end of each slat and corresponding slots in the rails (*drawing 10-G*). To lay out the biscuit slots I measure $1^{13}/_{16}$ in. from the shoulder of the rail tenon to mark the center of the first biscuit slot. Then I space the other slots $4^3/_{16}$ in. on center. The center of the slot at the opposite end of the rail should also be $1^{13}/_{16}$ in. from the tenon shoulder. I set the fence on my biscuit joiner so the face side of the slats will be recessed 1/4 in. from the face side of the rails.

With the slots complete, I install the slats in the bottom rail. The top rail goes on last (*photo 10-15*). I clamp the backrest together and measure the diagonals to check for square.

**10-14**   I have to cut an angled notch on the backrest bottom rail to fit around the post. I do this with my backsaw.

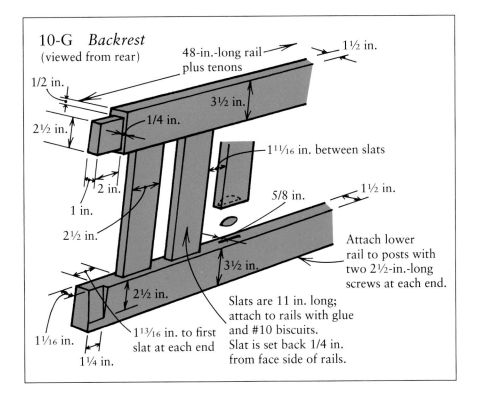

10-G  *Backrest*
(viewed from rear)

48-in.-long rail plus tenons

1½ in.

1/2 in.

2½ in.

1/4 in.

3½ in.

$1^{11}/_{16}$ in. between slats

2 in.

1 in.

2½ in.

5/8 in.

1½ in.

3½ in.

Attach lower rail to posts with two 2½-in.-long screws at each end.

2½ in.

$1^{1}/_{16}$ in.

$1^{13}/_{16}$ in. to first slat at each end

Slats are 11 in. long; attach to rails with glue and #10 biscuits. Slat is set back 1/4 in. from face side of rails.

1¼ in.

**10-15** Biscuits connect the backrest slats to the rails.

The seat support system comes next (*drawing 10-H*). The seat frame is made up of 2 × 4 redwood, and I've doubled up the 2 × 4 at the front of the bench to give it some added support. This frame is supported at each end by an angled brace, which rests against the back post and is fastened to the lower panel rail (*drawing 10-A*). The braces are joined to the ends of the seat frame with angled half-lap joints at the front. The end pieces are notched at the back end to fit around the post.

First I cut the angled braces. I cut the bottom end to a 45-degree angle and square off one corner to create a 1½-in.-wide flat (*drawing 10-H*). Then I measure 19¹³⁄₁₆ in. along the top edge to mark the long point of a second 45-degree-angle cut. After making the half lap on the angled brace, I need to cut a flat spot at this end too. This one is 1⁷⁄₁₆ in. wide.

To make the half laps in the angled braces and seat-frame end pieces, I set up my radial-arm saw with a stack dado head cutter. I set the blade to exactly half the stock thickness and set the saw to 45 degrees for the cut. Both the angled braces and the end pieces get 45-degree half laps (*photo 10-16*). At the back end of each end piece, I cut a 1¼-in. by 2½-in. notch to fit around the post (*drawing 10-H*). I mill these notches on the radial saw with the same dado head setup.

Next comes a 1½-in.-wide dado, 1/4 in. deep, on the inside of each end piece to receive the back rail of the seat frame. The front and back rails of the seat assembly also get shallow dadoes for the crosspieces (*drawing 10-H*). I mill all these joints on the radial-arm saw.

Now I can assemble the seat frame with waterproof glue and rust-resistant screws. The angled braces go on last. When the glue is dry, I'm ready to fasten the seat-frame assembly to the posts.

**10-H** *Seat*    Note: Frame is 2 × 4's. All dadoes and rabbets are 1/4 in. deep.

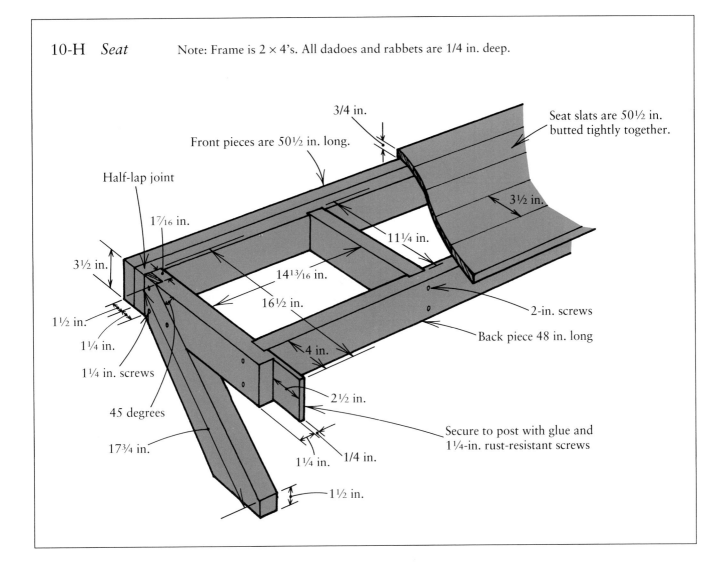

3/4 in.

Front pieces are 50½ in. long.

Seat slats are 50½ in. butted tightly together.

Half-lap joint

3½ in.

1⁷⁄₁₆ in.

11¼ in.

3½ in.

14¹³⁄₁₆ in.

16½ in.

1½ in.

1¼ in.

1¼ in. screws

2-in. screws

Back piece 48 in. long

45 degrees

4 in.

17¾ in.

2½ in.

Secure to post with glue and 1¼-in. rust-resistant screws

1¼ in.    1/4 in.

1½ in.

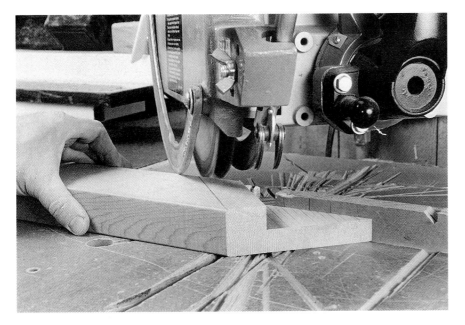

**10-16**    I cut half-lap joints in the angled seat braces with a stack dado head on my radial-arm saw.

## Installing the Seat

Now for a little assembly. I brush some waterproof glue on the tenons of the backrest top rail, in the mortise, and some in the notches of the bottom rail. I slip the tenons into their mortises in the posts and pull the joints together with a couple of long pipe clamps. I install two 2½-in. screws at each end of the bottom rail to fasten the rail to the post.

The seat assembly goes on next. I slip it in place between the posts, holding the top of the frame 15¼ in. from the bottom of the posts. Then I fasten it to the posts with glue and rust-resistant screws (*drawing 10-H*).

The seat slats are simply lengths of 1 × 4 redwood, cut to a 50½-in. length. I chamfer the edges slightly with a block plane and nail the slats in place across the seat frame with 4d galvanized nails.

## Arches and Rungs

The two arches are connected by 1½-in.-square rungs with 1-in.-square tenons on the ends (*drawing 10-I*). I cut the shoulders on the table saw using a gauge block as I did for the rails and cut the cheeks on the band saw. I round the corners of the tenons with a rasp so they'll fit into the mortises in the arches.

I assemble the rungs and the arches by gluing the tenons into the mortises in one arch. The other arch goes on top. It's a little bit tricky to get all the rungs seated in their mortises, but a tap or two with a mallet gets them aligned with the holes. I put on some clamps to pull the joints tight.

Once the glue is dry, I can install the arch assembly on top of the posts. No glue here — I want to be able to lift off the arch assembly so I can move the arbor.

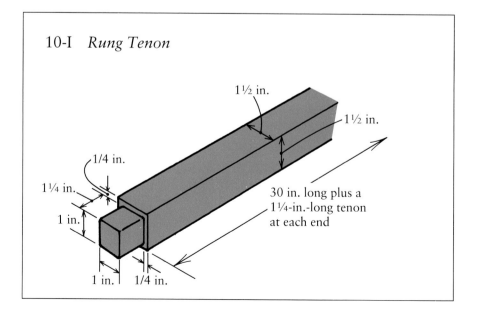

10-I  *Rung Tenon*

1½ in.

1½ in.

1/4 in.

1¼ in.

1 in.

30 in. long plus a 1¼-in.-long tenon at each end

1 in.    1/4 in.

**10-17** To cover the joint between the arches and posts, I nail on a small, chamfered molding, mitering the corners for a good-looking fit.

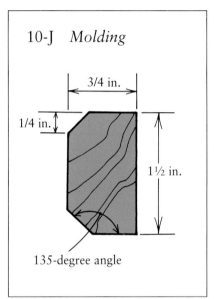

10-J  *Molding*

3/4 in.

1/4 in.

1½ in.

135-degree angle

All that's left for me to do is make some molding to cover the joints where the arch meets the posts. I mill some 3/4-in. by 1½-in. stock and chamfer 2 edges on the jointer (*drawing 10-J*). Then I "wrap" the posts with this molding, mitering the corners at a 45-degree angle on my miter box. I fasten the molding with some 4d finishing nails, nailing only into the posts, not the arches (*photo 10-17*).

That's about it. Now all I have to do is find the right place in the landscape to set up the arbor. It will look just great next summer when we train ivy or a morning glory to climb up over the top. It's going to be a terrific place to sit and read a book.

# *Index*

arches, for redwood arbor, 183–190

backsaw, 171, 190
bandsaw: for child's wagon, 139, 141; for garden swing, 98; for flame-top fence, 166; for redwood arbor, 197; for wheelbarrow, 69
belt sander: for gardener's workbench, 32, 40; for lidded bench, 149, 161; for picnic table, 79
bevel gauge, 184
bevels, for mortised fence, 175
biscuit joints, for redwood arbor, 193, 195, 197
block plane, 30, 95, 121, 126, 200
bow saw, 164
butt joints, 10, 193, 194

chamfers: for child's wagon, 134, 141; for large planter, 117; for lidded bench, 145, 154, 159; for redwood arbor, 190, 200
chemical preservatives for wood, 4
child's wagon, 123; bed, 123–127; finishing, 142–143; front steering mechanism, 123, 130–133; front wheel assembly, 130, 133–135; handle, 139–140; handle shaft assembly, 136–138; mortises, 123; project planner, 123–124; rear wheels, 123, 127–130; side boards, 126, 140–142; special tool, 123; support braces, 129–130
chlorofluorocarbons, 143
circular saw: for redwood arbor, 189, 190; for sandbox, 18, 21; for wheelbarrow, 63
counterbores and plugs, 77, 82, 91, 92, 100–101, 120–121, 124–126

dadoes: for child's wagon, 123, 124; for gardener's workbench, 29, 43; for garden swing, 89; for large planter, 107, 116; for picket fences, 167, 171, 181; for picnic table, 75–76; for wheelbarrow, 54, 55, 57, 58, 66
diamond-top fence, 163, 168; assembly, 168; pales, 168–171; posts, 171; project planner, 163–164; skirt board, 168, 171; stringers, 168
drill press: for child's wagon, 126, 139, 140, 141; for garden swing, 94, 95, 98, 104; for large planter, 118; for lidded bench, 159; for mortised fence, 173; for redwood arbor, 189, 192; for wheelbarrow, 59, 64
drum sander: for child's wagon, 126, 139; for gardener's workbench, 32; for garden swing, 98, 104; for lidded bench, 152, 159; for wheelbarrow, 59, 63, 70
dust collection chute on vacuum, 148

E.M.T. conduit, 92, 101, 102–103

fasteners, 3, 5, 6
finishes, 5; for picnic table, 83; for wheelbarrow, 71
flame-top fence, 163; pales, 167; posts, 167; project planner, 163; routing the flames, 164–167; stringer half laps, 167
forstner bit: for child's wagon, 124, 140; for garden swing, 92, 94, 95, 101; for mortised fence, 173; for picnic table, 77; for redwood arbor, 188, 189, 192

gardener's workbench, 27; backsplash, 27; bins, 42–45; project planner, 27, 29; shelves, 27, 32; side frame assembly, 29–

32; storage areas, 27; work surface assembly, 35–40; X-brace, 32–35
garden fence, 163, 179–181; posts, 181; project planner, 164
garden swing, 85; armrests, 98, 104; back slats, 104; back supports, 98, 100; eyebolts, 92–93; frame assembly, 90–92; frames, 85–90; platform, 101–102, 103–104; project planner, 85–86; seats, 98–101, 102–104; spacers, 104; squeaks, 105; vertical hangers, 93–95, 104; X-braces, 92
gauge block, 112, 124, 197
glue: construction adhesive, 5, 35; epoxy, 4, 5; hot-melt, 22, 25; resorcinol, 4–5; waterproof, 4–5, 119, 149, 160, 184, 193, 194, 198, 200; water-resistant, 3, 4, 5
ground-contact applications, 4

half-lap joints, 34, 35, 167, 198
hand saw, 34

jigsaw: for child's wagon, 123, 127, 139; for gardener's workbench, 34; for lidded bench, 152; for small planter, 115
jointer, 63–64, 119, 154
jointing with table saw, 149

laminate bending, 183
large planter, 117; assembly, 119–121; bottom slats, 121; posts, 117–118; project planner, 107–108; rails, 117–118; side slats, 118
lathe, for small planter, 109–111
lidded bench, 145; arch, 155, 158–159; back boards, 154–155; bottom

boards, 155; cleats, 153–154, 159–160; front boards, 159–160; gluing the panels, 149; jointing with table saw, 149; lid, 161; planing the boards, 147–148; project planner, 145; side panels, 149–153

linseed oil finish, 71

lumber, mail order, 147. *See also* wood

medium-density overlay (MDO) plywood, 40; for child's wagon, 123, 124, 127; for gardener's workbench, 27, 40; for wheelbarrow, 60, 63

miter box, power: for child's wagon, 130, 139; for garden swing, 86, 90, 98; for picket fence pales, 176; for large planter, 118; for lidded bench, 154; for redwood arbor, 193, 201; for wheelbarrow, 48, 53–54, 67

miter gauge: block, 112, 140; for child's wagon, 138, 140; for gardener's workbench, 29, 34; for small planter, 112; for wheelbarrow, 66

mitering, 12, 29

mortise-and-tenon joints: for child's wagon, 140–141; for mortised fence, 174; for small planter, 107, 111–112

mortised fence, 163, 173; assembly, 176; beveling the stringers, 175; pales, 176; posts, 176; project planner, 164; stringers, 173–174, 175; tenons, 174

mortises: for child's wagon, 123, 126, 142; hollow-chisel machine for, 112, 173, 176; for mortised fence, 173–174, 176; for redwood arbor, 188, 189, 190–192; for small planter, 111–112

nail gun, pneumatic, 90

paint: for child's wagon, 142–143; for lidded bench, 145; oil-based, 5

panel cutter, 149, 160

parting tool, 109, 110

pattern, poster-board, 152. *See also* template

picnic table, 73; center braces, 80–82; cleats, 75, 76, 79; crossmembers, 74–75, 76; finish, 83; legs, 74, 77; project planner, 73; top and seats, 79, 82–83

planer radius, 126; thickness, 79, 130, 133, 141, 147–148

plug-cutter, 118

rabbets: for gardener's workbench, 29, 43; for lidded bench, 145, 153; for wheelbarrow, 48, 51, 54–55, 57, 60, 63

radial-arm saw: for fences, 167, 168, 171, 174, 176; for gardener's workbench, 29, 32, 34; for garden swing, 86, 89, 90, 98; for lap joints, 54; for lidded bench, 154, 155; for picnic table, 74–75, 76, 79, 80–81; for rabbets, 63; for redwood arbor, 193, 198; for sandbox, 9, 12; for wheelbarrow, 54, 55, 57, 58, 60, 66, 69

radius plane, 126

random-orbit sander: for large planter, 121; for small planter, 112–115; for wheelbarrow, 60

redwood arbor, 183; arches, 183–190, 200–201; bench, 183; cleats, 195; corner posts, 190–192; lattice panels, 183, 193–196; molding, 201; project planner, 183–184; rungs, 200; seat, 196–200; side frames, 193, 194

refinishing, 5

resawing, 141

roughing gouge, 109, 110

roundover bit: for child's wagon, 140, 141; for lidded bench, 153, 159, 161; for picnic table, 83; for redwood arbor, 190, 192; for wheelbarrow, 59, 70

routers, 29; for child's wagon, 134; for flame-top fence, 166; for large planter, 117; minimizing tearouts, 159; plunge, 191; for redwood arbor, 187, 188–189, 190–192; for small planter, 112; table, 124, 141

safety tips: chemical preservatives, 4; recessed washers and nuts, 124; ripping short pieces, 132

sandbox, 9; canvas covering, 22–25; cleats for deck, 12–14; deck boards, 14–16; legs, 9–10, 12; project planner, 9–10; roof, 18–19; seats, 21–22; sides, 12; vertical standards, 20

sanding: child's wagon, 140; gardener's workbench, 32; by hand, 11; lidded bench, 152; small planter, 111, 115

sawdust, 154–55

shallow-flute spindle gouge, 109

sharpening tools, 109

skew chisel, 109, 110, 111

sliding bevel gauge, 69, 75–76, 98

small planter, 107; bottom slats, 116; finials, 108; legs, 107; mortises, 111; panels, 112–115; posts, 107–111; project planner, 107; rails, 107, 111, 112; sides, 116; tenons, 111–112; tools, 109

socket wrench, 77, 90, 102

spindle gouge, 110–111

spiral flute bits, 112

stains, 5; for picnic table, 73, 83

step drill, 129

straight flute bit, 117

stringers for fence support, 164, 167

table saw, 29; carbide-tipped blade, 115; for child's wagon, 124, 141; for gardener's workbench, 29, 42; for lidded bench, 149; for redwood arbor, 197; for sandbox, 15; for small planter, 107, 114, 115; for wheelbarrow, 48, 66–67

tapering jig, 37–38, 51

template: for picket fences, 164–166; for redwood arbor arch, 187–189; for turned balls, 111

tenoning jig, 48, 112, 140

tenons: for child's wagon, 140–141; for picket fence, 174; for redwood arbor, 188, 189–190, 191, 197; for small planter, 111–112

thickness planer, 79, 130, 133, 141, 147–148

varnish, marine spar, 5

vix bit, 45

warps and bows, 147, 149

wheelbarrow, 47; bed, 60–64; bending the braces, 68–69; finish, 71; frame, 48–51, 54–57, 59; front panel, 64–68; handles, 48, 58–60; lap joints, 54, 55, 60, 63; legs, 51–54, 60; project planner, 47–48; side boards and cleats, 69–70; stake brackets, 70–71; struts, 54, 55, 57, 60; wheel, 47, 60; X-brace, 57–58, 60

wood, 3–4; for arches, 183–184; cedar, 9, 73, 147, 164; chemical preservatives for, 4; cypress, 107, 109, 145–147, 161; for fences, 164; fir, 73; oak, 141, 142, 143; for picnic tables, 73; pine, 145, 164; pressure-treated, 3, 4, 5, 9, 15, 73, 164; red oak, 123, 124, 130; redwood, 73, 85, 147, 183–184; rot, 73, 85; rot/decay-resistant, 3, 4, 85, 107, 164; spruce, 73; teak, 4; unfinished, 5; warps and bows, 147, 149, 164; weather and, 3–4, 5, 73, 105, 107, 145

# New Yankee Workshop Project Index

All of the projects in the four *New Yankee Workshop* books are listed below:

Adirondack Chair (CL 31)
Bathroom Vanity (NY 76)
Bedside Table (NY 64)
Blanket Chest (NY 50)
Bookcase (NY 104)
Butler's Table (CL 47)
Candle Stand (NY 130)
Chest of Drawers (NY 116)
Chest on Chest (CL 153)
Child's Wagon (OP 123)
Chippendale Mirror (CL 137)
Corner Cupboard (MS 145)
Cricket Table (MS 167)
Drop-leaf Table (NY 38)
Entertainment Center (CL 195)
Four Colonial Fences (OP 163)
Garden Bench (CL 175)
Garden Swing (OP 85)
Gardener's Workbench (OP 27)
Harvest Table (MS 91)
Hearthside Settle (CL 79)
Hutch (NY 142)

Kitchen Cupboard (CL 61)
Kitchen Worktable (CL 115)
Library Table (MS 125)
Medicine Cabinet (NY 14)
Outdoor Lidded Bench (OP 145)
Outdoor Planters (OP 107)
Pencil-Post Bed (CL 97)
Picnic Table (OP 73)
Pie Safe (MS 185)
Redwood Arbor (OP 183)
Rocking Horse (CL 13)
Sandbox (OP 9)
Shaker Step Stools (MS 5)
Shaker Wall Clock (MS 71)
Shaker Washstand (MS 43)
Shaker Wood Box (MS 111)
Slant-front Desk (NY 156)
Trestle Table (NY 90)
Two-Drawer Shaker Blanket Chest (MS 23)
Wooden Wheelbarrow (OP 47)
Workbench (NY 26)

(CL): *Classics from the New Yankee Workshop*
(MS): *Mostly Shaker from the New Yankee Workshop*
(NY): *The New Yankee Workshop*
(OP): *The New Yankee Workshop Outdoor Projects*